Repression, Resistance, and Women in Afghanistan

Repression, Resistance, and Women in Afghanistan

Hafizullah Emadi

Westport, Connecticut
London

Library of Congress Cataloging-in-Publication Data

Emadi, Hafizullah.
   Repression, resistance, and women in Afghanistan / Hafizullah Emadi.
      p.   cm.
   Includes bibliographical references and index.
   ISBN 0–275–97671–8
   1. Women—Afghanistan—History—20th century.   2. Women in development—
Afghanistan—History—20th century.   3. Women—Afghanistan—Political activity—
History—20th century.   4. Patriarchy—Afghanistan.   5. Women in Islam—
Afghanistan.   I. Title.
   HQ1735.6.E46   2002
   305.4′09581′0904—dc21   2002025312

British Library Cataloguing in Publication Data is available.

Library of Congress Catalog Card Number: 2002025312
ISBN: 0–275–97671–8

First published in 2002

Praeger Publishers, 88 Post Road West, Westport, CT 06881
An imprint of Greenwood Publishing Group, Inc.
www.praeger.com

Printed in the United States of America

The paper used in this book complies with the
Permanent Paper Standard issued by the National
Information Standards Organization (Z39.48–1984).

10 9 8 7 6 5 4 3 2 1

This book is dedicated to my sisters, Nigar and Sanam, who could not acquire a formal education due to our family's economic situation and the prevailing cultural biases toward women's education, and to the oppressed women in Afghanistan.

Contents

Photos follow page 162

Tables

Acknowledgments

Repression, Resistance, and Women in Afghanistan is the product of several years of research on women and politics in the country. The leading factors that inspired me to conduct research on the subject were the influence of feminist politics in academic institutions in the Occident concerning the liberation of women and their perspective on women's liberation in peripheral social formations, and the tendency for existing literature on the national liberation struggle in Afghanistan to negate women's active role in the struggle during the nine years of the Soviet occupation of the country and their struggle for a new democratic society in the future in Afghanistan.

In order to render justice to women in Afghanistan, I intend my research to bring this neglected issue to international attention. Many people both in private and in academic institutions have graciously contributed to the writing of this book, although it appears to be a single author's work. It is difficult to find appropriate words to express gratitude to friends and colleagues for their scholarly contributions. My research and resulting work would truly be inadequate were it not for the illuminating remarks and insightful suggestions tendered by these scholars.

I am extremely indebted to Mohamed Alibhai for reviewing the first draft of the book and his thoughtful suggestions concerning how to improve it. My lifelong gratitude goes to Farooq Babrakzai. His thoughtful remarks on the first draft of the book, based on his experience in Afghanistan, were crucial to its final form. My special appreciation goes to Akram Gizabi, who took time out of his busy schedule to review an earlier version of the book. His unique insights on the topic enabled me to further expand on some issues discussed in this study. I would also like to thank the *Review of Radical Political Economics* for allowing me to incorporate my article "State, Modernization, and the Women's Movement in Afghanistan" (23, nos. 3–4 [Fall–Winter 1991]: 224–243) into this text. My appreciation also goes to the Revolutionary Association of Women of Afghanistan (RAWA; Jamiat-e-Enqilabi-e-Zanan-e-Afghanistan), for providing relevant literature and original photographs on women of Afghanistan.

I am much obliged to Rahima Sultani, Laila Sekandari, Zargham Ali Mayar, Iqbal Sheikhmiri, and Faqir Wais for their considerate support during my fieldwork in Pakistan. Among other people who assisted me in my research and to whom I owe boundless gratitude are Nazi Etemadi and Soraya Abachi, for providing me with relevant literature on the subject. Above all I am grateful to my wife, Lorilei, for her help during my research and preparation of the index. I tried my best to incorporate comments of the reviewers into my work to present a detailed and accurate view of the situation of women, but I am fully responsible for any errors that remain. Last but not least, I would also like to express my appreciation to Praeger Publishers for bringing this little-studied aspect of development and women in Afghanistan to public attention.

Introduction

One of the main characteristics of socioeconomic development in the West is that development in these societies did not originate from the top, as a result of state actions, but from below, as a consequence of choices made by members of society. At the beginning of the nineteenth century, capitalist development and modernization in the West had succeeded in transforming the feudal mode of production and its corresponding culture and politics into a new society that was based on a capitalist mode of production. This new era provided women with an opportunity to work outside their homes. Capitalist development in Afghanistan did not proceed from below, but rather was imposed from the top by the state apparatus. Imposed capitalism that succeeded in some of the developing nations did not alter the feudal mode of production or its corresponding ideology, politics, and cultural practices in Afghanistan. This trend of development, which began only in the post–World War II period, brought limited changes regarding women's status, and those at the forefront of this movement were mainly urban intellectuals. Capitalist development did not end women's oppression, and particularly in the rural areas the plight of women has remained a neglected issue in the literature devoted to social, economic, and political development in Afghanistan. Although a number of studies have been published discussing the status of women in both the private and the public arena in Afghanistan, most of these books examine the women's movements in isolation from international development and class struggle in the country.

Most scholars of modern Afghanistan have failed to reflect on the sub-ordinated position of women both at home and in society, and on the oppressive social norms that harness women's potential in societal development. A number of these scholars maintain that social and cultural traditions and Islamic laws protect women against any kind of injustices. They maintain that women are not seen as inferior to men and are treated with respect. For example, one scholar of modern Afghanistan described the status of women as follows:

The wife in the Afghan society of today is really the mistress of the household, usually wielding great influence over her husband and the young members of the family. Women are no longer considered inferior. Husband and wife discuss their family matters in an atmosphere of extreme friendliness and arrive at mutual decisions.[1]

Men often deny women's subordinated position and their suppression by men. Whenever someone questions a Muslim man regarding women's freedom and education, he immediately quotes verses from the Quran or Hadith, statements by the Prophet Muhammad, to show that Islam supports women's education and so forth. However, such an answer has nothing to do with the realities of women's life in modern Afghanistan and women's treatment as personal property to be sold and purchased by men.

Some scholars have relied on statements by men concerning the status of women both at home and in society. Such statements—for example, that women are "arch symbols of honor [whose] control and protection is essential to upholding *namaz,* prayer"—present a distorted picture of the reality with regard to women's status.[2] Although both men and women work outside the home, women are responsible for the household chores. This situation has led some scholars to argue that women are masters of the family and exercise full leadership in the management of the family's economy, their children's upbringing, and so forth. This line of thinking has been reflected in a study of women of the Sheikhanzi nomads of Western Afghanistan:

Women are neither submissive nor mere shadows in the society, and the means by which they contribute to a pastoral economy provide them with both control of resources and considerable power through such control. . . . In their roles as power-brokers, women also have power over their husband's reputations for hospitality and generosity through how skillfully food is prepared for guests, how much is available for sharing with others, and with whom this sharing takes place. In addition the prestige and power available to a man is related to the commodity and animal purchases he is able to make on the basis of sale or exchange of the dairy and other products contributed by the labor of women of household.[3]

Even though women may hold sway in the domestic arena and even manage the family's economy, this does not negate women's subordination to men. Such an analysis lacks a comprehensive examination of the socioeconomic system and the corresponding ideology and politics as prime factors that suppress women. The solution some scholars propose to facilitate women's equality with men is action by the government, that is, the introduction of more legislation for the involvement of women in public and private sectors of the national economy. The literature further maintains that equality for and liberation of women also require the transformation of traditional opinions and attitudes through the "creation of a viable ideology of modernism, balancing the traditional Islamic and innovative Western influences."[4] The literature also underestimates the significance of the active participation of women in the struggle for social change and indeed seems to ignore the abilities of women to do so.

Development during the Soviet occupation of Afghanistan often misled other scholars who argued that women had achieved some progress in social, political, and legal spheres. For example, Valentine Moghadam in her study of women in Afghanistan maintained that the status of women had enhanced considerably in the 1980s and attributed such improvements primarily to the existence of the pro-Soviet Sazman-e-Demokratik-e-Zanan-e-Afghanistan, Women's Democratic Organization of Afghanistan (WDOA). Moghadam stated:

As a result of the activities of the WDOA and the PDPA, women won the right to vote. . . . In the years before the *Saur* Revolution, the WDOA managed to win the legal right of women to study abroad. Another achievement was winning the right of women to work outside the home.[5]

Such an assertion by Moghadam distorts realities in Afghanistan. The pro-Soviet Hizb-e-Demokratik-e-Khalq-e-Afghanistan, People's Democratic Party of Afghanistan (PDPA), and its women's branch, WDOA, were formed after the promulgation of a new constitution in 1964. The constitution provided women with the opportunity to participate in the country's politics. Women were sent abroad for further education and training and were employed at public enterprises as early as the 1950s, and after the promulgation of the 1964 constitution women of various political orientations fought to further women's emancipation. In reality, during their rule the pro-Soviet PDPA and WDOA tortured, molested, and jailed many women who opposed their policies either vocally or by active opposition. They also shot and killed female students who demonstrated against the Soviet occupation.

Moghadam denied the fact that the pro-Soviet women's organization, WDOA, was a mouthpiece of the ruling party and the state whose main objective was to rally women in support of the government policies and Soviet occupation of Afghanistan. Appointments of a few women at various party and state positions is not a reflection of women's emancipation, liberation, and gender equality. Moghadam also wrongly justified sending a large number of youths and students to the Soviet Union and its bloc countries due to the political instability in Afghanistan in the 1980s that "made education even more precarious. This danger was the reason for the dispatch of students to the Soviet Union."[6] Moghadam denied the fact that the prime goal of sending youths to these countries was based on political consideration—to indoctrinate them with Soviet models of ethics, morality, and politics. Moghadam's recycling of the same article to various journals and chapters in books further contributed to misunderstanding of politics and women in Afghanistan.

This book differs from other studies of women and development in Afghanistan that precede it. It offers an empirical dimension concerning women and development in the country that is missing in other studies. The empirical quality can be justified, in my opinion, because there is no study of women in Afghanistan from the perspective of historical-political development in the twentieth century. This study explores this relatively uncharted terrain; it also serves as a map to guide the novice scholar in the field and to generate discussion and further study on the subject.

Materials that have been used in writing this book include documents and reports published by the governments of Afghanistan and international organizations, books and articles published by scholars on Afghanistan, and literature published by independent political organizations within and outside the country. Government-published materials are the sole sources of original documentation for most research on Afghanistan. However, the government in Afghanistan often manipulated data on demography, state achievements in economic and social progress, and the like, in order to demonstrate the steady progress that encourages international support for its development projects, to mislead potential sponsors. It is thus necessary to contrast these data with those of other governments and international organizations to extract relatively accurate information. Reports on Afghanistan by Western scholars, most of whom lived in the country and directly experienced developments in Afghanistan, are relatively reliable sources of information. Other useful sources for analyses and documentation, such as the literature published by political organizations both inside and outside the country, supplement existing information by providing data omitted in government publications for various national or security reasons.

APPROACHES TO THE STUDY OF WOMEN
AND DEVELOPMENT

There is no generally accepted definition of the word *development*. *Webster's Third New International Dictionary* defines the word as "the act, process or result of developing, the state of being developed, a gradual unfolding by which something . . . is developed . . . gradual advance or growth through progressive changes." Earlier scholars of the development paradigm argued that development was a process of growth and progress based on succession, in which the succeeding stage is far higher than the earlier stages. Prominent among them is Walt Rostow, who viewed development as growth through successive stages or change,[7] and Denis Goulet, who regarded modernization as a means of ascent and liberation of people.[8] Benjamin Higgins and Jean Higgins defined development as "increased productivity, i.e. increased capacity to provide whatever people want, whether it be food, leisure, temples, unpolluted sylvan scenes, ballet, heated houses, or national independence. To offer all these things to all people in the future will involve a great deal of economic ingenuity, political skill, and last, but not least, technological advancement."[9]

The word *development* is used in this study to refer to the process of change that occurs on a spiral basis within the economic, social, and cultural arena as well as within political consciousness. This study strongly disagrees with those who postulate that development necessitates changes in the infrastructure—the economy—and those who argue the opposite, or changes in the superstructure—the cultural arena. Both arguments have an Achilles heel in that each views the two interrelated aspects of development in isolation from each other. In a similar vein, this study also disagrees with cultural relativists who regard a culture in context to a particular environment and to the lives of its people. They maintain that "culture is environmentally relevant to the extent that it makes some contributions to issues important in our environment, issues pertaining to suicide, crime, health care, and among others, policing."[10] Such an argument justifies women's subjugation to men and subsequent male brutality toward them in many cultures around the world.

Scholars whose research focus has been international development have introduced the issue of women in various development forums. These development strategies have been characterized according to three main paradigms: the linear stage theory, the modernity theory, and the political economy theory. Proponents of the linear stage theory postulate that newly developing countries could transform and modernize their backward infrastructure simply through the appropriate application of capital and technology from developing nations.[11] This perspective also maintains that Western-oriented modernization equally benefits men and women in the developing nations because women in these countries face the same problems as men, for example, technological and institutional backwardness and poverty.[12]

The modernity theory, which often has been associated with the practices of Western democracy—constitutionalism, electoral participation, and competitive politics—reflects the conservative intellectual tradition of Western countries. Proponents of this theory maintain that the adoption of the modern values characteristic of developed nations by the developing countries is the essential component for development in these countries.

If the new institutions being widely adopted by developing countries, such as the factory, the school, the modern hospital, and the mass media, are thought of as Western, and if the habits, attitudes, values, and behaviors that are built into the social roles associated with these institutions are also defined as Western, then some sort of psychological Westernization may be a practical necessity for any country that seeks to modernize its institutions.[13]

The linear stage and modernity theories are inadequate because they regard development as an individual nation-state phenomenon and fail to comprehend the influence of international capital on the integration of developing nations into the fabric of the capitalist world economy and the resulting uneven development in the developing countries. The failure of these theories to explain the growing poverty and declining status of women in developing countries indicates that we must examine the issue by adopting the political economy approach as a more inclusive theoretical perspective.

The political economy theory regards development in terms of developments of the forces of production, albeit uneven, in most developing countries. It considers the control and use of economic surplus as the key to power and control of development.[14] The type of development varies from one socioeconomic formation to another, depending on which class controls this economic surplus. The study of political economy reveals that women's liberation and their achievement of equality with men cannot be accomplished through mechanical application of technology or capital, or through the imposition of cultural values of the developed nations on the developing countries. The subjugation of women, which began with the division of labor and emergence of classes, can only be eliminated by the destruction of the very fabric of class society and its corresponding ideology and politics, as well as by the active and determined participation in the process by women themselves.

There are two basic schools of thought within the political economy paradigm that attempt to provide an analysis of the problems of socioeconomic development in the developing countries: the development school and the underdevelopment school. Proponents of the development school, represented most prominently by the works of Bill Warren, maintain that capitalism has a progressive impact on socioeconomic development in the peripheries because it acts as

a powerful engine of progressive social change, advancing capitalist development far more rapidly than was conceivable in any other way. . . . [A]lthough introduced into the Third World externally, capitalism has struck deep roots there and developed its own increasingly rigorous internal dynamics.[15]

Scholars of the underdevelopment school argue that capitalism leads to underdevelopment in peripheral societies because it tends to develop those sectors of the economy in the developing nations that promote the priorities of the core over the needs of the periphery. The core engages in a system of production and other types of exchanges and trades that leads to its further development of the center, at the expense of the periphery.

Contemporary underdevelopment is in large part the historical product of past and continuing economic and other relations between the satellite underdeveloped and the now developed metropolitan countries. Furthermore, these relations are an essential part of the structure and development of the capitalist system on a world scale as a whole.[16]

Proponents of the world system theory further elaborate this type of analysis. They argue that in the world system, the core (center nations), requiring raw materials and markets for their commodity production, were able to control and dictate the economic operation of the world system, which led to significant disruption in local subsistence economies in the periphery.[17] The terms and conditions of trade and other exchange relations between the core and the periphery, decided largely by the center, lead to an unequal exchange of commodity between the center and the periphery. "Unequal exchange is the elementary transfer mechanism, and as such, it enables the developed countries to begin to give new impetus to that unevenness of development, which sets in motion all the other mechanisms of exploitation."[18] Scholars of the world system theory further argue that unequal specialization of production between the core and the periphery forms the basis of underdevelopment in the developing world, because a number of administrative measures have been employed compelling the developing world to produce what is expected.[19]

The proponents of both the development and underdevelopment paradigms fail to comprehend the contradictory effect of capitalism that simultaneously generates and retards growth processes, eventually resulting in uneven development and intensification of class struggle and national liberation movements in the developing countries. Based on this theoretical perspective, I have taken capitalism's often contradictory influences into account as I examine development and its impacts on the women's movement in Afghanistan.

Chapter 1 studies social formations and discusses capitalist development and its corresponding cultural influence in Afghanistan in the post–World War II period. Chapter 2 examines gender polity and the status of women, traditional male-female relations, and women's salient defiance and reaction to male domination and patriarchic cultural norms. Chapter

3 studies the role of the peripheral state and its top-down policies of social and economic transformation, and examines the state's policies concerning the gradual involvement of women in various state enterprises. Chapter 4 explores how development and modernization contributed to a new social and political consciousness among women of upper- and middle-class families and led to increased social, political, and class struggle in the country. It also studies women's participation in the anti-Soviet armed resistance, December 1979–February 1989. Chapter 5 studies developments in the post-Soviet era and analyzes the politics of the Islamic parties and the Taliban government toward women as well as the position of the revolutionary movement with regard to women's role in the reconstruction of Afghanistan. It also examines the exodus of refugees and problems they encountered in exile. Chapter 6 synthesizes the argument and attempts to discuss the prospect for women's liberation in Afghanistan in the future.

NOTES

1. Mohammed Ali, *Afghanistan: Land of Glorious Past and Bright Future* (Kabul: Franklin Book Programs, Education Press, 1969), p. 34.

2. For details, see Nancy H. Dupree, "The Afghan Refugee Family Abroad: A Focus on Pakistan," *The Afghanistan Studies Journal* 1:1 (Spring 1988): 31.

3. Bahram Tavakolian, "Women and Socio-Economic Change Among Sheikhanzai Nomads of Western Afghanistan," *The Middle East Journal* 38:3 (Summer 1984): 440–441.

4. Erika Knabe, "Afghan Women: Does Their Role Change?" in *Afghanistan in the 1970s*, Louis Dupree and Linette Albert (eds.) (New York: Praeger, 1974), p. 164.

5. Valentine M. Moghadam, *Modernizing Women: Gender and Social Change in the Middle East* (Boulder, Colo.: Lynne Rienner, 1993), p. 225.

6. Ibid., p. 240.

7. W. W. (Walt Whitman) Rostow, *The Stages of Economic Growth: A Non-Communist Manifesto* (Cambridge: Cambridge University Press, 1990).

8. Denis Goulet, "Development . . . or Liberation?" in *The Political Economy of Development and Underdevelopment*, 3rd ed., Charles K. Wilber (ed.) (New York: Random House, 1984), pp. 461–467.

9. Benjamin Higgins and Jean Downing Higgins, *Economic Development of a Small Planet* (New York: W. W. Norton, 1979), p. 23.

10. Morris Freilich, "Introduction: Is Culture Still Relevant?" in *The Relevance of Culture*, Morris Freilich (ed.) (New York: Bergin and Garvey, 1989), p. 18.

11. Alejandro Portes, "On the Sociology of National Development: Theories and Issues," *American Journal of Sociology* 82:1 (July 1976): 55–85; and Michael P. Todaro, *Economic Development in the Third World*, 3rd ed. (New York: Longman, 1985).

12. For details, see Jane S. Jaquette, "Women and Modernization Theory: A Decade of Feminist Criticism," *World Politics* 34:2 (1982): 269.

13. Alex Inkeles et al., *Exploring Individual Modernity* (New York: Columbia University Press, 1983), p. 11. See also Alex Inkeles and David Horton Smith, *Becoming Modern: Individual Change in Six Developing Countries* (Cambridge: Harvard University Press, 1974), p. 3.

14. Charles K. Wilber and Kenneth P. Jameson, "Paradigms of Economic Development and Beyond," in *The Political Economy of Development and Underdevelopment*, Wilber (ed.), pp. 13–14.

15. Bill Warren, *Imperialism: Pioneer of Capitalism*, edited by John Sender (London: NLB, 1980), p. 9.

16. Andre Gunder Frank, "The Development of Underdevelopment," *Monthly Review* 18:4 (September 1966): 18.

17. Immanuel Wallerstein, *The Capitalist World Economy* (Cambridge: Cambridge University Press, 1979).

18. Arghiri Emmanuel, *Unequal Exchange: A Study of the Imperialism of Trade* (New York: Monthly Review Press, 1972), p. 265.

19. Samir Amin, *Imperialism and Unequal Development* (New York: Monthly Review Press, 1977), p. 69.

1

Peripheral Social Formation: Drive for Modernity

Afghanistan, by virtue of its geographic location at the confluence of myriad cultures, has long been a crossroads of nations and religions, of traders and invaders. Sharp ethnic and linguistic differences have contributed to its turbulent history and often to violent economic and political developments. The outbreak of the war of national liberation in 1979, continuing civil strife in the post-Soviet occupation period, and the exodus of refugees both inside and outside the country have made it difficult to provide accurate data concerning the country's settled population. On the basis of data by the Kabul regime, the country population in 1985 was estimated at 14.7 million. One of the developing countries in Asia with a total area of 647,500 square kilometers, the country's population in 2000 was projected to be 25.9 million with a growth rate of 3.5 percent. Life expectancy was forty-six years for males and forty-five for females.[1]

SOCIAL STRUCTURE

Afghanistan is homeland to various ethnic communities: Pushtun (38 percent), Tajik (25 percent), Hazara (19 percent), Uzbek (6 percent), and several others such as Turkmen, Baluch, Aimaq, Qirghiz, Nuristani, Arab, Jewish, and Hindu.[2] The Jews came to Afghanistan from Mashhad, Iran, and settled in Herat, Balkh, and Kabul. The majority of this number emigrated to the United States and Israel beginning in 1948. In 2000, Rabbi Ishaq Levin was reported to be the only Jew residing in Kabul as caretaker of the only synagogue there. Incidents of harassment by Islamic militants and fear of further hostile actions caused a large number of Hindus and Sikhs to leave the country during the civil war of 1992–1996.

Every ethnic community has its unique culture and tradition. Pushtuns are the dominant ethnic group, but considering the total number of other ethnic communities they do not make up the majority of the country's population. All ethnic communities, to some extent, have equally participated in the country's social, political, and economic development; however, the word *Afghan* is often associated with Pushtuns. In ancient times the country was called Aryana and as early as the mid–eighteenth century the region that was called Khorasan formed the basis of today's Afghanistan. Since then all ethnic communities of the region have been identified by the name *Afghan,* and the word *Afghanistan* literally means "homeland of the Afghans." Although the word *Afghan* has been endorsed in the constitutions intended to apply to everyone residing in the country, other ethnic communities do not identify themselves as "Afghan" but by their respective ethnic names (i.e., Tajik, Hazara, Uzbek, etc.). There are no precise data on the ratio of religious denominations, but it is estimated that at least 75 percent of the people are Sunni and possibly as much as 24 percent are Shia, while less than 1 percent are followers of other faiths (i.e., Jews, Hindus, and Sikhs). A recent survey of literature on languages indicates that there are some forty-nine languages spoken by various ethnic groups,[3] but Persian and Pushtu are the two officially recognized languages, while more than 50 percent speak Persian. Table 1.1 shows the ethnic and religious composition of the country.

The country is fragmented not only by ethnolinguistic and religious differences but also on the basis of affiliation to different tribes and regions. The country's physical geography, and lack of adequate development projects in rural areas, have contributed to the persistence of tribalism, regionalism, and conflict among various ethnic communities. These factors hampered the emergence of a modern civil society and a nation-state. Political power remained the exclusive domain of the Sunni Pushtuns since the rise of Ahmad Shah Abdali to power in 1747, except for brief periods in 1929 and 1992–1996 when Tajiks seized power, suppressing the rights of other ethnic communities and causing them to fight for equality. The ruling circle within the state apparatus resorted to the colonial policy of "divide and conquer" to maintain their hold on power. Tribalism and regionalism constituted a major aspect of the country's social and political culture to the extent that individuals took enormous pride in their tribes and regions. The following Persian proverb aptly depicts tribalism and regionalism in Afghanistan:

> May the Lord grant that no person be without a nation,
> And that within this nation, no person should be without a tribe,
> And that within this tribe no person should be without a community of brothers
> And that within this community of brothers no person should be without
>   a son.[4]

Table 1.1
Afghanistan's Ethnic Communities

	Language	Religious Orientation
Pushtun	Pushtu (Indo-European-Iranian)	Hanifi Sunni (some Shia)
Tajik	Persian (Tajiki dialects)	Hanifi Sunni and Shia-Isma'ili
Hazara	Persian (Hazaragi dialects)	Shia, Isma'ili, a few Hanifi Sunni
Uzbek	Uzbeki (Jagatai) (Turkic dialects)	Hanifi Sunni
Aimaq	Persian with some Turkish	Hanifi Sunni
Farsiwan	Persian	Shia
Turkmen	Turkmani (Turkic dialects)	Hanifi Sunni
Qizilbash	Persian	Shia
Brahui	Brahui (Darvidian), Pushtu, or Baluchi	Hanifi Sunni
Baluch	Baluchi	Hanifi Sunni
Nuristani	Kafiri (Indo-Iranian)	Hanifi Sunni
Hindu	Persian and Pushtu; mother tongue is Hindi, Punjabi, or Lahnda	Hinduism
Sikh	Persian and Pushtu; mother tongue is Punjabi	Sikhism
Jew, Yahud	All speak Persian or Pushtu; mother tongue is Hebrew	Judaism
Pamiri	Indo-Iranian dialect (a group of six related dialects)	Hanifi Sunni and Isma'ili
Kohistani	Dardic dialect (Pashaei, Gawarbati, Sawoji, Deghani, and Kuwal)	Hanifi Sunni
Gujar	Indo-European (Pushtu)	Hanifi Sunni
Qirghiz	Turkic	Hanifi Sunni
Arab	Some Arabic but primarily Persian and Pushtu	Hanifi Sunni
Jat Guji	Jati, Indo-European (Dari and Pushtu)	Hanifi Sunni
Mongol	Persian with some Mongol words	Hanifi Sunni

Source: Adapted from Louis Dupree, *Afghanistan* (Princeton: Princeton University Press, 1973).

LANDOWNERS AND THE PEASANTRY

The country's economy is primarily based on agriculture, and agricultural products such as *qaraqul* fur, wool, cotton, and fruits compose the bulk of the country's exports. Local industries account for 20 percent of the country's gross domestic product (GDP), of which 10 percent comes from handicrafts and 1 percent from mining. Feudal modes of production dominate other types of productions such as prefeudalism, the Asiatic mode of production, and postfeudalism, mercantile and industrial capitalism. Four types of landownership exist in the country: *mulk-e-shakhsi,* private ownership; *mulk-e-khalisa,* joint ownership by lineage or by village residents related by blood; *mulk-e-ama,* public ownership; and *mulk-e-waqfa,* ownership by religious institutions.[5] In the case of landownership, tribal relationships can be transformed into a feudal relationship due to traditional methods of distributing land shares. In theory, public land is the collective property of the tribal clan. The rights of an individual family to share in its use or cultivation depend on the number of shares held by each family head. However, since the number of shares is tied to the number of family members, tribal chiefs, who commonly have the largest families, have the most shares.

"In certain regions tribal lands and flocks have become the property of the tribal chief, and members of the tribe have become tenant farmers on his lands and shepherds of his flocks. Their relationship with their tribal chief has been changed from one of kinship to one of occupation."[6] Income from land, whether individually or collectively owned, is divided on the basis of five traditional criteria: land, water, seeds, capital, and labor.

Water ownership, which is as important as landownership, follows a similar pattern. In many areas, landowners own the water and have exclusive rights to use or sell it to peasant farmers. In some areas, water rights are determined by the farmers, depending on the size of their land and traditional agricultural rules and regulations. The traditional system of irrigation is based largely on water from *kariz,* underground canals, *joi,* water channels, as well as springs and wells. The right to water from the public reservoir for irrigation purposes is only granted to married people; single people are regarded as dependents of their family and their parents have the right to retrieve water. To get more shares of the water, rich landowners often marry several wives and marry off their young sons. Feudal landowners commonly influenced rural politics in two ways: through their own economic positions and through their association with conservative mullahs, clerics. The influence of feudal landowners and tribal chiefs was so pervasive that local government officials often found it extremely difficult to collect taxes, recruit soldiers, or perform other duties without first consulting them and securing their cooperation.

In 1978 official government data indicated that total agricultural land amounted to 62.61 million hectares.[7] There were 7.91 million hectares of arable land, 3.75 million hectares were used for temporary crops, 0.14 million hectares were used for permanent crops, and 4.02 million hectares of land were left uncultivated. Another 54.7 million hectares were designated for pasture and meadows. Prior to the April 1978 coup, 5 percent of the feudal landowners possessed 45 percent of the country's most cultivable lands. Among the top 400 landowning families, who owned 20,000 villages, there were 30 families who owned between 200 and 20,250 hectares of agricultural land, including the families of the two influential religious figures in the Islamic movement, Mojaddadi and Sayed Ahmad Gilani. Twelve percent of the landowning families possessed 20 percent of the agricultural land, while 83 percent of peasant farmers owned 35 percent of the land, or about two to four hectares per farmer, and worked as either sharecroppers or tenant farmers.[8]

Feudal landowners, particularly absentee landowners, leased their land to farmers and poor peasants for a period of one year or more. There existed several types of land leases, all of which were designed to be favorable to the landowner. A leaseholder who owned his own agricultural equipment, seed-grains, and/or plow animals had to turn over one-half to two-thirds, the amount varied, of his annual output to the landowner. If the landowner supplied any, but not all, of these items, then the leaseholder had to turn over four-fifths of his annual output to the landowner. If the landowner supplied all equipment, animals, and seed-grains, the leaseholder became little more than a laborer hired to work the land, keeping only one-fifth of the annual output. In all cases, besides working on the land and turning over most of his output to the landowner, the leaseholder also had to perform various services for the landlord.[9] These services included repairing roads, cleaning ditches, and performing assorted household duties.

In most parts of the country agricultural activities were conducted using primitive methods of production. The instruments of agricultural production consisted of a single wooden plow, harrows, and sickles. Poor and lower-middle-class peasants helped each other by sharing other instruments of production, which included oxen, donkeys, and other animals. Farmers and peasants often worked in pairs and groups and shared labor and work in plowing their lands, preparing seed beds, and harvesting and threshing crops. In some areas the *purghu,* or shared oxen, system of farming is common. In the *purghu* system two farmers, each the owner of one ox, will use both oxen together for common plowing of their lands as well as for other aspects of farming involving animal power.[10] The system is based on necessity rather than profit; a farmer could not effectively plow his land with only one ox.

In addition to the settled population, a segment of Afghanistan's population consists of nomads of Pushtun background, whose number in 1978–1979 was estimated to be 2.5 million. At the turn of the twentieth century Afghanistan's ruler, Abd al-Rahman, settled a number of nomads in Ghazni and in Hazarajat, central regions in Afghanistan. The nomads were categorized into three distinct groups: nomads, semi-nomads, and local semi-nomads. The first group engaged in the purchase and sale of camels and other goods. They were mainly present in the southern regions and later most became wealthy by trading their camels for modern transportation systems (e.g., trucks and buses); most moved to Pakistan after the 1978 April coup. Semi-nomads were those who traveled from one region to another with their flocks of animals, and they too engaged in trade as well as in smuggling goods. Local semi-nomads, numbering an estimated 200,000 people, were found in eastern regions.[11]

THE CLERGY

Mullahs are in charge of mosques and conduct religious rituals, the five daily prayers, and other religious functions. Most mullahs are semiliterate and are able to teach children the art of Quranic recitation and basic reading and writing. They constitute a powerful group in the community and their power and authority often posed a threat to the central government. In the early twentieth century the ruler of Afghanistan, Abd al-Rahman (1880–1901), described the power of mullahs in these words:

Every priest, Mullah and chief of every tribe and village considered himself an independent king . . . the freedom and independence of many of these priests were never broken by their sovereigns. The Mirs of Turkistan, the Mir of Hazara, the Chiefs of Ghilzai were all stronger than their Amirs.[12]

Although Abd al-Rahman subjugated tribal chiefs, independent power centers, and religious leaders, he was not able to fully control the influence the mullahs had on the community of followers.

The status of the mullah and the imam is often interchangeable. In the Sunni tradition, an imam is a layman who conducts prayers in the absence of a mullah. A muazzin is a person who calls people for prayers from the minaret of a mosque. Influential mullahs are in charge of mosques of the highest grade, while ordinary mullahs attend mosques of lower grades. Other religious figures, such as the pir and the shaikh, also are important players in local political and social affairs. Since the vast majority of people are illiterate, they remain dependent on mullahs for reading and writing letters and performing religious ceremonies. Since Arabic is not a common language, a village mullah interprets religious scriptures the way he understands them and can easily silence opponents by reciting a verse from the Quran or a Hadith, statements by the Prophet Muhammad, in an interpretation to substantiate his point of view. If a mullah refuses to preside over a religious ceremony (e.g., refusing to pray for a dead person's soul at a funeral), the family of the deceased has no option but to submit to the mullah's conditions. While a mullah wields considerable influence in the Sunni community, his influence is not so pervasive in the Shiite and Isma'ili communities. Leadership in these communities is more hierarchical, and a mullah is subordinated to the person at the higher rung of the religious establishment (i.e., an ayatollah in the Shiite community and a mukhi in the Isma'ili community).

To placate influential religious leaders and mullahs and gain their support, the government had always sided with them. In 1931 the state established Jamiat-al-Ulama, the Society of Islamic Scholars, which had the authority to appoint mullahs to designated mosques and functioned as advisory board for the government. Members of the society were mainly affiliated with the ruling elites and preached in favor of government policies. The society shielded the government against attack by progressive clerics, radical Islam of the dispossessed, and marginalized social groups fighting for democratic rights. While most influential mullahs were on the government payroll, the community supported ordinary mullahs in charge of village mosques by providing them with some money, a house to live in, and a small share from the crops, for the religious services they performed. Some of these mullahs refused to compromise their principles, defended the interests of the poor, and did not endorse the ruling class's development programs.

Feudal landowners and tribal chiefs were the major contributors to a mullah's income. In exchange for this favor mullahs often used their religious authority to make the poor submit to the authority of feudal landowners. They often linked payments of debts and religious tax to gaining entrance to heaven upon death.[13] In return for the mullahs' help in influencing the local population to submit to their landlords, the feudal landowners set aside parcels of communal land for mullahs' use; and thus the mullahs were co-opted and became part of the country's feudal system. Conservative clerics vehemently opposed government policy on women's emancipation in the late 1950s; however, they were defeated because most die-hard clerics remained defiant of modernization programs. In the 1970s clerics again organized a rally in Kabul demanding a ban on Western cultural influence, coeducation, alcohol, and so forth. The number of mullahs at the end of the 1960s was estimated to be between 220,000 and 230,000.[14]

A significant number of Sunni clerics studied in religious schools in Islamic countries and a few even studied in institutions of higher education in the West. Clerics of the Shia community studied at religious schools in Qum, Iran, and Najaf, Iraq, and upon return home they taught at various private *madrasas*, religious schools, and some even attained the title of ayatollah. Prior to and during the Soviet occupation of Afghanistan a significant number of mullahs in both rural and urban areas collaborated with the Soviet-backed government while most others remained defiant of the regime. Some of the influential religious leaders and mullahs declared a holy war against the Soviet occupation and mobilized people to fight the invaders. Mullahs became major players in politics after the collapse of the Soviet-backed government in 1992, when Islamic parties seized power and Afghanistan was declared an Islamic state.

THE ELITE AND INTELLIGENTSIA

Prior to the April 1978 coup the elite who dominated the country's politics were mainly family members affiliated with former king Mohammad Zahir, 1933–1973, and Mohammad Daoud, 1973–1978, influential religious leaders, wealthy businessmen, and feudal nobility. Top posts in the state coercive apparatus (military, police, and intelligence agencies) and ideological apparatus (civil service, schools, etc.) were monopolized by intellectuals associated with them. A vast majority of these elites were primarily Persianized Pushtuns and Tajiks of the Sunni religious orientation. While a few intellectuals of the middle-class families of the Hazara, Uzbek, and other ethnic communities had been appointed to top positions in the bureaucracy, their roles were largely ceremonial and they lacked any real power and authority to influence decision-making mechanisms in the state apparatus.

A majority of upper-middle-class intellectuals received a modern education at home, but a significant number studied at institutions of higher education abroad. In 1970 there were 347 individuals with Ph.D., M.A., and M.S. degrees, and 3,593 persons with diplomas in vocational and technical training.[15] These intellectuals held leading positions within and outside the state apparatus and played important roles in formulating policies aimed at further accelerating modernization of the country. They espoused political ideologies such as liberalism, nationalism, and the doctrine of free market economy. However, a significant number of the intelligentsia also advocated alternative development strategies such as socialism and development strategies based on Islamic teachings.

Struggle for social, economic, and political reform, democratic rights, and social justice punctuated the country's politics in the post–World War II period. Intellectuals who came from lower middle classes and disadvantaged families fought for political equality and socioeconomic reforms, evidenced in the increased political activities in the 1940s and later in worker and student strikes in the 1960s and early 1970s.[16] Intellectuals who espoused socialist ideology were divided into two major groups: pro-Soviet reformists and revolutionaries.

Pro-Soviet forces supported building a socialist society based on the Soviet model of development and seized power in the 1978 April coup. The traditional elites were removed from positions of authority within and outside the state immediately after the coup and many left Afghanistan for Pakistan, Western Europe, North America, and elsewhere. The new ruling elites were mainly from the urbanite middle class and privileged families and ruled the country with active Soviet military intervention. Although most members of the PDPA were schooled in Afghanistan, a significant number of their leaders, particularly in the armed forces, had received professional and technical training in the Soviet Union and its bloc countries. In April 1992 the PDPA, also known as Hizb-e-Watan, the Party of the Homeland, was forced to transfer power to a coalition of Islamic parties and most of their erstwhile leaders left the country. PDPA elite, who earlier had brazenly condemned Western Europe and North American countries as "bloodthirsty imperialists," later sought asylum in these countries, considering them the most democratic societies that defended human rights.

The revolutionary groups advocated a radical transformation of the status quo, adhering to armed struggle and mass mobilization for social change. They opposed the Soviet invasion, participated in the war of national liberation, and suffered major casualties in the process. Intellectuals who advocated nationalist and liberal political ideologies also sustained major losses, and many were forced to leave Afghanistan and seek refuge in neighboring countries as well as in Western Europe, North America, and elsewhere. Intellectuals affiliated with various Islamic parties participated in the war of national liberation in the 1980s and a number of them gained prominent positions in the state bureaucracy in 1992 when Afghanistan was declared an Islamic State. Unlike traditional religious leaders who studied at the local madrasas, most cadres of the Islamic parties had graduated from the Abu Hanifa School in Kabul and a few had received higher education at Al-Azhar University in Cairo, Egypt. Most rank-and-file members of the group had attended public schools in Afghanistan, and a few had studied at the military academy in Kabul. A number of leading figures of the Islamic parties amassed substantial wealth during the war of national liberation in the form of monies appropriated from foreign aid from the West intended to fund the battle against the Soviet occupation forces. A significant number of others had prospered when the Islamic parties seized power in Kabul and fought each other for political and military domination of the country. Most of these intellectuals, single-minded in their pursuit of material gain and supported by regional and imperial powers, were party to or responsible for the destruction of the country and the ensuing war of ethnic cleansing that claimed the lives of thousands of innocent people.

THE ENTREPRENEURS

The entrepreneurs consisted of financial and commercial businessmen, industrialists, traders, merchants, and medium and small business owners. Since the state monopolized key industrial and commercial sectors of the economy, entrepreneurs in the private sector remained subordinated to those in the state apparatus. This factor stymied their efforts to significantly influence the direction of economic and political development in the country. This stratum often aspired to reform the status quo and lent support to forces fighting for liberal and democratic rights. The majority of entrepreneurs in both the state apparatus and the private sectors came mainly from the Pushtun community.

The private sector of the economy grew significantly in the post–World II period, evidenced in the growth of a number of light industrial, commercial, and trading centers throughout the country. Medium, small, and petty business strata also grew in the 1960s and afterward. The majority of this social group owned small retails shops such as food stores, drugstores, restaurants, and the like, and most employed a few workers on a full- or part-time basis.

After the 1978 April coup a significant number of local entrepreneurs left the country and settled in Pakistan, Western Europe, North America, and elsewhere. Those who remained in Afghanistan engaged in commercial trade with the Soviet Union and its bloc countries, and to a lesser degree with other countries in Asia, the Middle East, Western Europe, and North America. The majority of this group adopted conservative politics; however, some of them expressed sympathy with the Islamic parties, considering their political ideology to be compatible with their own and supportive of a free market economic system and its politics, culture, and ideology.

THE WORKING CLASS

Data from 1967 indicate that there were 48 private industries in Afghanistan that employed 3,417 workers and 85 state-owned industries employed 21,470 persons.[17] Although the numbers of the blue-collar workers were small compared to those of other social classes, the role that blue-collar workers played in the economic development of the country was of great significance, because any action such as a strike or work stoppage directly impacts the production process. Blue-collar workers had been active participants in the struggle for social transformation since the early 1960s. Table 1.2 shows the number of state industrial establishments and workers employed at various sectors of the economy in 1966.

The struggle of blue-collar workers for a radical transformation of the status quo failed in the 1960s and early 1970s because of their inability to

Table 1.2
State-Owned Industries, 1966

	No. of Industries	No. of Workers
Building materials		
Cement, tiles, marble, etc.	11	2,500
Food industry		
Flour mills, growing/processing		
foodstuffs, dried fruits, etc.	12	1,500
Cotton ginning and vegetables		
Oil mills	14	4,000
Manufacturing industry		
Leather and shoe	4	600
Chemicals, plastics, ceramics	7	200
Woodworking	6	670
Metal construction, motor repair, etc.	13	3,000
Textiles	18	9,000
Total	85	21,470

Source: Afghanistan Industrial Development Project, Checchi and Co. Final Report, Washington, D.C., and Kabul, September 1974.

combine their economic goals (e.g., demands for pay raises, worker compensation, etc.) with a political vision: the building of a neodemocratic society. This situation, together with workers' inability to form a union to defend their rights and guide their struggle, made it difficult for blue-collar workers to rise from a position of subordination to one of domination. The bureaucratic bourgeoisie and the feudal landowners thus retained their hold on the top rungs of the country's social ladder. Declining living standards at home and the oil-boom economy in the Middle East in the 1970s enticed an estimated 250,000 to 700,000 educated strata and laborers to leave Afghanistan. The majority of these people went to Iran, while others went to Saudi Arabia, Kuwait, and the United Arab Emirates. They sent money to their families in Afghanistan; remittance earnings of these laborers were estimated to be U.S.$20 million per month in 1979.[18]

Economic development did not occur evenly throughout the country, which exacerbated the dichotomy between rural and urban areas. The rural economy, which was primarily based on farming and animal husbandry, worsened and many agricultural laborers and rural poor migrated to urban centers in search of work, despite lacking the necessary skills to find employment. A vast majority of industrial and manufacturing industries were built in Kabul, with a limited number of such establishments in a few other provinces. By 1979 these industries employed an estimated 550,000 workers.[19]

The blue-collar workers suffered a major setback during the republican regime of 1973–1978 as the state banned political parties, assemblies, and labor unions. Political repression continued in the 1980s and the Soviet-installed government policy of "divide and conquer" led to the subjugation of the independent working-class movement. However, individual workers rallied in support of revolutionary organizations active in the liberation movement. Table 1.3 shows the composition of urban and rural populations in 1985.

AGRARIAN DEVELOPMENT PROGRAMS

Soon after the country's independence in 1919, the government, under the leadership of Amanullah, adopted new measures to reform the existing system of economy, which involved the introduction of the land tax and substitution of payments in kind with those of cash money. This measure was designed to promote money as the basis of exchange facilitating economic transaction throughout the country. The government also sold state-owned lands to government officials, moneylenders, and landlords and took steps to promote the development of local industries. Amanullah's modernization programs backfired when conservatives opposed his radical modernization programs. Conservatives incited public rebellion that eventually forced Amanullah to leave the country in 1929. The nine months of civil unrest following Amanullah's departure not only halted economic development but also affected the direction of modernization programs in the country.

Feudal oppression weighed heavily on the shoulders of the peasantry and sparked periodic peasant uprisings throughout the country. This situation prompted the state to embark upon policies aimed at providing land to landless peasants in order to deflect future uprisings. In the mid-1940s the state initiated agricultural development programs by bringing non-arable land under cultivation, and solicited financial aid and loans from the international community. The United States was a major donor of financial and technical aid to Afghanistan's economic development, evidenced in the building of the Hilmand Valley project in the southern region of Afghanistan. The project was designed to bring an estimated 300,000 hectares of land under cultivation for settling an estimated 15,000 farmers and nomads.[20]

The U.S.-based Morrison-Knudsen Company undertook construction of the project in 1945 and by 1952 it had completed the building of a 145-foot-high dam with a capacity of 157,085 hectare-feet of water.[21] When the

Table 1.3
Afghanistan's Population, 1985

Age	Total Population		Urban		Rural	
	Total	%	No.	%	No.	%
All ages	14,645,046	100.0	2,474,276	100.0	12,170,770	100.0
0–14	6,746,612	46.1	1,150,923	46.5	5,595,689	45.9
15–64	7,355,334	50.2	1,237,515	50.0	6,117,819	50.4
65+	543,100	3.7	85,838	3.5	457,262	3.7

Source: Central Statistics Office (CSO), *Statistical Yearbook 1985* (Kabul: CSO, 1986), pp. 16–17. Cited in Wali M. Rahimi, *Status of Women: Afghanistan* (Bangkok: UNESCO, Principal Regional Office for Asia and the Pacific, 1991), p. 20.

project was completed, the state settled an estimated 3,000 families, mainly Pushtuns, and about 1,200 nomads. The settlers were obligated to pay the balance of Afs. 16,800 (U.S.$320) over a twenty-year period. However, the project failed to produce the intended results of increased agricultural production to offset the high cost of the project. Although the state settled a number of farmers and nomads in the Hilmand Valley, problems soon emerged. The allotted land per family was too small to support a family and peasant residential housing was too far away from the land, which was inconvenient for tenants. In addition, the quality of the land in the area was poor, as plowed topsoil tended to wash away quickly or became saturated with salt.[22]

Development policies pursued by the state during three five-year plans, from 1956-1957 to 1971–1972, did not boost the country's economy but rather transformed the country's agricultural supply from surplus to self-sufficiency, and eventually to deficiency. The plight of the peasantry continued. Lack of financial institutions to lend money and credit to peasant farmers in times of need and crisis often forced them to mortgage their land to rich landowners. Rich landowners often provided loans to peasants at a high annual interest, and peasants who could not repay the loan had to forfeit their lands. In many instances rich landowners augmented the size of their land by purchasing land from poor peasants at a cheap price, often tricking them and sometimes forcing them to sell their land. In the event a peasant refused to sell his land, a feudal landowner might resort to underhanded tactics such as filing spurious lawsuits against the peasant. The exorbitant costs of lengthy litigation, resulting in lost income and lost time to work the land and maintain the family, often forced peasants to consider selling their lands. Local government officials often sided with feudal landowners against the peasants, leaving the latter with no other recourse but to submit to feudal landowners.

Afghanistan was declared a republic in the July 1973 coup, and the state announced progressive land taxes in July 1975. The land reform

[e]nvisaged the maximum size of holdings of 20 hectares for better lands and 40 hectares for poorer. Under the law the state redeemed surplus land from landowners over and above the established maximum on a deferred payment plan [over] the next twenty-five years, at two percent interest. The redeemed lands should be sold to landless peasants also on the deferred payment plan of twenty-five years and at the same interest rate.[23]

The Rural Development Board was established to conduct a survey of the land and categorize it into "better" and "poor" grades. The objective of issuing the progressive land tax was the imposition of exorbitant taxes on rich landowners, compelling them to sell their lands.[24] The land reform programs failed because the Cadastre Department had encountered numerous problems in implementing the reform and there was no uniform measurement of landholding throughout the country, making it difficult to determine exact plot sizes. Although President Mohammad Daoud issued edicts forbidding the sale of private land until after the completion of the land reform program, his brother, Mohammad Naim, sold his lands and transferred the proceeds to overseas bank accounts.[25] Furthermore, government officials in charge of land surveying used this opportunity to supplement their income by taking bribes and registering landholdings below the two categories of landholding proscribed by the state. For this reason many landowners registered their landholdings in the names of their children and successfully circumvented the reform. The government, however, distributed small plots of land to peasants and poor farmers. For example, in the Hilmand province, it provided 10,551 *jeribs* of land to 396 families in 1973 (5 *jeribs* = 1 hectare), 20,300 *jeribs* to 1,700 families in 1974, and 18,000 *jeribs* to 1,500 families in 1975.[26]

Modern agricultural production techniques were introduced in the early 1960s, when some 5,000 metric tons of chemical fertilizers were imported and distributed among a few lucky farmers in a few provinces. Most farmers and peasants did not understand the benefits of fertilizer, let alone how to apply it, and so were reluctant to use it at first, although modern methods of agriculture increased in subsequent years. In 1974 the use of chemical fertilizer increased from 78,000 to 80,000 metric tons, a 25 percent increase from the previous year, and the Agricultural Bank provided the sum of Afs. 763 million (U.S.$12.5 million) in loans to cooperatives, agricultural institutions, individual farmers, and groups of farmers, a rate increase of 44 percent from the previous year.[27] The amount of chemical fertilizers distributed to farmers increased from 9,000 metric tons in 1966–1967 to 100,027 tons in 1977–1978. Modern agricultural instruments also were introduced in some farming areas. By 1978 there were "253 tractors, 83 water pumps and 33 flour and rice mills. The distribution of agricultural machinery and tools [included] 283 diesel water pumps, 392 hand water pumps, 2,384 plows, 61 wheat cleaning machines, 12 threshing machines, 5 sprayers, 963 blade spades, 707 long point axes, 3,129 pitch forks, and 5,900 gate turnouts."[28]

Radical economic and agrarian reform was carried out soon after the 1978 April coup. The new regime issued two major decrees: Decree no. 6 was designed to reduce loans and mortgages. It exempted peasant farmers holding four hectares of land from paying debts and interests to landowners who mortgaged their land before 1975. Decree no. 8 limited the landholdings to six hectares of better land, with the rest being confiscated by the state. To implement the reform the regime dispatched young and inexperienced party members to the countryside, who confiscated lands from a few rich landowners and distributed them to peasants with certificates of entitlement. The methods by which the state carried out this land reform were severe and brutal and often resulted in the killing of those who resisted or opposed the reform. In most regions of the country people opposed the reform, considering it against their religious beliefs, and subsequently rebelled against the state.

The Kabul regime failed to fully implement its land reform programs because most peasants who received land lacked the necessary equipment to cultivate and harvest it and so remained dependent on landowners for seeds. In some cases when they were killed by feudal landowners the state failed to provide them protection. Nonetheless, the state declared the land reform a success. According to the government, a total of 739,000 hectares of land were distributed during the first phase of the land reform, which lasted from April 1978 to mid-December 1979. The primary recipients of the confiscated land were 300,000 landless or land-poor peasant families. They were allotted 665,000 hectares of mostly first-category (high grade) land. The remaining 74,000 hectares of land remained under state control, with 47,000 hectares earmarked for the establishment of new state farms and the remainder distributed to municipalities for urban development purposes.[29] Between 1978 and 1982, "The average farm size was 140 *jeribs* [5 *jeribs* = 1 hectare] in 1978, 131 *jeribs* in 1981 and 134 *jeribs* in 1982. The smallest average farm size was 10 *jeribs* in Kunar and the biggest was 1,226 *jeribs* in Farah. The average number of full-time farm workers was 4.6 in 1978, 2.9 in 1981 and 2.2 in 1982."[30]

The ruling party also declared that it had distributed approximately 80,000 hectares of first-category land to landless peasants in the period from mid-December 1979 to March 1984, and distributed about 112,000 metric tons of chemical fertilizers and 18,000 tons of improved seeds to farmers and peasants during the same period.[31] This claim could be an exaggeration; the war of national liberation could not help but interfere with such state programs.

GROWTH OF THE CAPITALIST ECONOMY

Although feudalism remained a dominant mode of production in Afghanistan, postfeudal modes of production such as commercial and industrial capitalism began to develop at the start of the twentieth century. The state encouraged the development of industries such as arms manufacturing, boot making, coin minting, textiles, and other ventures that served the interests of the country's armed forces. The native commercial bourgeoisie was not happy with the state policy of awarding privileges to foreign commercial bourgeoisie and wanted the state to abolish customs and tariffs and restrict the activities of their foreign counterparts, particularly the Indian merchants. This factor, together with growing disenchantment by patriotic and liberal-democratic forces agitating for political independence, led to King Habibullah's assassination on February 20,

1919, and the succession of his son Amanullah, who soon declared a war of independence from the British government. On August 8, 1919, the two countries signed the Rawalpindi Peace Treaty, which recognized Afghanistan's independence.

Modernization of the country's backward economic and social structure intensified soon after independence. To improve trade and commerce the state decided to build a railroad connecting the southern provinces to the northern provinces within a ten-year period, establish a communications line between Kabul and other provinces, and build power stations in Paghman, Jalalabad, and Qandahar. The state provided power to several existing industrial plants such as leather, cement, and match factories and built several other plants such as motor repair shops, hardware, soap, textile, carpentry, and so forth, in Qandahar and Herat provinces.[32]

State modernization programs suffered a setback in the mid-1920s when conservative forces opposed radical development policies, particularly those that restricted the privilege of clerics, a factor that compelled the state to rescind some of its reforms. The state devised policies that safeguarded and protected local mercantile classes and established the first *Shirkat,* a joint stock company whose partners were mainly members of the ruling elites and the king himself.[33] By the late 1920s there were an estimated twenty trade enterprises. The state granted the *shirkat*s

[m]onopoly rights to procure and market staple commodities. As a result, the position of foreign merchants in the country was somewhat weakened. [Amanullah] proposed that a state bank be set up, with a view to using merchant capital for the needs of the state. But the merchants, who feared to trust their money to the state, demanded that the bank be private, and did not support the proposal.[34]

After Amanullah's downfall in 1929 and Habibullah's seizure of power for nine months, political instability hampered sound economic development. However, the economy began to revive in the 1930s. Merchants and traders who suffered during the nine-month civil war, and who earlier had emphatically rejected state proposals to build *shirkat*s, now rallied in support of the new state headed by Mohammad Nadir, 1929–1933, as Nadir steadfastly defended their vested interests. Nadir not only abolished Amanullah's progressive social and cultural programs but also Amanullah's economic reforms. He introduced new measures that revived and protected the interests of feudal landowners and encouraged the growth of private entrepreneurs. State assurance to promote the private sector enticed a significant number of businessmen to engage in commercial and trade activities, and some of this group even formed partnerships with the ruling elites in the state bureaucracy. Abdul Majid Zabuli was a well-known businessman and with the support of the government he monopolized imports and exports in the country. The mercantile and trading strata had successfully strengthened their position to the extent that they could easily influence the direction of economic development. They achieved this by offering members of the ruling elites and top government officials expensive presents, interest-free loans, and other expensive gifts on occasions such as marriages, engagements of their children, and so on.

The ruling class in the state apparatus did not pay greater attention to further develop local industries except those that benefited their class. However, the state made some concerted efforts to develop the financial and commercial sectors of the economy. In 1930, Shirkat-e-Sahami, the Joint Stock Company, was established and two years later the company was transformed into Bank-e-Milli, the National Bank. The bank started its operation with an initial capital of U.S.$3.5 million and had an estimated 2,000 shareholders. Soon it opened branches both inside and outside the country and was in complete control of the country's trade and business sectors. The number of other private and joint stock ventures increased, and in 1932–1934 there were approximately thirty such ventures throughout the country. In Kabul, major companies that exported *qaraqul* fur included Sabir (initial capital Afs. 6 million), Tawakul and Baradaran (capital Afs. 1 million each), Ghanat (capital Afs. 1.25 million), and Khushish (capital Afs. 1.5 million). Companies in the northern areas of the country that exported lambskin were Aybak, Salamt, Saadat, Ikhlas, and Maimana, each with initial capital of Afs. 1 million. The Kabul Petroleum Company was the largest import enterprise, establishing its virtual monopoly on importing oil, and serving as a liaison to foreign companies. Other exporting companies included Etminan, in Herat, for export of wool and lambskin; Itihadiya-e-Shamali, for export of *qaraqul* fur and import of cement and other consumer items; and the Pushtun Company, in Qandahar, for export of dried fruits. To further stimulate growth of the private sectors of the economy the state leased the Jab al-Seraj Textile Mill, and match and leather factories, to private businessmen.[35] To centralize the country's financial activities, the state established Da Afghanistan Bank in 1939. It was the largest bank in the country and by 1972 it had 1,803 local and six foreign employees,[36] and had monopolized all foreign exchange transactions with branches both within and outside the country. Private capital holders were less interested in the development of production, as they saw their vested interest in trading with foreign countries.

In the mid-1950s the state supported foreign capital to boost the development of the local economy. Various expatriate capitals began investing in Afghanistan. For example, Pan-American, in partnership with local entrepreneurs, established the Aryana Airlines Company in 1954; Siemens, a West German electronics industry, exported goods and opened a maintenance and repair plant; Franklin Printing Press was established for the Ministry of Education; and a ceramic factory was built in Qunduz with Japanese aid.[37] Although the economic system was based on a mixture of laissez-faire and planned economy, the latter dominated economic development activities, especially during the rule of Prime Minister Mohammad Daoud, 1953–1963. The state devised a blueprint for economic development based on a five-year plan that lasted until 1963. During this period Afghanistan received substantial economic and technical aid from the Soviet Union to modernize its economy. Development from above paved the road for the bureaucratic bourgeoisie within the state apparatus to establish their monopoly on major light and heavy industries. Major local manufacturing plants included cotton, wool, rayon, textiles, casings, refined sugar, shoes, cement, and food processing. The country's endowed natural resources such as lapis lazuli, gold, chrome, lead, iron ore, zinc, talc, copper, sulfur, coal, salt, oil and natural gas, and precious and semiprecious gems also remained an exclusive monopoly of the state. Expansion of the finance economy during this period also led to the establishment in 1954 of a new bank, Bank-e-Tejarati Pashtany.

The laissez-faire policy created by the state in the mid-1960s and early 1970s led to significant growth of private sectors of the economy. New financial enterprises were established during this period, including the Afghan Insurance Company, 1963; Kohdamam Credit Cooperative, 1969; the Agricultural Development Bank, 1970; Baghlan Credit Cooperation, 1971; and the Three Insurance Agencies and the Industrial Development Bank, 1973. A new investment bill, which was approved by the state in the late 1960s, further stimulated the country's economic development. It encouraged greater foreign investment in Afghanistan and included among its advantages "[a] five-year tax holiday and duty-free imports of capital goods and raw materials. Investors were also exempted from corporate and personal income taxes. No export duties were levied on the export output of government approved projects. Foreign personnel of approved enterprises were allowed to repatriate 70 percent of their income after taxes."[38]

Economic development and expansion of trade necessitated building modern roads. The Kabul-Jalalabad road linked Kabul to Peshawar, Pakistan, and the road proceeding through the Salang pass connected Kabul to the southern borders of the Soviet Central Asian republics. Similarly the Kabul-Qandahar-Herat road connected Kabul to Iran through the border in Islam Qala and via Chaman to Quetta, Pakistan. Tribal communities in Qandahar, and the Mangal tribes who felt that modern roads would threaten their traditional autonomy and remove the income derived from the caravan traffic, revolted against government road-building in 1959; however, the state subdued the resistance.[39] Other modern plants built in the 1960s included

[t]he Naghlu Hydroelectric Power Station with a capacity of 100,000 kilowatts . . . the Jalalabad irrigation system with the Darunta power station, 1965, which made it possible to establish four farms in the region in subsequent years, gas fields in the north, and a 365-kilometer gas pipeline between Afghanistan and Soviet

Central Asia, 1968, after which Afghanistan began to export gas to the Soviet Union.[40]

The national bourgeoisie, who still had one foot on the land and the other in the business trade, could not effectively compete with the influx of foreign capital. It fell to a subordinate position and could no longer effect significant influence on the economic, social, and political development in the country. The bureaucratic bourgeoisie, however, supported by international capital, retained its dominant position in matters of economic development and requested aid, credits, and loans from a number of economically developed countries.

The terms and conditions of external aid changed from one plan to another. During the first plan, interest rates averaged 1.85 percent, with a grace period of about 9 to 10 years and repayment periods extending to 25 years. During the second plan these terms changed to an interest rate of 1.59 percent with a grace period of 11 years and a repayment period of 20 years. Terms and conditions became more difficult during the third plan, when average interest rates increased to 2.19 percent; the grace period was cut to 5 years and repayment period reduced to 15–16 years.[41]

By 1965 repayment of foreign loans was running as high as U.S.$7 million annually and within five years repayment on earlier loans were estimated to be U.S.$25 million, roughly equal to or over 30 percent of Afghanistan's export earnings.[42] Table 1.4 lists foreign loans and grants to Afghanistan between 1952 and 1972.

New economic development policies, based on a seven-year plan, were formulated during the republican regime, 1973–1978. The state relied on foreign loans and grants for implementation of its development projects, which included building a railroad connecting Kabul to Pakistan via Chaman in Qandahar, and to Iran via the Islam Qala border in Herat, as well as the building of several new plants such as textile, cement, sugar, and the like. However, the state could not implement most of the projects due to lack of financial resources.

Between 1973 and 1976 Afghanistan received U.S.$80.7 million from the United States and U.S.$1.03 billion from the Soviet Union for its development projects.[43] The country's repayment of interests from foreign loans in 1975 alone was estimated at U.S.$7.3 million.[44] In 1975 Afghanistan's exports were mainly animal casings, fruits, oil seeds, skin (raw leather), rugs and carpets, natural gas, cement, medical herbs, fur coats, urea fertilizer, and the like, with a total value of U.S.$225 million. Its imports were sugar, tobacco, tea, vegetable oil, medicine, textiles, metal, vehicles and machinery, shoes, spare parts, and the like, valued at U.S.$220.7 million, of which U.S.$2 million was used clothing and U.S.$21 million was tex-

Table 1.4
Foreign Loans and Grants, 1952–1972 (in U.S.$ millions)

	Total Loans	Total Grants
USSR	572.0	100.0
USA	99.3	313.5
West Germany	67.3	31.0
China	33.6	—
Czechoslovakia	12.0	—
Yugoslavia	8.0	—
World Bank	10.0	—
France	10.0	14.0
India	5.4	2.0
Japan	3.0	—
Asian Development Bank	2.2	—
United Kingdom	1.0	1.0

Source: Mohammad Siddiq Farhang, *Afghanistan dar Panj Qarn-e-Akhir* [Afghanistan in the Last Five Centuries], vol. 2 (Peshawar, Pakistan: Author, 1373/1994), p. 777.

tile products.[45] The state failed to devise and implement economic programs to augment the production capacity of the manufacturing and industrial establishments to effectively compete for markets.

After the 1978 April coup the new regime devised radical development programs that stressed state control of the economy and collectivization of private land. The country's agricultural productivity declined in the 1980s because of state collectivization of agricultural farms and the escalating war of national liberation and fell even further in the post-Soviet era when civil war raged throughout the country. In 1990 agriculture accounted for 53 percent of the country's GDP, while industry and service sectors accounted for 28.5 and 18.5 percent respectively.[46] Through most of the 1990s a major source of farmers' income was derived from cultivation of poppies, which led to Afghanistan becoming a major opium-producing nation.

WESTERN CULTURAL INFLUENCE

Capitalist development not only integrated Afghanistan's economy with the world economy but also paved the road for capitalist ideological and cultural influences. Western technologies and industries required the training of professional workers, managers, and administrators. A great number of the country's intellectuals were sent to Europe, the United States, and other countries to acquire modern skills and technical knowledge. Western culture also established its influence in Afghanistan because of a massive influx of foreign consumer items, including used clothing.

A number of small businessmen were engaged in the import of used Western clothes and their customers were mainly people of low-income families. In Kabul and several other major cities there were many stores selling used clothes. One of the centers in Kabul was pejoratively called the "Nixon Market" (the name changed with the U.S. presidents until the 1978 April coup, which declared Afghanistan a democratic republic). Used clothes constituted one of the country's import items from the United States, and the effect of this clothing on local textile industries has been described in these words:

Last year [1976] the leading US export to Afghanistan was used clothing, totaling about $900,000. But like the irate tribesmen at the annual bazaar, traditionalists are quick to see the destructive nature of such trends. Though insignificant for the US, the influence of old clothes here has all but killed Afghanistan's age-old hand-loom industry. . . . The more expensive home-spun clothes simply cannot compete with the cheap machine-sewn foreign castoffs that seem to herald the first invasion of Western industrialism into this remote land.[47]

The period of 1955–1973 is considered to be the peak period of Western cultural influences in the country, which manifested itself in terms of dress, eating habits, lifestyle, and so on. This trend of development led to changes in consumption patterns and lifestyle, reinforced by advertising agencies, and to changes in the attitudes of the professional and technocratic elites toward identifying themselves with the culture and lifestyle of the metropole, the United States, and the Soviet Union and its respective blocs.

Modern nightclubs and hotels opened in Kabul. Fashion shows featuring Western dress were held in most of Kabul's prestigious hotels, such as the Intercontinental Hotel, the Spinzar Hotel, and the Kabul Hotel. A well-known historian graphically described Western capitalist cultural influence on women in Afghanistan in the following words:

[The] Afghan girl is experiencing a new freedom in living and in new ways of dressing. Instead of dressing in the ways her mother did at her age, an educated Afghan girl slips quickly into exactly the kind of costume worn by her counterpart in London, Paris or New York. Instead of plaiting her hair, she bobs it in European fashion, pulls on some fine nylon stockings, pushes her feet into moccasins, and dabs her smiling lips with bright red lipsticks.[48]

The local press and other media also began to promote the modern lifestyle through writings and advertisements. One of the latest features of the Western-oriented modernization projects carried out in the local press was the promotion of beauty pageants in Kabul. The weekly *Juwandun* initiated the project with the approval of the ruling-class families. A committee composed of several men and women was delegated the task of selecting the most beautiful girl from among hundreds of contestants, to be named "Girl of the Year."[49]

Women of ruling-class and upper-middle-class families usually identified themselves with Occidental culture and were eager to emulate elements of Western lifestyles. These privileged families usually delegated most of the domestic chores such as cooking, cleaning, and care of the children to servants. In Kabul, these women spent much of their leisure time discussing the latest fashions and participated in various outdoor recreational activities such as volleyball, basketball, swimming, and tennis. By the 1960s all types of Western cultural shows (e.g., pop music, rock and roll, and jazz) flourished in Kabul, and the upper and middle classes often attended them:

The younger generation has listened to overseas broadcasts and, in local record shops, has access to a large stock of relatively recent records and tapes from Europe and the United States. The audience at the rock festival reflected this generation gap. A vast majority of the audience was Afghan, and all were young. . . . The Afghans were almost equally divided between male and female, many unaccompanied. Several women wore *chadari* . . . but most sported the latest Western fashions, including high, platform shoes. The audience consisted mainly of Kabul University and High School students, members of the growing, urban middle class in Kabul where the overwhelming majority were born and bred. At first quiet and subdued (and physically cold), the crowd warmed up as the concert progressed. It never exhibited the frenzies of crowds at similar concerts in the West, but hand clapping, foot stomping and cries of delight punctuated the performances.[50]

One of the most swiftly growing trends of Westernization in Kabul during this period was fashion. Fashion addicts spent huge sums of money to purchase modern Western outfits. Western clothes such as miniskirts and sleeveless dresses were seen on the streets of the capital. Many fashionable items were available in the "Nixon Market" as well as in many other shopping centers in urban areas. Women of upper-middle-class backgrounds purchased brand-new Western-imported clothing from various department stores in Kabul. Others bought the material and took it to a tailor to have dresses custom-made in the latest styles. Women from lower-class families who could not afford to purchase new items, bought used clothing and altered them in an attempt to look elegant and fashionable. This semi-modernization trend and change in lifestyle of the urban population did not spread into rural areas, but nonetheless provoked hostility by clerics and religious fundamentalists in all regions.

In the spring of 1970, more than 2,000 mullahs, clergy and *qazi,* judges from every section of the country converged on the capital. Parading almost daily to the Wulusi Jirgah (the house of representatives), they demanded a crackdown on Marxist influence and Western immorality, specifically miniskirts, coeducation, and alcohol. Subsequent riots by mullahs in the cities of Jalalabad and Ghazni revived memoirs of the forces that ousted King Amanullah in 1929, although a loyal and well-equipped army barred any replay in 1970.[51]

Despite opposition by clerics and conservatives, modernization programs continued throughout the 1970s. Modernization and women's emancipation meant different things for two groups of women—the revolutionaries and the liberals. Women's emancipation to the first group meant a complete rupture in the system and its ideology, politics, and culture. To the liberals, who primarily belonged to upper- and middle-class families, it simply meant cosmetic changes resulting in mimicry of the more ostentatious features of Western cultural behaviors and lifestyles (e.g., wearing form-fitting or revealing clothing, styling hair, wearing cosmetics and perfume). Such views have been vividly reflected in complaints by three female students of Kabul University whose families hosted three American female exchange students in 1974. The girls decried what they saw as degeneration of women's emancipation, stating that "these American girls did not wear bras, shaved under their arms, and always wore blue jeans."[52]

In the 1980s a new political culture emerged when the Kabul regime made a concerted effort to indoctrinate youths and state employees with their new outlook. The ruling PDPA party banned independent political and civic organizations, viewing them as a threat to Soviet-style socialism and its corresponding cultural values, and arrested and executed members and activists of the countercultural movement. To popularize Soviet-style culture the Kabul regime opened new cultural centers and sent children and youths for political and cultural orientation to the Soviet Union and its bloc countries. However, the PDPA failed to maintain its domination and eventually was forced to transfer power to a coalition of Islamic parties in 1992.

When the Islamic parties seized power they articulated a new policy aimed at building an Islamic society and its corresponding culture and politics. The new era required women to wear a *hijab,* a veil covering their bodies from head to toe. The new measure only affected a small stratum of educated women in urban areas. It also forced men to grow thick beards, discard Western clothes, and wear traditional long shirts, loose pants, and turbans. Nightclubs and theaters were closed and other forms of popular entertainment were banned; books and printed media perceived to be anti-Islamic were removed from public libraries.

Islamicization of an already Muslim society was furthered when the Taliban seized Kabul in 1996 and expanded their domination over other regions of the country. The Taliban declared that they would observe strict adherence to the Sharia, as they perceived it, mandating an army of enforcers to do everything at their disposal to implement it. A culture and politics emerged that denounced non-Islamic cultural heritage of the country's past era and condoned its destruction, exemplified in the pulverization in March 2001 of the two historic statues of the Buddha carved into the cliff-face in Bamiyan province around A.D. 250–300. The new culture defied diversity and cultural pluralism, viewing the country's diverse ethnic culture and traditions as a potential threat to consolidation of Islamic rule rather than viewing diversity as a source of strength. A culture began to take shape that had no regard for individual freedom but aspired to build a highly regimented Islamic society that was perceived to be a model of Islamic purity in the twenty-first century.

NOTES

1. U.S. Central Intelligence Agency, *The World Factbook 2000* (Washington, D.C.: CIA, 2000), p. 1.

2. Ibid., p. 1.

3. For details, see Barbara F. Grimes (ed.), *Ethnologue: Languages of the World*, 13th ed. (Dallas: Summer Institute of Linguistics, 1996).

4. Maliha Zulfacar, *Afghan Immigrants in the USA and Germany: A Comparative Analysis of the Use of Ethnic Social Capital* (Munster: Lit Verlag, 1998), p. i.

5. Harvey H. Smith et al. (eds.), *Area Handbook for Afghanistan* (Washington, D.C.: U.S. Government Printing Office, 1973), p. 271.

6. Ibid., p. 272.

7. Hafizullah Emadi, *State, Revolution, and Superpowers in Afghanistan* (New York: Praeger, 1990). For more details, see Ministry of Planning, *Afghan Agriculture in Figures*, Qaus 1357 (Kabul: Government Printing House, 1978), p. 21.

8. Raja Anwar, *The Tragedy of Afghanistan: A First Hand Account*, translated from the Urdu by Khalid Hasan (London: Verso, 1988), p. 130.

9. Ghulam Omar Saleh, "The Economical Geography of Afghanistan," *Afghanistan* 19:3 (July–September 1963): 38.

10. Sayed Bahaouddin Majrooh and Sayed Mohammad Yusuf Elmi, *The Sovietization of Afghanistan* (Peshawar, Pakistan: Afghan Information Center, 1986), pp. 163–164.

11. Anwar, *Tragedy of Afghanistan*, p. 129.

12. Cited in Fazal-ur-Rahman Marwat, *The Evolution and Growth of Communism in Afghanistan, 1917–1979: An Appraisal* (Karachi: Royal Book Company, 1997), p. 20.

13. This comment was made by a local cleric when he addressed an audience in a private house in Kabul, 1978.

14. Yuri V. Gankovsky et al., *A History of Afghanistan*, translated from the Russian by Vitaly Baskakov (Moscow: Progress Publishers, 1985), p. 280.

15. Mir-Ahmed B. Zekrya, "Planning and Development in Afghanistan: A Case of Maximum Foreign Aid and Minimum Growth" (Ph.D. thesis, Johns Hopkins University, 1976), p. 23.

16. For details, see Emadi, *State, Revolution, and Superpowers*.

17. *Afghanistan Industrial Development Projects*, Checchi and Co. Final Report, Washington, D.C., and Kabul, September 1974.

18. Richard F. Nyrop and Donald M. Seekins, *Afghanistan: A Country Study*, Foreign Area Studies, the American University (Washington, D.C.: U.S. Government Printing Office, 1986), p. 173.

19. International Labor Organization, *Yearbook of Labour Statistics* (Geneva: 1982), p. 52.

20. Mir Ghulam Mohammad Ghubar, *Afghanistan dar Msir-e-Tarikh* [Afghanistan in the Path of History], vol. 2 (Herndon, Va.: Hishmat Khalil Ghubar, 1999), p. 221.

21. Louis Dupree, *Afghanistan* (Princeton: Princeton University Press, 1973), p. 484.

22. Ibid., p. 504.

23. Vladimir Glukhoded, "The Economy of Independent Afghanistan," in *Afghanistan: Past and Present*, 2nd ed., Oriental Studies in the USSR, no. 3 (Moscow: Academy of Sciences, 1981), p. 234.

24. Mir Mohammad Siddiq Farhang, *Afghanistan dar Panj Qarn-e-Akhir* [Afghanistan in the Last Five Centuries], vol. 3 (Peshawar, Pakistan: 1373/1994), p. 20.

25. Ibid., pp. 20–21.

26. *Social, Economic, and Development Plan: Republic of Afghanistan, 1354* [1975], translated and edited by the UN Development Program (UNDP) (Kabul: UNDP, November 3, 1975), p. 98.

27. Ibid., p. 6.

28. Majrooh and Elmi, *The Sovietization of Afghanistan*, p. 165.

29. Ministry of Foreign Affairs, *Achievements of the April Revolution in Afghanistan* (Kabul: Ministry of Foreign Affairs, 1984), pp. 15–18.

30. Mohammad Qasim Yusufi, "Effects of the War on Agriculture," in *The Tragedy of Afghanistan: The Social, Cultural, and Political Impact of the Soviet Invasion*, Bo Huldt and Erland Jansson (eds.) (London: Croom Helm, 1988), p. 205.

31. Ministry of Foreign Affairs, *Achievements of the April Revolution*, p. 20.

32. Mir Ghulam Mohammad Ghubar, *Afghanistan dar Masir-e-Tarikh* [Afghanistan in the Path of History] (Qum, Iran: Payam-e-Muhajir, 1359/1980), p. 791. Critical of the regime, this book was seized by the government immediately after it was published in 1346/1967. It was not made available to the public until the pro-Soviet PDPA seized power in April 1978.

33. Gankovsky, *History of Afghanistan*, p. 215.

34. Ibid., p. 216.

35. Vartan Gregorian, *The Emergence of Modern Afghanistan: Politics of Reform and Modernization, 1880–1946* (Stanford, Calif.: Stanford University Press, 1969), pp. 315–316. The exchange value of U.S.$1 was estimated at Afs. 10–12 between 1932 and 1934.

36. Maxwell J. Fry, *The Afghan Economy: Money, Finance, and the Critical Constraints to Economic Development* (Leiden: E. J. Brill, 1974), p. 96.

37. Gankovsky, *History of Afghanistan*, p. 252.

38. *Quarterly Economic Review: Pakistan, Bangladesh, Afghanistan*, no. 2 (London: Economist Intelligence Unit, 1967), p. 15.

39. Andrew Wilson, "Inside Afghanistan: A Background to Recent Troubles," *Royal Central Asian Journal* 47:3–4 (July–October 1960): 288.

40. Gankovsky, *History of Afghanistan*, p. 269.

41. Zekrya, "Planning and Development in Afghanistan," p. 73.

42. Anthony Hyman, *Afghanistan Under Soviet Domination, 1964–91*, 3rd ed. (London: Macmillan Press, 1992), p. 34.

43. U.S. Agency for International Development, *Helping People* (Kabul: USAID, April 1976), p. 35; and *Quarterly Economic Review*, 1976, p. 18; 1977, p. 17.

44. *Social, Economic, and Development Plan*, statistical app., tab. 6.

45. Ibid., tabs. 7–8.

46. U.S. Central Intelligence Agency, *World Factbook.*

47. Harry Kramer, "Out of Isolation: Afghanistan Is Pushing Toward the Twentieth Century with Bold Spending Plan, but Tribesmen Resist," *The Wall Street Journal*, September 2, 1977, p. 22.

48. Mohammed Ali, *The Afghans*, 3rd ed. (Kabul: Kabul University, 1969), pp. 77–78.

49. Author's personal notes and observation of developments in Kabul.

50. Louis Dupree, "It Wasn't Woodstock, But: The First International Rock Festival in Kabul," *AUFS Reports* 20:2 (May 1976): 6.

51. Marvin G. Weinbaum, "Afghanistan: Nonparty Parliamentary Democracy," *The Journal of Developing Areas* 7:1 (October 1972): 71.

52. Sondra Howell Bechhoefer, "Education and the Advancement of Women in Afghanistan" (M.A. thesis, University of Maryland, 1975), p. 222.

2

Gender Polity:
The Status of Women

The status of women is manifested in women's access to economic, political, educational, and organizational resources outside the home. With the emergence of classes and division of labor, men gained control of the resources in the public realm and women's role was to increase production and reproduction. Modernization policies to end gender-based inequalities since the country's independence in 1919 were often resisted by conservative tribal leaders, clerics, and feudal landlords. Although the government succeeded in consolidating its authority by assimilating some of these forces into its power structure, building roads, and improving communications networks to link villages to urban centers, tribalism and regionalism continued to hamper modernization. And although local customs and traditions varied from one region to another and from one tribe to the next, women's subordination to men is a common feature in all the diverse segments of the country's population.

IMAGES OF WOMEN IN THE GENDER SYSTEM

Afghanistan is a mosaic of various ethnic and linguistic communities. Despite their cultural and linguistic differences, their attitude toward women, to a large extent, is similar. The perception of women's role in society is largely determined by a combination of tribal cultural mores and religious precepts as understood by men. Although some tribes treat women with some respect and impose fewer restrictions on them, this

does not negate the fact that patriarchy and its prevailing culture and traditions dictate moral codes of conduct for women.

Central to the patriarchal systems is the universal intellectual paradigm
of androcentrism, which rests on the common belief that maleness is the
natural order of things. In Abrahamic tradition God is male and created
the female after his own image, sanctioning women to submit to men and
obey their orders and leadership because men are considered superior to
women. In Islamic traditions men are not only required to support women
but are also responsible for disciplining them.

Women who are virtuous are obedient to God and guard the hidden as God has
guarded it. As for women you feel are averse, talk to them suasively; then leave
them alone in bed (without molesting them) and go to bed with them (when they
are willing). If they open out to you, do not seek an excuse for blaming them
(4:34). If any of your women is guilty of fornication, bring four of your men to
give evidence; if they testify against them, retain them in the houses until death,
or until God provide some other way for them (4:15).[1]

Although women work outside the home and contribute to the family's
income, men are regarded as the sole provider and guardian of the family.
Men are described with attributes such as *asl*, noble by birth, *baghayrat*,
brave, and *banamus*, a term used to denote a man's ability to discipline
women of the family. Women who are submissive to men are referred to
as *pakdaman*, pure, *bahaya*, modest, *padardar*, noble, and so on. Intellectuals
of the patriarchal system vigorously defend male superiority and women's
inferior position. For example, the following poems by an acclaimed
Persian poet, Muslihuddin Sa'di (born A.D. 1175), instruct the husband concerning his obligations toward the wife:

Dar-e-khurami bar saray-i buband	Close the door of happiness in a house,
Ki bangi zan az way bar ayad buland	Where one hears women's loud voices
Chu zan ray-e-bazaar girad bezan	If a woman visits the market you beat her,
Wagarna tu dar khana benshin chu zan.[2]	Otherwise you stay home like a woman.

Despite prescribing harsh discipline for women who talk to strangers and
chastising men for lack of courage in controlling their women, Sa'di also
instructed men how to enjoy themselves by marrying a new wife. He
wrote:

Chu dar roye bigana khandid zan	When a woman smiles to a stranger
Digar mard gu lafi mardi mazan	Tell him [husband] not to brag about his manliness
Ze biganagan chashmi zan kur bad	Blind be the eyes of women to strangers

Chu birun shud az khana dar gur bad   If they leave the homes they would
rather be dead

Zan-e-naw kun ay dust har naw bahar   Oh friend, marry a new wife in every
spring

Ke taqwim-e-parina nayad bakar.[3]   An old calendar ought to be discarded.

Other poems composed by men use abusive language toward women and regard women who visit markets not as decent women but as crude animals:

Zan ke dar kochaha butak bashad   A woman on the street is just [an attractive] doll

Zan nabashad chu macha sag bashad.[4]   She is not a woman, but a female dog.

The comparison of women to dolls and animals reflects a mindset in backward communities that regarded women as useless creatures of lowly position prone to senseless acts if left to their own devices.

The patriarchal society views women as inferior to men in both intellect and nature. Women in general are referred to as *naqis-e-aql*, lacking wisdom, *badal*, impure, *kam asl*, imperfect by birth, and so on. The position of women is so low that the term *woman* is often used by men to insult opponents who lack courage and initiative, and so forth. Women are discriminated against even from birth. If a boy is born, the family celebrates the occasion because a son in a patriarchal society is considered to be a preserver of the family's name and inherits the property. If the baby is a girl, the occasion goes without notice because a girl is considered to be disposable property destined to enter another's home upon marriage.

Women are treated as personal chattel to be sold and purchased by men. Although women have personal names, upon marriage they are not called by their own names but by their husband's or sometimes by their eldest son's name. Society and its cultural traditions have inculcated the concept of self-denial to women to the extent that most women do not even introduce themselves or call each other by their personal names but by their husband's or their father's name. A woman is prohibited from addressing an older man by his name, nor should she be addressed by her own name by anyone younger than she. She may not walk ahead of her husband or an elder male family member. In general, she is prohibited from direct speech or actions of any kind. Men use indirect language when they refer to female members of the family, and it is construed as an unpardonable insult if a man inquires after or mentions another man's female relatives by their personal names. They use oblique phrases such as *khanawada*, family, when inquiring about female members of the household. Women are raised to depend on men and even women who head a household need men to mediate with the outside world if the husband is not home. Women are brought up to believe in their own natural inferiority and even feel shame and disgust regarding their menstruation. A woman of the Maduzai, a subtribe of the Durani tribes in the Saripul region in northern areas of Afghanistan, described the mistaken belief in women's innate inferiority in her own words:

Why aren't women free? Because they have many devils, while men have few. In the beginning women went to the mosques but then one woman was obscene and insulted the Mullah, and the women were sent away. Men among themselves would not behave like this; women are corrupt, putrid. Women are not clean in the eyes of religion because they menstruate and bear children. If the women went to the mosque, then they and the men would desire each other, and if a devil messed up the prayers it would be blasphemous. And too, if women gathered in mosques, there would certainly be fighting; men don't fight even if there are twenty of them, but three women fight, and if there are twenty women, then there are twenty fights. . . . Men fight about the government and so on, but it doesn't matter—they do not gossip.[5]

Society has unwritten rules concerning female morals and codes of conduct. It requires that a woman should be quiet, retiring, and modest. Demonstrative mannerisms, laughing, or speaking loudly are considered social offenses, as is approaching or speaking to an unrelated male or a stranger under any circumstances. Women are considered to be less valuable than animals in some rural areas. For example, in the northern part of the country, some wealthy Turkmen regard their horses to be more important than their wives. The *bays*, rich landowners who in the past kept horses for the purpose of launching quick raids on their enemies, now regard horses as an indispensable asset in the political rivalry during the *buzkashi*, a game popular among the wealthy.[6] A Turkman proverb portrays a Turkman's attitude toward horses and women: "If you have one day left of your life, take a horse; if you have two days left, take a woman." In a similar vein, nomads, who keep camels and use them as a means of transportation, consider camels to be at least as important and valuable as women. According to them, "a good woman is like a transport-camel. She is sturdily built, has big, strong legs, a steady gait and is clean."[7] Such a physically strong woman plays a major role in loading and unloading animals and doing heavy-duty chores and is regarded as beautiful, and a prospective husband is often required to pay a higher bridal price to marry her.

The concept of women as a private property is extremely strong among some nomadic tribes; indeed, some tribes even tattoo their women with the same marks they put on their animals.[8] The prevailing practice of treating women as personal belongings is particularly pervasive among the illiterate rural populace, who simply ignore the existence of women in society. For example, it has been observed that some men deposit their women in a designated public area when they visit the city to attend to business, and the women must wait for their husbands for an hour or longer until they return. Although there is no designated public space catering to women's needs, men are largely to be blamed for neglecting their wives. Women cannot wait for their husbands in restaurants and teahouses that cater mostly to male customers. There have been instances where men simply "parked their wives like cars when they went somewhere, eyes facing the wall, and left them there for two hours."[9]

SECLUSION AND RESTRICTIONS

The culture of treating women as personal property necessitated ways and means of their protection, which often resulted in the confinement of women at home and their isolation from men who are not related to the family. Although there are references in the Quran regarding etiquette and modesty for women, men often quote such verses to justify women's seclusion:

Tell the believing women to lower their eyes, guard their private parts, and not display their charms except what is apparent outwardly, and cover their bosoms with their veils and not to show their finery except to their husbands or their fathers or fathers-in-law, their sons or step-sons, brothers, or their brothers' and sisters' sons, or their women attendants or captives, or male attendants who do not have any need (for women), or boys not yet aware of sex. They should not walk stomping their feet lest they make known what they hide of their ornaments (24:31).[10]

Based on individual understanding of religious scriptures and tribal codes of conduct, men forbade their women from talking to men other than immediate relatives. Prevailing cultural norms demanded that women cover themselves whenever they encountered strangers. In urban areas, women of conservative and traditional families wear a *chadari*, veil, when they leave home to visit relatives or go shopping. The veil covers their bodies from head to toe, with only a small textile net for them to see through. Some women use a *chadari* but underneath wear Western clothing, such as skirts and slacks. In rural areas where men are more self-restrained and families know one another, women do not wear a *chadari* when they go out to visit relatives or work on the farm. Whenever these women encounter a stranger they run away and hide if possible; otherwise they wrap a *chadar*, the long scarf that is part of their costume, around themselves and turn their backs until the stranger passed. However, a few men in the rural areas who become economically prosperous insist that their wives observe *hijab* (seclusion), as they no longer see the need for them to work outside the home. Wearing a *chadari* or observing seclusion was alien to the culture of nomadic women, who did not cover their face when they encountered strangers.

Strict social traditions and customs restrict women's mobility in public spheres. Sexual segregation of space exists in most public areas. For instance, women are allotted special places in public transport, and the first few seats in the front row of every type of public transportation are reserved for women. Some restaurants and teahouses have special curtained rooms for women, but not many women dine in such places. Women are restricted from participation in the formal communal observances of religious rituals such as *namaz*, five daily prayers, when men are in the same room. They perform the *namaz* and say the *dua*, prayers of wishes and supplication to God, in their homes.

Women's spiritual life mostly centers around the local *ziyaratgah*s (shrines), cooking and preparing ritual food and bringing votive offerings.[11] However, a few women of affluent families make the *hajj*, pilgrimage, to Mecca. Prior to the outbreak of the civil war in 1992, in certain urban areas women visited *ziyaratgah*s on specific days designated as "women's day." On these days women would normally begin assembling at these places early in the morning and by the late morning all women might be present in the surrounding courtyard. The women would arrive swathed in the traditional *chadar*, but threw back the veils from their faces as they entered the compound, one of the few places where they could do so. Both women and children would dress in their best finery; it was as much a rare social occasion as a religious event.[12]

Although traditional families do not allow women to leave their homes without a legitimate reason, women are allowed to visit places such as women's public baths, women's hospitals and clinics, and the houses of their immediate relatives and very close female friends, known as *khahar khanda*. They may attend engagement and wedding parties, which are as a rule segregated by sex. Women are excluded from social gatherings with men in their own homes. If a family receives a guest who is not an immediate relation of the family, female members of the family are not permitted to entertain the guest. This tradition is relatively relaxed among some ethnic and tribal communities, but very strict among others. A recent study of the Durani tribe in the northern regions of Afghanistan indicated that a Durani woman was less restricted in her environment and that, "within the household, Durani women expressed little sexual segregation and women were able to entertain male guests when a man was not present or available to do so."[13] However, women are more restricted among many other Pushtun tribes. The seclusion of Pushtun women from the public has been described in these words:

A [Pushtun] may also invite you to his home, but either he or another man will carry in the food that has been prepared in the women's quarters. The food, in turn, is often the traveler's only clue to the presence of a woman nearby. If the dish is relatively clean and the meal appetizing, it means there is a woman in the adjoining room who cooked it, if the food is inedible, a [Pushtun] man did the deed. A [Pushtun] won't even tell you the names of his wife and mother. . . . Women are as private to a [Pushtun] as his private parts.[14]

CULTURE OF REPRESSION AND DOMINATION

Society denies women the right to define their future, particularly the freedom to marry men of their choice. They are also forbidden to marry non-Muslim men; however, men are allowed to marry non-Muslim women. Women who defy such strict traditions and marry foreign nationals are disowned by their family and forced to leave the country, even if their husbands were converted to Islam. Women who are already abroad who marry non-Muslim men are denied the right to Afghan citizenship and allowed to return home only with the passport of their husband's country.

Women suffer both from societal injustices and from male oppression and brutality. Their suffering ranges from physical abuse such as beating and stabbing, to crippling and even death. For instance, if a woman talks to a stranger or is suspected of complicity in a sexual affair, she can be condemned to death. Women are occasionally killed by influential and respected men of the community. For example, a woman was molested and subsequently killed by a cleric in Bamiyan when her brother left her in his care until his return from a visit abroad:

Shaikh Barsia was a holy man who prayed a lot and therefore was considered a perfectly reliable person. A man going on the pilgrimage wanted to leave his sister, who was very beautiful, with someone trustworthy while he was away, so he decided that there could be no place safer for her than the house of Shaikh Barsia. But while she was staying in the house, Shaikh Barsia noticed her, loved her, and finally took her by force. She became pregnant so he killed and buried her. When her brother finally returned from the pilgrimage the Shaikh told him she had died of a disease.[15]

Women are also murdered by their fathers or husbands, often with the support of the community, for reasons such as infidelity, whether proven or only suspected. In the Muhmand region in eastern Afghanistan, for example, a married woman had become pregnant while her husband was away from home. Accusing her of "waywardness," her husband's family brought her to her father's house where, in accordance with tribal tradition, he was expected to preserve his and his family's honor by killing her for her crime. He killed her with his own hands without hesitation; had he balked, however, her in-laws would have done the deed themselves, for their honor was also at stake. After she was killed, people from neighboring villages visited the father to offer their congratulations for the honorable deed he had performed. Even the *alaqadar,* local administration head, came to offer his congratulations. No accusation of murder was registered against him, nor was he questioned or arrested by the authorities. The fact of his daughter's murder was superseded by what he and society saw as the greater crime.[16]

Coercive social traditions sometimes compelled unmarried women to rebel and take their destiny in their own hands by running away with men they loved. This type of behavior often provoked familial and tribal war if not settled in a manner acceptable to the contending parties, particularly the woman's father. Women have long been used as negotiable items in settling such tribal and familial disputes. For example, if a man commits an offense or violates the social order regarding another family or tribe, he commonly settles the dispute by offering a woman from his family to the offended family or tribe. In the early 1970s an incident occurred in which a Maduzai girl, Kafter, fell in love with a Hazara man who worked as a servant for her father, Toryaley. One evening Kafter camouflaged herself in Hazara clothing and ran away with her inamorato. When her father was informed about it he sought the support of the tribal chief, who organized armed and mounted men to force the Hazaras to return the girl. The Maduzai refused a settlement of four girls and Afs. 400,000 (U.S.$5,037 in 1972) by the Hazaras and demanded that Kafter be returned. A hefty bribe convinced the Maduzai chief to accept the handover of the couple to the custody of a local police commandant. When the Hazaras refused to hand over the girl a fight broke out, the commandant sustained severe injuries, and the case later was transferred to authorities in Kabul.[17] Kafter's community regarded her as a lustful girl and condemned her for running away with a Hazara, whom they considered to be inferior to Pushtuns. They believed that her action shamed and dishonored the family. They demonized Kafter for her brave action:

After she had eloped, her shame was conceived in such a way that it completely distorted the memory of her physical appearance, and she was often described . . . as if she were a monster or a freak: with a blackened face, a crooked mouth and speckled, shifty eyes.[18]

Patriarchal traditions require women to be completely submissive to men. It is a disgrace for a woman to protest any physical or mental abuse by her father, brother, or husband. Women are not only sentenced to death for sexual impropriety but may also be killed if they contradict or disobey a man of the family. For example, a father murdered his daughter when she refused to marry the man he chose for her. She was in love with another man, whom she called upon to rescue her, but her father killed her before she or her inamorato could do anything.[19]

Although women are entitled to inherit property and land according to Islamic Sharia, tradition dictates that they may not own land or property. After marriage, most women leave any inherited shares to their brothers to enable them to sustain the family's name. In Islamic tradition a woman inherits only half the amount of her brother upon the death of the father, and a widow receives less than her daughters. According to Islam:

As for the children, God decrees that the share of the male is equivalent to that of two females. If they consist of women only, and of them more than two, they will get two-thirds of the inheritance; but in case there is one, she will inherit one half. The parents will each inherit a sixth of the estate if it happens the deceased has left a child; but if he has left no children, and his parents are his heirs, then the mother will inherit one-third; but if he has left brothers, the mother will inherit one-sixth after payment of legacies and debts (4:11).[20]

Despite women's rights to inheritance, Islamic laws also entitle them to *mahr,* the amount of money determined by the husband at the time of a marriage contract. *Mahr* is regarded as social insurance for women in case the husband divorces her at a later time, but in reality it is often difficult for women to claim the full amount of *mahr* upon divorce. Women are so powerless that they cannot even dispose of household items, goods, or even their own trousseau, let alone the *mahr,* without approval of the husband.

ENGAGEMENT AND MARRIAGE

Patriarchal culture treats women as creatures who lack wisdom, foresight, and judgment and who therefore cannot decide matters related to their lives. Thus men are entitled to make decisions for them, particularly on issues such as engagement, marriage, and divorce. The tradition of arranged marriage is a common practice among all ethnic and tribal communities. Young and beautiful girls are married much earlier to wealthy men without regard to their age. Families often agree to marry their sons and daughters to each other and arrange their engagements even while they are still infants or children. The reasons for these arrangements are usually political or economic in origin. For example, a marriage between two families can be arranged as a way to combine landholdings, or to gain influence in the community. A father may also wish his son or daughter to live nearby, and will select for them a spouse from the same village.

Some children are engaged even before they are born, during the pregnancy of the mother. Two friends or two relatives will sometimes pledge that when their children, if one has a boy and the other has a girl, are born to them they will be married to each other. When this happens, both sides invite their relatives and announce the engagement, sometimes simultaneously with the births. Another reason for arranging a marriage is to reciprocate a favor received during a time of need. A man may give his daughter in marriage as a token of gratitude to the person who did him the favor, or to that person's son. A girl with prospects of inheritance is often sought after by her relatives or outsiders who have in mind the property that she will bring with her. Profit is the leading motive for this type of arranged marriage. Likewise, a "connecting engagement" occurs when a family seeks a profitable linkage by marrying their daughter into a more influential family.

An "engagement by bequest" may take place in order to ensure continuing good relations between families, or to heal an existing rift; a man may announce such an engagement between two persons on his deathbed. Some engagements are made by force: an influential man may coerce, trick, or bribe parents or their daughter if he desires her. To express his loyalty to a family, a man may marry his daughter to a member of that family; this is called a "charitable engagement." A "punitive engagement" can take place in order to penalize a female who resists the patriarch by insisting on making her own choice. The patriarch may impose his will by suddenly announcing her engagement to another man, and forcing her to go through with it. A family may sometimes have difficulty in making a rational choice among several candidates and may decide by relying on vague feelings, assuming that the man they select will later prove to be most worthy. This is referred to as an "engagement by fate."[21] On rare occasions, and only among certain tribes, a poor and indebted man who cannot pay his financial dues to his creditor may agree to give his daughter in marriage to a member of his creditor's family.

When an engagement is contracted, the parties are socially and culturally obligated to honor it, particularly the bride's family. An incident that occurred in Herat provides a better understanding of such a commitment. A young girl was engaged while she was still a child and the groom's family left the town permanently without staying in touch with the bride's family. The girl was not allowed to marry another man and this uncertainty compelled her parents to consult a local religious judge to find out how much longer they had to wait before marrying her off to another man. The judge told them to "hang the young girl's *chadari* on the wall and when it disintegrated and fell off the hook, she should be released to marry someone else."[22] It is rare to see termination of engagement by either family. If an engaged girl dies prior to her marriage, her family is required to give her sister as a bride or to find another suitable replacement.

Another form of arranged marriage that has become popular recently is called "parceled marriage." It is arranged between a wealthy man who migrated to the West and a girl who still lives in Afghanistan or in refugee communities in Iran and Pakistan. The would-be husband, who may be old, sends a photograph depicting his young age and money to the bride's family. When the bride's family sees the photograph, they may be induced by financial incentive and the promise of a better life for their daughter to agree to engage and marry off their daughter to him. When a deal is struck between them the groom visits the bride's family to get married. The girl has no option but to submit to her family's decision. If for some reason the husband does not like the girl, he returns to the West never to be heard from again and the wife remains behind leading the life of a widow.[23]

Gender ideology reinforces the inferior position of women, particularly when it concerns the future of widowed women. Based on levirate tradition, widowed women are compelled by the family to marry the younger brother of her deceased husband. The death of her husband does not set her free to leave unless she is old and has adult sons. So any male in the family, young or old, single or married, will marry the widow. This tradition is common among most tribal communities who try to keep and protect women within the extended family. Such a tradition sometimes leads to disputes over who has the right to have the widowed women. For example, in Bamiyan a dispute arose between two *qawm,* communities, Maya and Lablabu, over a woman from Lablabu whose husband from Maya had died and who had returned to her native community. In her hometown several men proposed to marry this woman, who was still young, and eventually she was engaged to one of the men.

The brother of the first husband, who of course belonged to Maya *qawm* community, tried to break up the engagement by claiming he had a prior right to her. But the Lablabu qawm community insisted on keeping her, under the excuse that her father had already promised her and this could not be changed. They agreed that if he had claimed her earlier, he could have had her. A group of elders from Maya qawm came to Lablabu to make their claim on her and take her away, but after a great argument they agreed to accept a payment of cash from her *qawm* instead.[24]

THE BRIDE PRICE

The culturally held perceptions of female inferiority transform women into chattel in which dowry constitutes an integral component of marriage transactions. Men pay the bride's family certain amounts of dowry, and the amount given by families varies from one region to another. On average, it amounted to Afs. 40,000–100,000 (U.S.$790-1,976 in 1983). In some regions people paid the required sum in kind, such as with cows, bulls, sheep, goats, and furniture. The lowest amount of dowry paid by low-income families in the Hazarajat regions was estimated at Afs. 10,000–20,000 (U.S.$197-395 in 1983). Payment in kind was common among low-income families in most parts of the country. The amount of dowry is negotiated between the respective heads of the families, and is regarded as compensation for the money expended on the girl's care and upbringing before she is married off and becomes (completely) the property of her new family.

The following is an account of an engagement ceremony that occurred in the house of a district chief in Laghman in August 1983. The parties involved were the families of a boy of six and a girl of three:

The girl's family was demanding 100,000 Afs. while the boy's family wanted to pay less. Finally, a deal was struck at 70,000 Afs. In accordance with custom, the boy's family was to pay this sum in installments to the girl's family until she reached the age of ten or twelve when she would be handed over to the boy's family. The Mullah who helped make the settlement raised his hands solemnly in prayer afterwards. . . . The two little children, quite unaware of what was happening, meanwhile kept playing in a corner of the room.[25]

Occasionally, poverty or greed will drive a father to betroth his daughters to potential grooms and collect the dowry from each of them. Such cases eventually end up in court and sometimes escalate into violence. Settlement of these cases usually involves appeasement with further offerings of women. In 1972 an actual case involved a man, Khaliqdad, who contracted an engagement between his daughter, Bibi Khanum, and a man named Hussein. But he also arranged for her marriage to another man, Sardar, and collected her bride price of Afs. 50,000 (U.S.$630 in 1972) from both men. Hussein sued Sardar for marrying Bibi Khanum. According to Hussein, to avoid being sued also, Khaliqdad offered his other daughter, Bobo Gul, to Hussein for the same bride price. Hussein agreed, only to find later that Bobo Gul was to be married to yet another man, Allah Nur. He sued Khaliqdad, but since Hussein in this instance did not have a valid *nika khat*, marriage license, to support his claim, both the primary court and the provincial court denied his suit.[26]

Since the dowry and other marriage-related expenses are high, some poor men cannot marry their fiancées until they are middle-aged, and many are forced into a celibate life. Financial obstructions like these are one of the factors that have contributed to occurrences of homosexuality, as boredom, frustration while waiting for marriage, and the severely restricted access to women compel some men to engage in homosexual behavior.[27] Homosexuality is common among a small segment of the population, but remains hidden. A recent article detailed homosexuality in Afghanistan in these words:

Love between men, is in fact, exalted, and tenderness, affection, and deep friendships are not uncommon. . . . Men frequently hold hands while walking, and it is not uncommon to see men embracing. Poetry and popular songs use the male gender as the object of affection. This is generally interpreted as a coy reference to women, but songs that talk of undying friendship between men are part of the repertoire of popular verse. . . . Notions of male bonding remain strong in most rural communities, including the fierce Pathan [Pushtun] tribesmen. (This is the same ethnic group that is settled in Afghanistan . . .). Alexander the Great was unable to conquer them; so he married a tribe's woman to gain safe passage to the rich land.[28] Sir Richard Burton, famed researcher of things sexual, refers to an ancient Pathan proverb . . . 'Women for breeding, boys for pleasure, but melons for sheer delight.'[29]

During the civil war of 1992–1996 there were occasions in which a number of warlords fought gun battles that involved disputes over the possession of handsome young boys. For example, in July 1994 there was "a marriage between two boys, celebrated with a great deal of jubilation in Qandahar."[30] Despite this rare public incident, homosexuality remains forbidden and subject to severe punishment. Since it is not safe for homosexuals to publicly express their feelings, they rarely reveal themselves to anyone other than trusted friends, with the result that researchers often must refer to folktales dealing with homosexuality to infer its existence. For example, in one such tale a man laments because "a beautiful boy with a bottom like a peach stands across the river, and I cannot swim."[31]

SEXUAL ABSTINENCE AND MODESTY

One of the culturally accepted ideals of honorable females is modesty, and their honor is defined in maintenance of virginity prior to marriage. Although women are expected to be shy and refrain from talking about sexuality, women often defy such social norms and express their sensual feelings with intimate friends, and make innuendoes and joke about sexuality. A study of Farghanachi women settled in Qunduz revealed that women sometimes jokingly talk about sex:

For example, one little girl did not like carrots and picked them off her pillow. A woman jokingly explained that virgins should not eat carrots; the joke being a reference to the penis as a carrot and sexual intercourse. Another joke was referring to baby girls as *pista* bazaar, pistachio nuts, because their genitals were said to resemble the nuts.[32]

A woman's social and cultural milieu is restricted to the household, where close female friends socialize and gossip about various things both mundane and intimate. A study of the Maduzai tribes also indicated that women had no inhibition about discussing sexuality. They talked and joked about sex "either laughing at the nuisance of having intercourse and babies or joking that barren women are well-loved by their husbands because their vaginas are tight like a young girl's."[33]

Premarital sex and cohabitation of unmarried people are forbidden by Islamic laws. The preservation of patrilineal bloodlines and identity is a strong motive for safeguarding a woman's virginity. A woman's virginity is also considered to be the family's symbol of honor. Fathers and brothers are deeply concerned with the virginity of their daughters and sisters. A girl's virginity must be proved on the wedding night; women are usually involved in the inspection or proof of virginity, and their bedding is checked the next morning for the bloodstains that signify former virginity. A family in the United States even sent proof of the bride's virginity to her family through Federal Express:

We happened to come to California for a visit and stayed with our paternal aunts. We had met their elder son while we were living in refugee camps in Peshawar, Pakistan. Already at that time we were thinking of him becoming our son-in-law. During this visit our daughter and her present husband got to meet each other, and they liked each other, and his family proposed an engagement. The engagement and wedding was all done and we are proud of her being *sar-bayland*, virgin. The groom's family had mailed the blood of her purity through Federal Express to us.[34]

If a girl is even suspected not to be a virgin, she is returned to her parents amid great scandal.[35] It is because of this fear of scandal and dishonor that conservative parents avoid taking girls suffering from genital disorders to medical doctors. In one account, a woman whose infant daughter had no opening in her *parda-e-bekarat or dukhtari,* hymen, sought advice from another, older woman. She was told that a medical doctor could cut a small opening in the hymen, and that the pain for her daughter would be minimized if it were done while she was still a baby. This procedure was also necessary for the girl's health, as the lack of an opening would prevent her from menstruating when she grew older. Although the mother was made aware of these facts, she still delayed taking her daughter to a doctor because she was more concerned about the possible damage to her daughter's virginity (if the doctor made the opening too big) than she was about her daughter's health.[36]

Because sanctions against women who fail to remain virgins are harsh, premarital sex occurs infrequently and most often happens between a man and his fiancée. If the girl becomes pregnant, the couple try to marry as soon as possible to avoid discovery. If for some reason the parents delay the date, the girl is forced to abort her baby in order to avoid the public scandal and shame associated with premarital sex. It is rare to find families who did not hand down the death sentence to their daughters for having sex prior to marriage. If there is a pregnancy, these parents will try to hide it until they can either abort the baby or dispose of it after the birth.

POLYGAMY

The culture of polygamy is common among all ethnic communities. Islamic laws permit men to marry up to four wives, on the condition that they treat their wives without discrimination. Many factors have contributed to the practice of polygamy. For example, a woman's infertility may cause a man to take another wife, or in the case of younger couples, irreconcilable differences may develop over time, compelling the man to marry another woman; divorce is not a viable option because of the stigma attached to it.

Polygamy is a common practice among wealthy men who marry several wives not only to acquire more land shares, property, and wealth but also to have more children. Having many children increases one's influence in society. Although a polygamous man may be content with his lifestyle, the relationship among the *ambaq,* cowives, living under one roof is nothing but constant hostility. A Persian saying aptly depicts the life of a polygamous man: *du zan kardi du gham kardi,* two women and two worries. Polygamy also is considered to be economically profitable to men, especially when a woman possesses certain marketable skills such as weaving or embroidery. In the northern part of the country, women are traditionally known for their expertly woven carpets and rugs, which greatly contribute to the family's income. It is chiefly due to this reason that polygamy is occasionally practiced by some poor men in this region as well as other parts of the country. Most polygamous men are generally old and marry young girls; after their death the widowed women, often with several children, are forced to remarry. This factor, together with lack of rigorous legislation to prohibit such cultural practices, sustains the culture of polygamy.

WOMEN AND DIVORCE

Social and cultural norms combined with Islamic Sharia laws have institutionalized women's subordinated position. Men often have the exclusive right to *talaq,* divorce, without prior consent from the wife. Although Islamic and civil laws stipulate certain conditions in which a woman can initiate *talaq,* social and cultural traditions make it rather impossible for a woman to initiate divorce and it is considered shameful for a woman to seek it. Dissolution of marriage either by men or by women is regarded as a disgrace, and it is due to this reason that Afghanistan's divorce rate is extremely low. Official government data indicate that in 1975, a mere 0.1 percent of the total population of the country had even sought divorce.[37]

In the case of divorce, men take custody of adult children and a mother receives custody of babies until they reach adulthood; the father is responsible for child support. If the mother remarries she loses custody of the children and the father's immediate relatives will take care of the children until he remarries. Although divorce is considered a dishonor, a husband's brutality sometimes compels a wife to initiate a divorce proceeding in spite of her fear of retaliation from the community. The legal system also presents a woman seeking divorce with serious obstacles. She often has extreme difficulty proving her claim regarding mistreatment by her husband. Since most women do not possess identification cards, a result of the traditional identification with one's husband, a woman must have two (male) witnesses testify on her behalf. The first witness must testify as to the identity of the plaintiff (the wife) and the second man must testify as to the identity of the first witness. A woman who spends her life sequestered from the presence of men other than close family members will find it very difficult, if not impossible, to find even a single male willing to do such a thing.

According to local traditions, a man can divorce his wife without filing an application and registering it in court. He needs only to say *"talaq"* three times to her. In the eyes of the law, however, they will still be married. This represents another dilemma for the woman, since her ex-husband is still her legal husband in the eyes of the court, and therefore can at any time return and harass or assault her, and she will have no recourse against him. She will not be able to substantiate any claims against him since she is still legally his wife. An example of the problems a woman in this situation faces can be found in the case of Niyaz Bibi's claim against her husband, Mohammad Zahir, in a primary court in Qandahar. He divorced her verbally but did not file formal divorce papers. Subsequently he continued to harass her. Niyaz Bibi appealed to the primary court to issue a restraining order against her husband. The court required her to substantiate her claim. Niyaz Bibi was unable to provide any of the required forms of evidence to support her claim, but she requested the court to force Mohammad Zahir to tell the truth under oath. Zahir took the oath, but then denied all of Niyaz Bibi's allegations. On his words, the court decided that no divorce had taken place. Therefore, the harassment claim had no grounds, and they ordered Niyaz Bibi to abide by her marital vows. She then appealed before the provincial court of Qandahar. Her appeal was summarily denied; the provincial court confirmed the decision of the primary court. Niyaz Bibi then appealed to the cassation court, Afghanistan's highest court, which referred her application for review by a court equivalent to the provincial court, but in the province of Hilmand. Again, Niyaz Bibi was not able to secure two male witnesses willing to testify on her behalf and she was again ordered to abide by her marital obligations. Another appeal to the cassation court resulted in the confirmation of the Hilmand provincial court decision.[38]

Table 2.1
Marital Status by Age Group (both sexes), 1980

	Single	Married	Widowed	Divorced
0–7	46.0	0.0	0.0	0.0
8–9	9.8	0.1	0.1	0.0
10–14	20.9	0.7	0.2	1.7
15–19	12.6	8.3	0.5	8.7
20–24	5.7	14.2	1.5	16.3
25–29	2.5	15.2	2.5	10.7
30–34	1.0	14.2	3.7	12.4
35–39	0.5	12.2	5.1	12.2
40–44	0.3	9.9	7.9	9.7
45–49	0.2	8.0	9.3	7.9
50–54	0.1	6.0	12.2	5.4
55–59	0.1	4.5	12.9	4.1
60–64	0.1	3.0	14.6	5.4
65+	0.1	3.7	29.5	5.3

Source: Central Statistics Office (CSO), *Preliminary Results of the First Afghan Population Census* (Kabul: CSO, 1981), p. 61. Cited in Wali M. Rahimi, *Status of Women: Afghanistan* (Bangkok: UNESCO, Principal Regional Office for Asia and the Pacific, 1991), p. 29.

Table 2.1 shows marital status of both sexes by age group in 1980, during which time the highest rate of marriage and divorce among the settled population of both sexes was between the ages of 20 and 39 years. Unsatisfactory marriage, disappointment in love, illegitimate pregnancy, and domestic abuse sometimes compel women to commit suicide as the only way out of such oppressive relationships, since most women cannot overcome the legal barrier for divorce. Available data indicate that in 1968 there were 32 cases of suicide, 28 males and 4 females, throughout the country.[39] The ratio of suicide was extremely low, 0.2 per 100,000 population. It is suggested that the rate of suicide considerably increased in the 1980s and 1990s, as many young girls and women committed suicide in order to avoid rape and abduction by militias affiliated with various Islamic parties fighting for domination of the country.

SEXUAL LIAISON

Sexual impropriety is strictly prohibited in Islamic tradition. Those who fail to uphold religious norms with regard to sexual behaviors are subject to severe punishment. Despite stringent rules, premarital sexual affairs and adultery continue to occur. When a girl loses her virginity prior to marriage she often loses her family's support and has no possibility of finding a man who is willing to marry her. This situation sometimes compels her to resort to prostitution, which is illegal; those caught face severe punishment. However, official policy toward prostitution was lenient in the past, as "certain people called *Kanjars* brought *Kafir* girls and used them as prostitutes in Jalalabad."[40] Despite stringent rules by the Islamists, the culture of prostitution continues to survive. Underground brothels exist both in big cities and in small towns and are managed either by men or women referred to as *murdagaw* and *khala kharabati*, respectively. A recent study of the Maduzai tribe reveals the operation of a brothel in one of the villages. For example, in a brothel run by a man named Majid:

He summons women by sending his wife Tajbibi after them. She fixes them up and then he gets some money for it. . . . If a woman goes from house to house, people don't worry as they do if a man does. We call her *ruybar,* a woman sent by her husband to another man to fix it up between him and another woman. So she does *ruybari* for them and brings them face to face. Majid and his wife use their own house, and when she has the woman inside she locks the door. Some women are not accustomed to this kind of business and get angry, but the man is stronger than her and he may cover her mouth, then what can the woman do? If a woman isn't agreeable then either they will find some present to please her, or they won't approach her next time.[41]

Female prostitutes either operate independently by visiting the client's house or work with one of the underground brothels. These houses often change location to avoid detection by security agencies. Males or females in charge of the brothels negotiate the deal and make necessary arrangements for the male customer and the female prostitute to meet.

Data on crimes and other acts of misdemeanor committed by women are not well documented by government agencies; however, a few incomplete statistics reveal that a small number of women have been involved in acts and behaviors defined as criminal by the law. A study of the Maduzai tribe shows that a significant number of women had committed physical violence toward their husbands. For example, in the early 1970s two women physically assaulted their husbands and as many as a hundred women inmates in the provincial jail were charged for murder and attempted murder of their husbands, often with the support of an inamorato.[42] In 1976 there were 170 women inmates in Kabul's Central Jail, including 17 girls with no programs for rehabilitation.[43] Table 2.2 shows the number of women inmates imprisoned in jails in Kabul for various crimes and misdemeanor acts in 1980–1985.

Table 2.2
Women Jailed for Crimes in Kabul, 1980–1985

	1980–1982	1984	1985	Total
Sexual	27	21	63	111
Theft	11	5	8	24
Murder	2	2	1	5
Pick-pocketing	2	—	3	5
Drug abuse	—	3	—	3
Total	42	31	75	148

Source: Wali M. Rahimi, *Status of Women: Afghanistan* (Bangkok: UNESCO, Principal
Regional Office for Asia and the Pacific, 1991), p. 35.

WOMEN AND HEALTH

Gender ideology has greatly affected the status of women's health.
There are a limited number of health centers in the capital of every province, and women are generally neglected by their husbands and excluded
from healthcare. A vast majority of poor families cannot afford to visit a
medical center or a hospital. Fathers and husbands continue to take their
daughters and wives to shrines and known *pirs* (spiritual masters) for
spiritual healing, or to a local *hakim,* a practitioner of holistic medicine,
for treatment involving traditional local medicine. The available data indicate that in 1976–1977 there were 176 female government-licensed physicians and nurses throughout the entire country. It is estimated that 150
of these female professionals worked in health centers in the capital. Although there were 76 auxiliary nurse-midwives, 23 of them were in
Kabul.[44] The lack of female professionals in health-related areas discour-
ages conservatives from allowing their wives and daughters to visit health
centers. Even in cases of emergency, medical treatment is conducted in
absentia when the medical doctor is a man and the patient is a woman.
In these situations the husband or father will act as an intermediary between the doctor and the patient, relaying the doctor's questions and the
patient's responses. The doctor must thus diagnose the patient's condition and recommend treatment, often without meeting the woman face
to face.[45]

Patriarchal tradition, combined with the necessity to have children to
supplement the family's income in an agricultural or cash economy,
imposes on women a duty to reproduce and maintain a high fertility rate.
Birth rates are estimated to average 6.9 babies per woman. This figure is

relatively lower in urban areas (5.8) and higher in rural areas (7.3). In other words, a woman will usually give birth to six or seven babies during her fertile years. The statistics indicate that the majority of women spend most of their time and energy engaged in childbearing and childrearing activities.

Table 2.3 shows fertility rates of women between the ages of 15 and 49 in 1979, indicating that fertility rates reach their highest peak when a woman is between the ages of 20 and 30, and then gradually decline. The period between each birth is also very short. Since the majority of women of low-income families cannot provide proper nutrition for their children, infant mortality is high, particularly in rural areas. In addition to the lack of nutritional food, men's negligence of the health of female members of the family is also a contributing factor in both infant and female mortality.

Mary McMorrow, a nurse who worked for an international agency helping refugees in Pakistan, described the attitude of men toward women's health issues in these words:

The women are the most neglected, the women are the most anemic, the women have the highest level of tuberculosis; the women in general are in pretty bad shape. . . . Traditionally, the Afghan men get the best of the food, which is then passed down to the children, and the women eat last, what's left over, if anything. There are certain long-standing taboos: women in some of the tribes won't eat meat or vegetables, because they think they are bad for them. So what they basi-

Table 2.3
Estimated Fertility Rates, 1979 (per 1,000 women)

Age	Urban	Rural
All ages	189.6	240.3
15–19	120.3	168.6
20–24	262.9	346.9
25–29	285.5	362.6
30–34	249.3	264.9
35–39	183.8	238.5
40–44	74.6	108.2
45–49	47.5	85.6

Source: United Nations, *Demographic Yearbook 1987* (New York: Department of International Economic and Social Affairs, Statistical Office, 1989), p. 368.

cally live on is sweet bread and green tea. . . . You cannot get a husband to do-
nate blood for his wife because if you take his blood you take his life, but if she
dies he can always get another wife.[46]

Malnutrition of mother and child, lack of health awareness, and insuf-
ficiency of health centers and medical facilities, coupled with men's refusal to take their wives to medical centers, if one exists in the vicinity,
have greatly contributed to the high rate of infant mortality. Table 2.4
shows infant mortality in 1979, indicating that female infant mortality was
considerably lower than male mortality. However, this may not be an accurate figure. One possible explanation was the practice of underreporting
female mortality. The birth or death of a female was not considered note-
worthy because it had no economic impact on the family. Reporting of
male mortality, however, was relatively accurate because of the political
incentive to report it. The military expected all adult males to serve, and
a family that did not report the death of a son would sooner or later be
expected to provide a male for service.

High mortality rates and health-related illnesses could also be attributed to the lack of educational institutions geared to promoting topics
related to women's health. Although there were schools for women, the
majority of low-income and poor families could not afford education for
all their children. Those who could did not regard girls' education to be
as important as boys' education. The overwhelming majority of women
were illiterate and did not approve of their daughters' education after they
reached puberty. They did not perceive any material rewards to be gained
from their daughters' attendance at school. A dearth of employment opportunities for educated rural women also discouraged families from supporting education for girls. The lack of education and health awareness

Table 2.4
Infant Mortality (age 0–1), 1979

	Male	Female
Urban	6,313	4,722
Rural	50,747	44,545
Total	57,060	49,267

Source: United Nations, *Demographic Yearbook
1987* (New York: Department of International Economic and Social Affairs, Statistical Office, 1989), p. 446.

programs has largely contributed to poor health, high mortality, and life-threatening diseases. Nonetheless, some girls managed to obtain educations at varying levels.

Table 2.5 shows female enrollment in various school levels in Afghanistan. Female students in most rural areas did not continue their studies beyond the elementary level of education and during their studies they did not learn anything about health and nutrition and other issues that affected women's lives. Although a few enlightened families permitted their daughters to attend school with boys until the sixth grade, they were kept home afterward and soon forgot whatever they had learned. Some families believed that higher education alienates their children and opposed sending their daughters to a high school, college, or professional and vocational school. A few educated girls often preferred to stay in urban areas in hopes of finding suitable employment rather then returning to their home villages, which further discouraged conservative families from approving their daughters' higher education.

Parents' attitudes toward education for women in the early 1970s ranged from allowing it as an "indulgence" for a few years at most, to viewing it as a complete waste of time that did not help their daughters' future life as a wife and mother. For example, in Nangarhar, boys attended school from elementary to the secondary level but girls attended a village school only up to the third grade. Girls in some affluent and progressive families were able to continue schooling up to the sixth grade at a school for boys. Parents in Herat did not view education as a useful thing for their daughters. They were of the opinion that the girls would soon forget what they had learned if they were not able to continue beyond basic levels of education. In the northern provinces of Qunduz and Balkh, Turkmen and Uzbek parents were against the idea of girls attending school at all, considering it as a waste of time for them. They preferred their daughters learn from the age of seven or eight how to weave carpets and rugs and how to cook and raise children.[47]

Although the state of rural education improved somewhat in the 1960s and 1970s, no significant efforts were made to introduce subjects to help women learn the fundamentals of rural health and nutrition. What little progress and improvement that was made in education was lost during the ensuing armed insurgency soon after the 1978 April coup, which led to the closure of most schools in the rural areas. Educational institutions sustained major damage in the 1980s as armed struggle intensified between the insurgents and the Kabul government. Table 2.6 shows women's educational attainment in 1979.

WOMEN'S DEFIANCE OF PATRIARCHY

Since the majority of women are illiterate and their access to legal institutions is extremely limited, they are at a disadvantage to fight

Table 2.5
Women's Enrollment in Schools and Universities, 1951–1971

	1951	1955	1958	1961	1968	1971
Village	—	—	224	4,659	9,993	13,885
Primary	5,048	9,036	12,022	23,735	52,577	64,856
Middle	202	763	1,427	2,431	8,541	11,409
High school	81	124	299	628	2,353	4,642
University	41	41	61	213	753	664
Total	5,372	9,964	14,033	31,666	74,217	95,456

Source: Sondra Howell Bechhoefer, "Education and the Advancement of Women in Afghanistan" (M.A. thesis, University of Maryland, 1975), p. 83.

Table 2.6
Women's Educational Attainment (age 25+), 1979

| | Total | % No Schooling | Primary | | Secondary | |
			% Incomplete	% Completed	% Lower Secondary	% Postsecondary
Urban						
Total	717,983	72.1	12.1	1.1	3.5	11.4
Female	335,968	88.2	5.7	0.8	1.6	3.7
Rural						
Total	4,173,490	92.0	5.5	0.2	0.7	1.6
Female	2,069,219	99.2	0.7	0.0	0.0	0.0
Total	4,891,473	89.0	6.5	0.3	1.1	3.0
Female	2,405,187	97.6	1.4	0.1	0.3	0.6

Source: UN Educational, Scientific, and Cultural Organization (UNESCO), *Statistical Yearbook 1999* (Paris: UNESCO, 1999), p. II-56.

injustices, discrimination, and physical abuse by men through legal means. One of the few options open to them to express their outrage and anger over societal and male oppression is through singing songs and behaving in a manner that subtly reflects their defiance of the social rules.

In the past women did not actively fight social injustices and male oppression, but occasionally individual women did defy patriarchal traditions and revolt against social oppression. Folklore and legend are replete with women's bravery and struggles for freedom. Rabia Balkhi (tenth century) was a well-known poet of a ruling family in Balkh who fell in love with Baktash, one of the slaves of her brother, Haris. She defied the values cherished by the ruling class, refused to marry the man chosen for her by her brother, and paid for her love for Baktash with her life. Her resistance led to her imprisonment until she died in prison. Prior to her death, Rabia wrote a poem in Persian on the prison wall with her own blood, in which she condemned society for not allowing her to marry the man of her choice. The poem reads as follows:

> I am caught in love's web so deceitful
> None of my endeavours turned fruitful,
> I knew not when I rode the high-blooded steed.
> The harder I pulled its reins the less it would heed.
> Love is an ocean with such a vast space
> No wise man can swim it in any place.
> A true lover should be faithful till the end
> And face life's reprobated trend.
> When you see things hideous, fancy them neat,
> Eat poison but taste sugar sweet.[48]

Another courageous and popular woman who despised rigid social and cultural traditions that denied women the right and freedom to decide their lives on their own was Mahboob. She was born in Herat into a middle-class family and was supported by her brother in her endeavor for learning. She was a poet who expressed her dismay of the patriarchal tradition of arranged marriage. In one of her poems, she wrote:

> Oh, friends, this love-sick one is nearly dying
> Who's to tell that merciless one about her condition
> Neither luck nor my beloved help me,
> How difficult it is to lead such a life
> You, oh, enticer, remember the enticed;
> Free the enslaved.
> You wronged me much, now learn to be good.
> Soothe my wounds, don't irritate the sore spots.
> When you pass by Mahboob's place,
> If you like,

It would not hurt you to put a heart
Back into her chest.[49]

Women often despised men's control of their lives and sexuality but did not have the power to confront men and fight for their rights. Some women engaged in illicit sexual affairs as a way to fight men's domination of their lives and their *khahar khanda*s often helped hide their acts. Women also have expressed their feelings of defiance in local folk songs, songs that reveal their romantic and sensual fantasies, as well as their frustration and anger at their lowly position in society. Such songs could be viewed as a challenge to the social system, and are sung by women only among fellow women. A folk song that portrays a woman's desire for freedom reads as follows:

God knows, there is no way,
to climb the sky.
And the earth, you've made it
A blazing fire for me.
The moon rises over my head
In the center of the sky
Is there no sleep without one's lover
Or is it only I who cannot sleep.[50]

There are songs that reflect a young girl's contempt for being forced to marry an old man of fifty or sixty. These songs express the woman's resentment and hatred toward her old husband, and her desire for a young man closer to her age. One of the reasons that young women are unhappy with an arranged marriage with elderly men is because their aged husbands are often impotent. The following song portrays a woman's complaint about her elderly husband:

Carrots do not grow on mountaintops,
The young girl's heart
Pine not for an old man.
The old man is a father to me
But the young man a light in my eyes.
The old man has no fault
Except weak sinews and no erection.[51]

There are also other folk songs that express a woman's desire to meet a man she loves but cannot visit in his house nor receive him in her house. They content themselves with a visit far away from their homes. One such song reads:

My beloved
Allowed not to visit me,

> My parents permit me not
> To leave the house.
> I can go out only
> When girls go to the spring nearby
> To fetch water.
> My beloved you must pass by
> So we can catch a glimpse of one another.[52]

Women express their anger and frustration not only in private but sometimes also at public social gatherings such as weddings and cultural festivities by singing songs, performing dances, and playing music that satirize social and cultural traditions that oppress women. For instance, during a wedding in Herat a woman minstrel, Jamilah, sang the song "The Knife-Sharpener's Wife." The song reflects the anger of a woman who loves the knife-sharpener but has been forced to marry a carpenter instead. The song portrays this woman as a defiant and spirited woman who is exhausted by frustration and anger, and who pines for freedom. As a sign of defiance, "She slams the tool of that profession [carpentry] down upon [her husband's] head . . . . the carpenter's saw, the mullah's book, the tea-house proprietor's teapot, even the hash-smoker's pipe." The women loved the song because it claimed the lowly knife-sharpener as an ideal husband and made fun of the serious world of men. Another song specifically sung by women was "The Widow," a variant of an ordinary love song. In it the widow flirtatiously shows off various parts of her body—lips, eyes, eyebrows, bottom—demonstrating that she is ready to marry again.[53]

Minstrel women generally perform music that is secular and does not manifest any devotional feelings. They play music and sing songs that are mostly concerned with women and their desire for freedom. This scandalous action of publicly expressing women's feelings of resentment and anger was tolerated only because it was performed only at special occasions and only in the women's quarters, not amid the main party, and this occurred in the relatively liberal environment of the 1960s and 1970s. Islamic insurgency prior to and during the Soviet occupation period of 1979–1989, the establishment of an Islamic regime in 1992, and the rise and consolidation of the Taliban rule have effectively put an end to such cultural activities.

NOTES

1. *Al-Qu'ran*, a commentary translation by Ahmed Ali (Princeton: Princeton University Press, 1984), pp. 75–78.

2. Muslihuddin Sa'di, *Sharh-i Bustan*, Muhammad Khaza'ili, ed. (Tehran: Sazman-i Intisharat-i Javidan, 1362/1983), p. 327.

3. Ibid., pp. 327–328.

4. Bibi Khanum Astarabadi, *Ma'ayib al-rijal: Dar Pasikh ba Ta'dib al-Nisvan* [Vices of Men: In Response to Disciplining Women], edited with an introduction by Afsaneh Najmabadi (Chicago: Midland, 1992), p. 82.

5. Nancy Tapper, *Bartered Brides: Politics, Gender, and Marriage in an Afghan Tribal Society* (Cambridge: Cambridge University Press, 1991), p. 210.

6. Contrary to the popular belief that it is an Afghanistan version of polo, *buzkashi* is a much rougher game of skill that involves two teams on horseback bent on snatching a calf or goat carcass by hand from a shallow ditch surrounded by a circle and fighting to carry it to the far end of a field, which can be several miles long, and deposit it back into the original circle goal, called a *halal*. No instruments are used during the game, and it is played at a breakneck pace, requiring significant skill and agility on the part of the rider, who must be able to throw himself to the side of the horse to retrieve the carcass while moving at high speeds and fending off opposing players, as well as skill and agility on the part of the horse, which must be able to start and stop abruptly and bend its forelegs quickly to help its rider to pick up the carcass. This game effectively fosters teamwork as well; once a player has acquired the carcass, his teammates immediately rally to defend him to the *halal*.

7. Anneliese Stucki, "Horses and Women: Some Thoughts on the Life Cycle of Ersari Turkmen Women," *Afghanistan Journal* 5:4 (1978): 140.

8. John C. Griffiths, *Afghanistan: Key to a Continent* (Boulder, Colo.: Westview Press, 1981), p. 97.

9. William T. Vollmann, *An Afghanistan Picture Show, or How I Saved the World* (New York: Farrar, Straus, and Giroux, 1992), p. 125.

10. *Al-Qu'ran*, pp. 300–301.

11. Veronica Doubleday, *Three Women of Herat* (London: Jonathan Cape, 1988), pp. 45–46.

12. Pamela A. Hunte, *Women and Development Process in Afghanistan*, project for the U.S. Agency for International Development (USAID) (USAID, 1978), p. 63.

13. Nancy Lindisfarne, "Women Organized in Groups: Expanding the Terms of the Debate," in *Organizing Women: Formal and Informal Women's Groups in the Middle East*, Dawn Chatty and Annika Rabo (eds.) (Oxford: Berg, 1997), pp. 211–238.

14. Robert D. Kaplan, *Soldiers of God: With the Mujahidin in Afghanistan* (Boston: Houghton Mifflin, 1990), p. 50.

15. Robert L. Canfield, *Faction and Conversion in a Plural Society: Religious Alignments in the Hindu Kush* (Ann Arbor: University of Michigan Press, 1973), pp. 37–38.

16. Raja Anwar, *The Tragedy of Afghanistan: A First-Hand Account*, translated from the Urdu by Khalid Hasan (London: Verso, 1988), p. 128.

17. Tapper, *Bartered Brides*, pp. 61–62.

18. Ibid., p. 226.

19. Ibid., p. 225.

20. *Al-Qu'ran*, pp. 74–75.

21. Mohammad Hashim Kamali, *Law in Afghanistan: A Study of the Constitutions, Matrimonial Law, and the Judiciary* (Leiden: E. J. Brill, 1985), pp. 109–110.

22. Margaret A. Mills, "Of the Dust and the Wind: Arranged Marriages in

Afghanistan," in *Everyday Life in the Muslim Middle East,* Donna Lee Bowen and Evelyn A. Early (eds.) (Bloomington: Indiana University Press, 1993), p. 54.

23. Author's observation of developments among refugee communities in Pakistan, 1999 and March 2000.

24. Canfield, *Faction and Conversion,* p. 50.

25. Anwar, *Tragedy of Afghanistan,* p. 265.

26. Kamali, *Law in Afghanistan,* p. 90.

27. Discussion with two college students (male and female) at Kabul University, 1976. The students wished to remain anonymous.

28. Badruddin Khan, "Not-So-Gay Life in Karachi: A View of a Pakistani Living in Toronto," in *Sexuality and Eroticism Among Males in Moslem Societies,* Arno Schmit and Jehoeda Sofer (eds.) (New York: Haworth Press, 1992), p. 99. This quote is contained within the larger quote cited with endnote no. 29.

29. Ibid., pp. 93–94.

30. Kamal Matinuddin, *The Taliban Phenomenon: Afghanistan 1994–1997* (Karachi, Pakistan: Oxford University Press, 1999), p. 23.

31. Louis Dupree, *Afghanistan* (Princeton: Princeton University Press, 1973), p. 198.

32. Audrey C. Shalinsky, *Long Years of Exile: Central Asian Refugees in Afghanistan and Pakistan* (Lanham, Md.: University Press of America, 1994), p. 87.

33. Tapper, *Bartered Brides,* p. 124.

34. Maliha Zulfacar, *Afghan Immigrants in the USA and Germany: A Comparative Analysis of the Use of Ethnic Social Capital* (Munster: Lit Verlag, 1998), p. 164.

35. Discussion with a high school graduate in Kabul. The man, who wished to remain anonymous, not only returned his wife to her family after the wedding night when he suspected that his wife was not a virgin, but also tried to take revenge against those he suspected had deflowered his bride, which he regarded as a personal attack on his honor.

36. Audrey C. Shalinsky, "Learning Sexual Identity: Parents and Children in Northern Afghanistan," *Anthropology and Education Quarterly* 11:4 (Winter 1980): 257.

37. Afghan Demographic Studies, *National Demographic and Family Guidance Survey of the Settled Population of Afghanistan,* vol. 1, *Demography and Knowledge, Attitudes and Practices of Family Guidance* (Buffalo: State University of New York Press, 1975), p. 62.

38. Kamali, *Law in Afghanistan,* p. 176.

39. Asad Hassan Gobar, "Suicide in Afghanistan," *The British Journal of Psychiatry* 116:534 (May 1970): 495.

40. Hasan Kakar, *Government and Society in Afghanistan: The Reign of Amir Abd al-Rahman Khan* (Austin: University of Texas Press, 1979), p. 175.

41. Tapper, *Bartered Brides,* p. 236.

42. Ibid., p. 213.

43. Fahima Rahimi, *Women in Afghanistan* (Liestal: Stiftung Foundation, Stiftung Bibliotheca Afghanica, 1986), p. 102.

44. Hunte, *Women and Development Process,* p. 17.

45. Griffiths, *Afghanistan,* p. 99.

46. Vollmann, *Afghanistan Picture Show,* p. 126.

47. Sondra Howell Bechhoefer, "Education and the Advancement of Women in Afghanistan" (M.A. thesis, University of Maryland, 1975), pp. 139–140.

48. K. Habibi, "A Glance at Literature: A Box of Jewels," *Kabul Times* 3:75 (1967): 3. Cited in Dupree, *Afghanistan*, p. 78.

49. Rahimi, *Women in Afghanistan*, p. 32.

50. Saduddin Shpoon, "Paxto Folklore and the Landey," *Afghanistan* 20:4 (Winter 1968): 46.

51. Common folk songs among the Hazara community; English translation by the author.

52. Ibid.

53. Doubleday, *Three Women of Herat*, p. 182.

3

Peripheral State: Politics of Modernization

Liberal political discourse views the state as an autonomous institution that serves the interests of all social classes, mediates class conflicts, supports individual rights, and promotes services that the community as a whole needs. The Marxist paradigm regards the state fundamentally as an instrument of class domination. The ruling class uses both the coercive state apparatus (military, police, etc.) and ideological state apparatus (schools, mosques, civic centers, etc.) to maintain its domination. State and development are virtually joined at the hip. The ruling class articulates development strategies to regulate labor productivity and consolidates its rule by establishing schools and other institutions to promote its ideology, ethics, and values.

THE STATE AS AN AGENT OF CHANGE

Prior to Afghanistan's independence in 1919, the state was little more than a loose tribal confederation. The emerging bourgeoisie, still linked to the land, could not play a significant role in the process of modern development. Religious teachings served as a guiding principle for both the state and society. Educational institutions were under the influence of clerics. There were no schools for girls, but families of upper- and middle-class backgrounds allowed their daughters to acquire a rudimentary education at home. After Afghanistan achieved its independence in 1919, the state under the leadership of Amanullah tried to modernize the country and free women from age-old social and cultural oppression. During a speech he stated:

At present I abolish at the outset the system of *begar,* impressed labor, in the country. Henceforth no labor will be impressed, and not a single individual will be employed by force from among you in making roads, working on public works, tree-cutting, etc. And by the grace of God our sublime government will employ such measures of reform as may prove suitable and useful to the country and nation so that the Government and nation of Afghanistan may make and gain great renown in the civilized world and take its proper place among the civilized powers of the world. For the rest, I pray to God for his favors and mercy and seek his help for the welfare and prosperity of you Muslims and all mankind.[1]

To achieve this, Amanullah initiated a number of reforms aimed at building a modern society based on a European model of development. On April 9, 1923, he promulgated a new constitution, *Nizamnamah-ye-Asasi-e-Dawlat-e-Aliyah-e-Afghanistan, 20 Hamal 1302* [April 9, 1923], which consisted of 73 articles. It provided a blueprint for building a modern civil society and delineated the responsibilities of the king and state officials. The constitution was a progressive national document that stressed local economic development, defined the rights of individual citizens and the state, and abolished slavery. Articles 8 and 10 stated:

Article 8: All persons residing in the kingdom of Afghanistan, without respect to religious or sectarian differences, are considered to be subjects of Afghanistan. Afghan citizenship may be obtained or lost in accordance with the provisions of the appropriate law. **Article 10:** Personal freedom is immune from all forms of violation or encroachment. No person may be arrested or punished other than pursuant to an order issued by a *Sharia* court or in accordance with the provisions of appropriate laws. The principle of slavery is completely abolished. No man or woman can employ others as slaves.[2]

This new development led to the freedom of an estimated 700 Hazara slaves in Kabul alone who were enslaved during the reign of Amanullah's grandfather, Abd al-Rahman. The enslaved Hazaras were sold at a fixed price of fifty rupees for twelve-year-olds and thirty rupees for boys and girls over twelve years of age. Subsequently the price was lowered to the extent that every affluent family owned one or more slaves and friends and state functionaries were offering slaves as gifts to each other. Abd al-Rahman and his successor Habibullah continued to receive slaves as before. Odalisques known as *kaniz, surati,* and *eunuch* are referred to as *ghulam bacha* and were assigned to the palace's harem.[3] Amanullah not only abolished such practices but also granted freedom to minority religious communities as well as non-Muslim communities, Jews, Hindus, and Sikhs to practice their faith. The state admitted children of Hindus and Sikhs to military schools, who subsequently became army officers.[4]

In the social arena Amanullah strove to end illiteracy by establishing adult classes, with Amanullah himself participating in teaching some classes, and by recruiting itinerant teachers to serve nomadic citizens. Amanullah also established modern schools for training of new generations of state and civil service personnel. The Amaniya School, founded in 1922, followed the French educational models; the Amani School, built in 1923, was patterned after the German educational system; and the Ghazi School, established in 1927, followed the British model of education, with classes taught in English. By introducing modern education Amanullah did not intend to dismiss religious education but expected that modern education would broaden the horizon of religious teachers and clerics. Stressing the importance of modern education, Amanullah stated:

We are keenly alive to the value of education. But to bring learning to my people must be a slow process. . . . We hope to lay our plans well and truly, but not too fast. Religion must march hand in hand with learning, else both fall into the ditch. This country is rich in fine men and magnificent material resources, both as yet undeveloped. It is my hope to invite experts from all over the world—including America—to help me in my plans. But, frankly, Afghanistan is for the Afghans, and I intend my people to enjoy the fruits of their labors, not foreign capitalists.[5]

Although conservatives and traditionalists did not approve of Amanullah's educational programs, he insisted on building modern educational institutions. Elementary education was made compulsory and free of charge for both sexes, and the state provided some stipends and clothes to students beyond primary education to encourage poor and marginalized families to send their children to school. In 1921 the state sent forty-four students to France for higher education; a year later it sent another forty students to Germany and several other students were sent to Turkey, Iran, Switzerland, and the United Kingdom.[6]

The state also established schools for girls. The first primary school for girls, Masturat School, was established in 1921 in Kabul under patronage of Amanullah's wife, Soraya. Soraya's mother, Asma Rasmiyah Tarzi, born in Syria, was the principal of the school, assisted by her two nieces, Belqis and Rohafza.[7] The state encouraged people to send their daughters to school, and civil service personnel in particular were persuaded to send their daughters to school so that they could set an example for other people to follow. During the same year the state also established the first women's theater in Paghman, Kabul, with the objective being to break women's isolation, as women spent most of their time looking after children and performing household chores and had to deal with boredom associated with such routine works. To raise women's social awareness the state established the weekly *Irshad-e-Niswan*, the Guide for Women, in 1921, which was edited by Amanullah's mother-in-law, Asma Rasmiyah Tarzi. The paper's main theme revolved around social, political, and international issues, but it also provided recipes and useful tips to women regarding homemaking and fashion.[8]

To improve women's health the state established the first women's hospital, Masturat Hospital, in Kabul, which was administered by Amanullah's sister, Bibi Gul, known as Seraj al-Banat. Al-Banat was also active in social works and often participated in campaigns aimed at raising social awareness among women. In 1923 she addressed a public gathering in Kabul in which she criticized the prevailing concept of women's inferiority:

> Some people are laughing at us, saying that women know only how to eat and drink. Old women discourage young women by saying their mothers never starved to death because they could not read or write. . . . But knowledge is not man's monopoly. Women also deserve to be knowledgeable. We must on the one hand bring up healthy children and, on the other hand, help men in their work. We must read about famous women in this world, to know that women can achieve exactly what men can achieve.[9]

Amanullah discouraged polygamy and remained monogamous after his two earlier marriages arranged by his mother, Sarwar Sultan. His first marriage lasted for a few days and then Amanullah married Pari Gul, known as Shahzada Khanum, who died shortly after giving birth to a boy, Hidayatullah, and at the age of twenty-one Amanullah married Soraya Tarzi, a marriage of mutual choice.[10] One of the major achievements of the state under Amanullah's leadership was the introduction of the *Nizamnamah-ye-Arusi* and the *Nikah wa Khatnasuri*, laws concerning engagements, marriages, and circumcision in August 1924. The *Nizamnamah* stressed gender equality and established a minimum age for marriage. Girls were encouraged to choose their marriage partners without their parents' interference and women were urged to take legal action if their husbands did not treat them well. The *Nizamnamah* stated:

> If the wife of a polygamist man feels that her husband has failed to treat all of his wives fairly and equally, she can file a complaint against her husband in a court of *Sharia,* so that the unjust husbands should be punished accordingly. Moreover, punishment was prescribed for husbands who would prevent their wives from petitioning against them. . . . Article 18 of this document prohibits a forced marriage between adults; it calls the arranger of such a forceful marriage *jabir,* tyrant, and states that the *qazi* [judge] who presides over this contract is to be reprimanded.[11]

Queen Soraya and her supporters also campaigned to advance the cause of women's freedom. During the seventh anniversary of the country's independence, Soraya delivered a public speech in which she harshly criticized those who viewed women's equality as anti-Islamic:

Independence has been achieved. It belongs to all of us. . . . Do not think, however, that our nation needs only men to serve it. Women should also take part as women did in the early years of Islam. The valuable services rendered by women are recounted throughout history, from which we learn that women were not created solely for pleasure and comfort. From their examples we learn that we must all contribute toward the development of our nation and that this cannot be done without being equipped with knowledge. So we should all attempt to acquire as much knowledge as possible in order that we may render our services to society in the manner of the women of early Islam.[12]

To further advance the women's cause, Amanullah announced that he would establish five additional schools for girls in Kabul. Modern education grew to the extent that in Kabul in the period 1920–1927 there were two primary schools and one middle school for girls, with an estimated 700 students. Amanullah promoted a co-education system and the Amaniya School, which was named for him, admitted a few girls as well as boys and encouraged female instructors from France, Germany, Turkey, and India to teach foreign languages and science classes. In 1928 Amanullah sent fifteen female graduates of the Masturat middle school, mainly daughters of the royal family and government officials, to Turkey for higher education.[13]

Conservatives opposed Amanullah's radical social, political, and economic reforms. A major rebellion broke out in Khost in March 1924 but was immediately suppressed by the state's armed forces. However, the threat of rebellion compelled Amanullah to temporarily rescind some of his reforms and modify several others, for example, directing women to receive schooling at home, encouraging religious studies prior to learning foreign languages, allowing men to marry four wives, establishing Arabic classes, and substituting cash or commodity in exchange for service in the army.[14] After Amanullah suppressed the rebellion his modernization programs moved at a slower rate.

Between December 1927 and June 1928 Amanullah, his wife, Soraya, and a number of his entourage visited several countries, including British-controlled India, Egypt, Italy, France, Germany, England, and the Soviet Union. On his way home Amanullah visited Turkey and Iran and was impressed by the efforts of the Turkish leadership in modernizing Turkey. The objective of Amanullah's long visit abroad was twofold: to project a new image of Afghanistan abroad, and to observe Western developments with the intention of implementing them in Afghanistan. When Amanullah returned home he delivered this speech to a public gathering in Kabul:

My beloved people! I can hardly express to you the measure of my devotion to my country, and to you. I have seen most of Europe, and you will be pleased to know that I was every where warmly welcomed and esteemed. But it was not my personality that was so highly honored: rather it was in the fullest sense the Afghan nation. My purpose in going was to understand thoroughly the secrets of Europe's wonderful progress, my one idea being to formulate the proper means for our own advancement. I earnestly desire to see our sacred country progressing in every way by leaps and bounds. It was my part to chart the path of progress, to devise measures for the uplift of our general condition—moral, mental, social, economic. . . . The surest way [to progress] is to make every effort to have our sons and daughters educated according to modern standards. I am compelled to say that the great secret of progress for our country lies in discarding old, outworn ideas and customs, and as the proverb goes, march with the times. Rest assured that it rests with our generation to rebuild this country in the fullest sense. In truth, the rise or fall of our country depends largely upon our rising generation, and you are in duty bound to bring up your children in the light of modern education. Therefore, I ask you to make a solemn promise that you will do your best to support the cause of education throughout the length and breadth of Afghanistan. We must show [other countries] that we are no longer an ignorant people and that we are determined to stand upon our own feet, without leaning upon others.[15]

Amanullah vigorously pursued his premature modernization programs, some of which had no practical application to the daily lives of common people. For example, ordering residents of Kabul to wear Western dress and hats—such a measure caused much distress among conservatives and poor people who could not afford such expenses, and most stores in Kabul had few European clothes in stock. To ensure its implementation, harsh measures were adopted—signs were posted in certain areas in the city that prohibited entry to veiled women and law enforcement officers fined anyone who did not obey orders.[16]

To further enhance the status of women and defend their rights, Amanullah established Anjuman-e-Himayat-e-Niswan, the Association for Protection of Women, in 1928 and appointed his other sister, Kubra, head of the association to coordinate, supervise, and guide its work concerning women's liberation. The association had twelve active members who worked to promote women's welfare and encouraged women to protest to the society if their husbands, brothers, and fathers mistreated them.[17]

On August 29, 1928, Amanullah convened a Loya Jirgah, a Grand Assembly of Tribal Elders, that lasted until September 2 of that year, to endorse his development programs. The 1,100 delegates were required to wear European clothes that were provided for them by the state.[18] Amanullah addressed the delegates and demanded new taxes for the implementation of his social, economic, and political reforms. The reforms included a campaign to reduce and eventually abolish stipends and privileges of tribal chiefs and distant members of the king's family, as well as subsidies and salaries of religious leaders. The reform also aimed at terminating the system of *muhtasib,* religious police who were delegated the task of enforcing religious observances; and establishing schools to train qualified religious leaders and to ban students of the India-based Deoband School of Islamic Theology from teaching in Afghanistan.[19]

Amanullah argued for women's rights to education and equality and asked his wife, who accompanied him to the Loya Jirgah, to discard her veil. After that, Soraya appeared in public without a veil and an estimated 100 women, mainly wives of government employees who supported her, also discarded their veils.[20] Progressive delegates applauded when Soraya discarded her veil, but conservatives and traditionalists were scandalized by such an action. Conservatives objected to the unveiling of women, regarding it a violation of Islamic values, and opposed other propositions that concerned abolishment of honorary titles and privileges of clerics and the ban on clerics of the Deoband School to teach in Afghanistan. Although the conservatives reluctantly endorsed Amanullah's proposals, upon their return home they began to mobilize public opinion against him on the grounds that his policies were anti-Islamic.

In September 1928 Mohammad Sadiq Mojaddadi, the brother of influential religious leader Fazl Omar Mojaddadi, collected signatures of 400 clerics declaring Amanullah anti-Islamic and organized a rebellion in Paktiya. The state suppressed the uprising, executed four clerics, and sentenced members of the Mojaddadi family to life imprisonment.[21] As opposition mounted against Amanullah, a number of people within the state apparatus also turned against him. To convince the public that Amanullah had violated Islamic values, the opposition reproduced copies of Soraya's photographs published in various European newspapers during Amanullah's official visit to Europe. In the photographs Soraya was depicted wearing a low-cut gown at various official meetings and ceremonies. The opposition then distributed these photographs among the tribal peoples in the frontier areas in an effort to turn public opinion against Amanullah, claiming that he and his wife had undermined the Islamic way of life by promoting Western culture, and called for a *jihad,* holy war, as a necessary means to restore Islamic order. In November 1928 the Shinwari tribes rebelled against Amanullah.

In order to placate his opponents and restore stability, on January 6, 1929, Amanullah temporarily canceled most of his reforms. For example, girls studying in Constantinople were recalled and schools for girls were closed. Religious teachers of the India-based Deoband School were again allowed the right of residence in Afghanistan. Women were again prohibited from appearing unveiled and cutting their hair. Old tribal systems were reinstated; compulsory military enrollment was abandoned; *muhtasib*s were reinstated and appointed for each province to ensure the strict observance of religious precepts. Clerics were no longer required to obtain teaching certificates in order to teach religion. Religious leaders, including Mojaddadi, were released from jail as a gesture of goodwill by the state in an attempt to defuse the volatile political situation.[22]

These concessions and the others did not appease the tribal chiefs and conservative clerics. Aided and abetted by the British government of India, they opposed Amanullah's policies and demanded that he divorce his wife and close all foreign missions except those of the British. Amanullah's refusal to accede to these demands escalated social tension. It was during this time that Habibullah organized a group of armed men to overthrow Amanullah. Habibullah was known by the name of Bacha-e-Saqaw, meaning "son of a water carrier" by his detractors, a reference to his father, who was a water carrier for his town (an occupation similar to an American milkman). Habibullah was born and raised in Kalakan district, a few miles north of Kabul, and was recruited as a soldier in the king's army, Qita-e-Namuna, model battalion. During the Khost rebellion in 1924, Habibullah deserted the army and went to British India. In Peshawar he ran a teahouse. A few years later he returned to his native town, Kalakan, and was warmly greeted by his friends. Soon Habibullah's fame spread throughout the country because he had amassed considerable wealth through attacking and plundering caravans. In his autobiography he stated: "I was Lord of Kohistan, and ruler of the caravans, and my name was known throughout Afghanistan. . . . I realized that to enhance and sustain my position, I must not rest on my laurels. Moreover, I could not continue indefinitely as a mere robber of the trade routes. . . . I must do more than that."[23]

On January 14, 1929, Habibullah and his supporters launched a frontal assault on Kabul. Amanullah was forced to abdicate the throne in favor of his elder brother, Enayatullah, and retreated to Qandahar. A few days later Enayatullah also left Kabul for Peshawar and then joined Amanullah in Qandahar. In Qandahar, Amanullah tried to recruit support, but the city's population only reluctantly responded to his call. He managed to organize a small force to recapture Kabul but was defeated and left his country for Italy in March 1929. Amanullah did not wish to fight further, as he believed that the bloodshed would exacerbate the situation and inflict further disaster on the nation.[24]

REGRESSIVE DEVELOPMENT POLICY

Habibullah seized state and political power and ruled the country for nine months. He took the honorific appellation of Khadim-e-Din-e-Rasul Allah, Servant of the Faith of the Prophet, and was known as Habibullah Ghazi. Habibullah promised a complete return to an Islamic way of life. Most religious leaders who were disenchanted with Amanullah's modernization programs supported Habibullah. To consolidate his position, Habibullah relied on his brothers and close aides. He appointed his brother Hamidullah as his deputy and his other brother, Ata al-Haq, as his foreign minister. His trusted aide Sayed Hussein was appointed minister of war and Shir Jan was appointed chamberlain. Habibullah published a newspaper, *Habib-ul-Islam*, Friend of Islam, that propagated conservative social and political agendas. He closed all the modern schools and reinstated laws that facilitated polygamy.[25] During his final days of rule he also declared that he planned to reopen some of the schools in Kabul. During the reopening ceremonies of a school for foreign-language instruction his close aide Qiyamuddin stressed the importance of learning "the language of the unbelievers, without the knowledge of which it was impossible to have normal relations with foreign states."[26]

Rebellion against Habibullah's rule broke out in regions where the people still remained loyal to Amanullah. Mohammad Nadir was Afghanistan's ambassador to France in 1924–1926 but remained in France until 1929. Soon after his return Nadir began anti-Habibullah campaigns, calling him a Tajik bandit who usurped power from the Pushtuns. By capitalizing on Habibullah's ethnicity, Nadir tried to stir nationalist emotions among the Pushtuns and garner their support in his bid for power. In October 1929 Nadir and his four brothers organized a volunteer tribal army from among some of the Pushtun tribes of Paktiya to overthrow Habibullah. They fought Habibullah, defeated him, and proclaimed Nadir the new king.

Nadir was born in 1883 in British India, where his family was forced into exile by King Abd al-Rahman, but he and his family returned after Abd al-Rahman's successor, Habibullah, declared a general amnesty. Nadir became a brigadier-general in the army in 1906 and commander in chief in 1913. He was a conservative man who opposed Amanullah's modernization programs and was sent into diplomatic exile. To consolidate his power base, Nadir arrested and executed a number of Amanullah's supporters and crushed local uprisings to his rule. He relied on his brothers and appointed Mohammad Hashim prime minister, Shah Mahmood minister of war, Shah Wali his deputy, and Mohammad Aziz ambassador to Moscow and later to Germany, and appointed other family members to key government posts.[27] Nadir also allied with conservative clerics and tribal chiefs and appointed some of them to key positions in the state bureaucracy. He appointed Mojaddadi's brother, Shir Agha, minister of justice and his other brother, Mohammad Sayed, minister of state, and made Hazarat his ambassador to Egypt.[28]

To legitimize his rule Nadir convened a Loya Jirgah in September 1930 that was composed of 301 delegates, including 200 government officials and 18 foreign diplomats. The Loya Jirgah, which was dominated by handpicked representatives, recognized Nadir as the king, approved his policies, and revived the awarding of honorary titles to clerics and government officials that Amanullah had abolished as part of his modernization project. The Loya Jirgah also charged 105 of its members, called the Shura-e-Milli or National Assembly, with the task to draft a new constitution. On October 31, 1931, the new constitution, *Usul-e-Asasi-ye-Dawlat-e-Aliyya-e-Afghanistan*, the Fundamental Principals of the Higher State of Afghanistan, was promulgated. The constitution contained 110 articles, some of which were retained from the 1923 constitution. It restricted civic and political liberties and the freedom of other faith-based communities to practice their faiths. Article 1 of the constitution stipulated that the Hanifi School of Islam must be the official religion and that the king must be of the Hanifi Sunni background. Article 5 confirmed Nadir as the king and the succession of leadership to his family, and Article 22 brought all educational institutions under state control.[29]

In 1932 Nadir introduced additional statutes, one of which concerned citizenship and the status of women and prohibited marriage between Muslim women and non-Muslim men. It stated that foreign women legally married to the citizens of Afghanistan were considered to be the country's citizens. If widowed, and if they were born into the Muslim faith, they were free to revert to their original nationality. But a widow who had converted to the Muslim faith could revert to her original nationality only after the government had assured itself that upon returning to her native country she would not repudiate the Muslim faith. Non-Muslim widows were not allowed to repudiate Afghanistan citizenship. Article 97 stated that women who were married to non-Muslims were not regarded as citizens unless their husbands became naturalized citizens. If widowed, they were allowed to regain Afghanistan's citizenship by petitioning the government. Article 100 stated that women married to foreign citizens were excluded from all privileges of Afghanistan citizenship. Article 101 ordered that women who possessed property in Afghanistan must sell their property and land upon their marriage to a foreigner.[30]

A return to an Islamic way of life required desecularization of education, and Nadir delegated the task of supervision over educational materials to clerics to ensure that school curricula would be developed in accord with Islamic teachings. Nadir's policy of promoting Islamic education did not apply to the children of his immediate family members, who were sent to non-Islamic schools abroad. Duplicity was a common practice among leaderships who wanted others to abide by strict Islamic codes of conduct but did not extend such practices to their own family. Nadir closed the schools for girls, recalled all female students who had been sent abroad for higher education during the reign of Amanullah, and reinstated the practice of polygamy. The Hanifi School of Islamic Jurisprudence became the basis of civil and criminal laws. Women were forced to dress according to Islamic teachings and laws were enacted that prohibited the sale and production of alcoholic beverages and proscribed severe punishment to those who drank alcohol.[31] The Ministry of Justice was authorized to strictly enforce Islamic laws and *muhtasib*s were given full responsibility to ensure strict adherence to Islamic rules and codes of conduct.

Nadir erased any symbols of progress identified with Amanullah, for example, by renaming the Amaniya School as Estiqlal, Independence, and the Amani School as Nijat, Salvation. He reopened one of the schools for girls, Esmat, and converted it to a nursing school. To placate clerics and conservatives within and outside the state apparatus Nadir justified the opening of this school on the grounds that its function was primarily to train female nurses and midwives. Later Nadir also established a thirty-bed women's sanatorium and laid the foundation for a medical school in Kabul. In the final years of his rule, 1931–1933, girls were allowed to attend schools separate from men. There were 5,941 male and female students in high schools and other institutions of higher education.[32]

Nadir's pro-British and conservative policies generated dismay among progressives and pro-Amanullah intellectuals fighting to alter the status quo. In July 1933 Sayed Kamal assassinated Nadir's brother, Mohammad Aziz, who was ambassador to Germany. Soon afterward Mohammad Azim entered the British mission in Kabul with the intention to kill the chief of the mission. Unable to reach him he killed three employees of the mission and was arrested and sentenced to fourteen years in jail. Nadir's opponents finally succeeded in their objective. On November 8, 1933, Abdul Khaliq, a student at the Nijat School in Kabul, assassinated Nadir during a student award-distribution ceremony.

POST–WORLD WAR II PROGRAMS OF MODERNIZATION

Mohammad Zahir succeeded his father and ruled the country until July 1973. Zahir was young at the time of succession, so his uncles, Mohammad Hashim and Shah Mahmood, effectively ruled the country until 1953. Fearing opposition from clerics and conservative tribal chiefs and haunted by the experience of Amanullah's educational programs for women, Zahir adopted a cautious approach regarding women's education. A few separate schools for girls were established, including Zarghuna in 1941; Rabia-e-Balkhi in 1948; the Women's College in 1950, on the premises of the Malalay School, formerly called Masturat; and the first girls high school, the Lycee Mehri, in Herat in 1957.[33] The state encouraged employment of women in professions that were considered appropriate for women, such as teaching and healthcare. Since the overthrow of Amanullah, women once again remained in seclusion and wore the veil. Wives of high government officials who went unveiled to attend conferences abroad had to wear the veil upon their return home in order not to antagonize the conservative social strata and clerics. Some women did not always carry their *chadar,* and upon arrival at the Kabul International Airport such women were often met by servants running up to the stairs of the airplane to deliver a *chadar.*[34]

Intellectuals of upper-middle-class families were dismayed by the plight of women and began agitating for women's emancipation. These intellectuals still did not regard women's oppression as part of the social, political, and economic structure but rather attributed it to people's ignorance and the prevailing cultural traditions. Most of these intellectuals were male, and while they did not believe in women's equality to men, they did support education for women. Poet Fekri Saljuqi emphasized education for women as a prerequisite in preparing future leaders, and poet Shayeq denounced the treatment of women as second-class Muslims. He condemned:

The laxity of the courts in enforcing the legal rights of women in regard to marriage, divorce and property, attacking the tyranny of mother-in-law and sister-in-law in this connection. He even made an indirect attack on *purda,* which he found discriminatory and non-Islamic, placing women in the position of second-class Muslims.[35]

The ruling elite cautiously moved toward a gradual involvement of women in the public sectors. The first female announcer, Latifa Kabir Seraj, was employed at the Radio Station in 1947, and the first female singer, Parwin, who came from an influential family in Badakhshan, was also employed at the Radio Station in 1951. Habiba Askar was the first female actress and began her career in 1958 when she was twelve years old.[36] Prior to this time female entertainers performed in women-only theaters, while males dressed as women characters to entertain male audiences in theaters. Women performers gradually appeared in front of male audiences. Although there was some initial protest to women's work as singers and announcers, it gradually died out.

The decade of Prime Minister Daoud's administration, 1953–1963, was considered by most scholars to be a decade of modernization and women's emancipation. Having achieved stability and modernized the army with new weaponry capable of crushing any rebellion, the ruling elite were ready to support greater participation of women in the public and political arena. For example, in 1958 a women's delegation attended a conference of Asian women in Ceylon. Members of the delegation included Homaira Saljuqi, Kubra Noorzayi, Anahita Kiramuddin (Ratibzad), and Ayesha Mohammad Ali. Another woman, Mahbuba, was sent as a member of a delegation to the United Nations.[37] The government further tested public reaction to women's emancipation by employing a few women as receptionists and telephone operators in the Tele-Communications agency and employing other women, Najeya Wali, Zayeda Ata, and Fazila Ataye, as hostesses for Aryana Airlines.[38]

No large-scale opposition to this initial stage of women's liberation emerged. This convinced Daoud and the ruling class within the state apparatus to embark upon a major program of modernization, including the unveiling of women. During a military parade celebrating the country's independence anniversary on August 24, 1959, "the ladies of the royal family and wives of officials led a movement to end the use of the veil."[39] Some senior army officers who refused to bring their wives unveiled to the review podium during the military parade were relieved from their posts and some were arrested. However, women of the upper and middle classes and the intelligentsia supported the unveiling of women on the grounds that it was a step toward women's freedom. Daoud tried to implement his modernization project in the countryside. In the city of Pul-e-Khumri, taxi and cart drivers were fined if they gave rides to veiled female passengers, and the wives of factory workers who did not discard their veil were refused admission to the cooperative society to buy tea, flour, and other necessities.[40]

Daoud's policy of women's emancipation sparked opposition and rebellion by tribal chiefs and religious leaders in several southern provinces such as Qandahar, Jalalabad, and Wardak. Conservative clerics staged massive protest demonstrations and attacked various state-owned institutions in these cities with the intention of forcing the government to retract its women's rights program. In some of these cities the demonstrators beat to death women who removed their veils. Daoud used the military to crush opposition to his "women's movement." Within two days the government forces crushed the resistance, imprisoned approximately 600 people, and executed some of the key organizers.[41] To further humiliate the clerics still in jail, Daoud challenged them in the ideological arena and had his aides debate the issue of women with them:

He sent Musa Shafiq, the senior mullah of the royal family's palace mosque, to debate them on Quranic law. Shafiq, who would later become Afghanistan's prime minister, held a law degree from Columbia University, and was also a graduate of al-Azhar University in Cairo. He was considered one of the country's highest authorities on Islam at the time. Daoud ordered him to challenge the imprisoned mullahs to find Quranic support for their insistence that women's faces should be covered. The clerics failed to do so, and Daoud's modernization program continued unhindered.[42]

After crushing the opposition, the state moved forward with its programs of women's emancipation. During an anniversary of the country's independence celebration in 1962, three women, Sayed Bibi, Saleha

Farooq, and Simin Askar, became the first group to participate in a public parade. Similarly, a delegation from the Women's Institute visited the Soviet Union in 1962; a year later another women's delegation participated at the Women's International Congress in Moscow, and two members of the Women's Institute participated at the Women's International Congress in Helsinki.[43]

Scholars of the development school in Afghanistan attribute the unveiling of women to Daoud's leadership, but downplay the influence of capitalist development on the freedom of women to adopt Western culture and dress. Foreign products, including luxury items, flooded internal markets, and merchants needed consumers to buy those products. Local entrepreneurs and merchants regarded women as a potential consumer market, so they joined with the government to press for women's liberation. Daoud reflected on the power of conservatives and clerics and their opposition to women's emancipation:

At times up to eighty percent of the village mullahs, especially in the south of Afghanistan, have been graduates of a special high school in another country. . . . When a picture of the king first appeared on paper money, the cry went up that the Royal Family would force the Muslim population to accept idolatry, also anathema to Islam. The first school of higher education for girls in Kabul had to be disguised under the name of School for Midwifery. For ten years, because of pressure from the clergy, all students taking human anatomy in the Faculty of Medicine had to travel to Bombay in order to dissect a cadaver.[44]

Opposition to Daoud's strategies of modernization and his repressive administration grew both within and outside the state apparatus. A power struggle within the ruling family led to his resignation in 1963 and Mohammad Yusuf, minister of mines and industries, became the new prime minister.

WOMEN AND MODERN EDUCATION

Modern educational institutions gradually expanded in the post–World War II period. Not only was there an increase in the number of schools, but efforts were made to introduce a coeducational system. In 1958 the first experimental coeducational school was established for teachers training in Kabul. In the late 1950s the state also took calculated steps to send female students to study abroad in institutions of higher education. In 1957 Mahgul M. Ali went to the United States to study medicine and became the first female physician in Afghanistan. Asadullah Seraj was appointed Afghanistan's ambassador to Turkey in 1951, enabling his daughter, Mahbuba Rafiq, to study in Ankara. She was the first woman to obtain a doctoral degree in literature and worked at the Ministry of

Foreign Affairs. Two other women of upper-class families, Homaira Hamidi, a teacher and editor of a women's magazine, and Maryam Shah, who was also a teacher in one of the schools in Kabul, also went to the United States for higher studies.[45]

In the 1960s capitalist development and industrialization also expanded, to the extent that by 1966 there were 85 industrial complexes with a total number of 21,470 workers.[46] New industries, banks, and other technical projects required professional and skilled labor forces. This situation led to a steady expansion in educational establishments as well as technical and vocational schools and an increase in enrollment of students. In 1968 there were 111 primary coeducational schools, 51 of which were in Kabul with the rest in other provinces.[47] During the same period there existed 36 middle schools for girls in 19 provinces, and 11 high schools in 10 provinces, with 7 middle and 5 high schools for girls in Kabul.[48] Education was free of charge from elementary school up to the university level. Girls were required to wear uniforms, which consisted of a single dark blouse and skirt, black stockings, and a white scarf. Wearing uniforms relatively declined in the late 1960s and mid-1970s. Although boys and girls attended the same classes in the elementary grades, they usually sat on separate sides of the room. Boys and girls attended separate schools after graduating from elementary schools, but they were united again in college. Table 3.1 shows the number of female students in schools in 1975–1995.

Table 3.1
School Enrollment, 1975–1995

		1975	1985	1995
Preprimary	Total	1,891	17,000	—
	Female	919	7,545	—
	% Female	49	44	—
Primary	Total	784,568	580,499	1,312,197
	Female	115,795	179,027	420,270
	% Female	15	31	32
Secondary	Total	93,497	105,032	512,851
	Female	10,505	33,248	130,136
	% Female	11	32	25

Source: UN Educational, Scientific, and Cultural Organization (UNESCO), *Statistical Yearbook 1988* (Paris: UNESCO, 1988), pp. 3-75, 3-92, 3-130; and UNESCO, *Statistical Yearbook 1999* (Paris: UNESCO, 1999), pp. 3-83, 3-102, 3-178.

Enrollment at colleges and universities increased in the 1960s and 1970s, and substantially increased during the Soviet occupation of Afghanistan, December 1979 to February 1989. Attending school was one of the ways that young students could avoid being drafted into the army. The rate of school attendance declined after the Islamic parties seized power in 1992 and the subsequent war of ethnic cleansing shut down most educational institutions.

Rural areas have few high schools and colleges except in the capital of each province. The overwhelming majority of girls in rural areas could not continue their education after elementary school because strict traditions forbid girls to live anywhere but with their parents until their marriage. Thus, unless a rural family could arrange some kind of accommodation for their daughters with relatives who lived in a city, their daughters would end their education with elementary school. Furthermore, the vast majority of people were poor and could not afford further education for their children. Children of working-class families could not spend many years in school, for they had to work to supplement the family's income. Their participation in economic activities depended on what type of employment was available to them. In cities they generally worked in small shops doing cobbling, tailoring, carpentry, brass work, copper work, blacksmithing, automobile repair, and the like. Girls usually assisted in domestic work such as cooking, sewing, weaving, and housecleaning. The realities of their economic situation compelled most working-class children, especially girls, to drop out of school and marry. Few schools would admit married women; the exceptions were two schools in Kabul: the Jamhuriyat Vocational School, with 935 students in 1978, and the Afghanistan Women's Democratic Association Vocational School, with 987 students in 1978.[49] Table 3.2 shows student enrollment in universities and vocational and technical schools in 1986.

The number of female students continued to be smaller compared to the number of male students in most vocational and technical schools and colleges because most parents preferred that their daughters end school at an early age, and because working-class families were compelled by economic necessity to withdraw their daughters from school; girls, whether educated or not, had few opportunities for employment. Basically, working-class and low-income families considered education for girls unimportant in light of their poverty and struggle for survival. There were certain educational institutes that did not admit women, such as the School of Aviation and the School of Land Surveying. For these reasons, a very limited number of women attended vocational schools and universities. Table 3.3 shows the number of female students in various educational departments at Kabul University in 1956–1990.

Educated women consider the tradition and practices of arranged marriage to be a thing of the past, but many still consult their parents and seek

Table 3.2
Enrollment at Institutions of Higher Education, 1986

	Male	Female	Total
Institutions of higher learning			
Kabul University	2,503	3,148	5,651
Nangarhar University	885	197	1,082
Polytechnic Institute	1,797	556	2,353
Medical Institute	1,740	1,328	3,068
Kabul Pediatric Institute	365	603	968
Teachers Training Institutes	290	1,162	1,452
Total	7,580	6,994	14,574
Vocational and technical schools			
Kabul City	3,860	1,277	5,137
All provinces	2,976	74	3,050
Technical craft school	1,872	24	1,896
Total	8,708	1,375	10,083

Source: Wali M. Rahimi, *Status of Women: Afghanistan* (Bangkok: UNESCO, Principal Regional Office for Asia and the Pacific, 1991), pp. 44–46.

their approval when they want to marry. Parents continue to make sure that their daughters and sons marry someone of the same class and ethnoreligious affiliation. Most female college students hope that prospective marriage partners would possess "T, Kh, and M," *tahsil* (education), *khana* (house), and *motar* (car). A significant number of these women did not place too much stress on wealth as the basis of a good marriage but attached great importance to education in a prospective husband.

The number of female teachers was very small compared to that of males throughout the country. The figure was low due to a number of factors, but social discrimination against women was the most significant. Women could only teach in girls' schools, and there were many fewer girls' schools than boys' schools. Table 3.4 shows the number of female teachers in schools and universities in 1975–1994.

The number of faculty and teachers had gradually declined after the 1978 April coup. A significant number of them were either expelled from the colleges or imprisoned due to their political beliefs and subsequently replaced by party members and sympathizers, many of whom lacked the necessary academic qualifications to teach at institutions of higher education. The Kabul regime's repressive policies forced many faculty and instructors to flee the country. Available data indicate that approximately

Table 3.3
University Enrollment by Field of Study, 1956–1990

		1956	1965	1975	1986	1990
Education sciences	Total	—	451	3,740	3,351	739
	Female	—	208	904	—	525
Humanities, religion, theology	Total	98	555	807	236	755
	Female	—	150	163	152	154
Fine and applied arts	Total	—	—	—	284	23
	Female	—	—	33	135	9
Law	Total	197	509	464	613	157
	Female	—	51	29	337	87
Social and behavioral sciences	Total	103	460	1,047	634	87
	Female	18	58	98	301	56
Business administration	Total	—	—	—	—	148
	Female	—	—	—	—	53

Communications and documentation	Total	—	—	—	—	75
	Female	—	—	—	—	47
Natural sciences	Total	132	417	1,101	1,205	163
	Female	26	88	221	960	141
Medicine and health programs	Total	186	617	1,876	2,395	110
	Female	—	86	123	748	52
Engineering	Total	30	293	2,130	436	47
	Female	—	5	118	50	32
Agriculture, forestry, fishery	Total	24	140	1,052	1,135	125
	Female	—	—	35	441	41
Others not specified	Total	124	9	—	12,017	—
	Female	—	—	—	441	—

Source: UN Educational, Scientific, and Cultural Organization (UNESCO), *Statistical Yearbook 1968* (Paris: UNESCO, 1968); UNESCO, *Statistical Yearbook 1977* (Paris: UNESCO, 1977); UNESCO, *Statistical Yearbook 1988* (Paris: UNESCO, 1988), p. 3-231; and UNESCO, *Statistical Yearbook 1997* (Paris: UNESCO, 1997), p. 3-350.

Table 3.4
Number of Teaching Staff in Schools, 1975–1994

		1975	1985	1990	1994
Preprimary	Total	95	837	—	—
	Female	95	837	—	—
	% Female	100	100	—	—
Primary	Total	18,555	15,581	—	20,055
	Female	3,353	8,223	—	7,557
	% Female	18	53	—	38
Secondary	Total	8,089	5,715	—	17,548
	Female	1,090	1,887	—	6,042
	% Female		33	—	34
Two-year colleges and technical schools	Total	982	—	1,342	—
	Female	64	—	323	—
	% Female	6.5	—	24	—
Universities	Total	737	—	444	—
	Female	42	—	97	—
	% Female	5.6	—	22	—

Source: UN Educational, Scientific, and Cultural Organization (UNESCO), *Statistical Yearbook 1988* (Paris: UNESCO, 1988), pp. 3-75, 3-92, 3-130; and UNESCO, *Statistical Yearbook 1999* (Paris: UNESCO, 1999), pp. II-234, 3-83, 3-102, 3-178.

36 teachers from various colleges of Kabul University were executed between the 1978 April coup and the period of the Soviet invasion, December 1979. Of 258 faculty members, 238 males and 20 females, who fled to various countries in the West, 133 of them sought and received refuge in the United States.[50]

WOMEN IN THE PUBLIC ARENA

The number of women in other professions was also very small. There were few women doctors, nurses, engineers, and other personnel from the public health department. In 1976, there were 150 female physicians, 572 nurses, 400 midwifes, and a few in other health-related areas. Women's employment in occupations that require overnight travel to distant villages was very limited because of security considerations; fathers, brothers, and husbands generally refused to let a woman stay away from home overnight. Although women's employment in various industrial and manufacturing establishments was on the rise, their number was still very small in terms of the total female population in the country, because of lack of employment in general and job discrimination against women in particular.

Most industrial establishments are labor-intensive and tend to call for extreme physical effort. This in turn limited women's entry into such industries. On the other hand, women's labor is cheap compared to that of men, which led a number of companies and manufacturing industries to begin hiring female workers in the early 1960s. The Cottage Industries Bank established the Women's Handicraft Center in Kabul. The center consisted of a number of different sections, such as embroidery, tailoring, weaving, printing, leathercraft, and doll making. Available data indicate that female workers were dominant in the areas of embroidery and carpet and rug weaving. Table 3.5 shows women's employment in various handicraft centers in 1975–1976.

Although the main objective of these companies was to exploit cheap female labor, they claimed that their policies were to provide employment for women and involve them in the socioeconomic development of the country. The number of women employed by the state and the private sectors was relatively smaller in the rural areas because of the limited number of such projects there. The bulk of state-owned light and labor-intensive industries were in Kabul, with a few more such establishments in other provinces. Table 3.6 shows female employment in rural areas in 1972–1973. More women were employed in light industries because such industries (carpet and rug weaving, embroidery, textiles, etc.) required less physical strength. Women were underrepresented in agriculture, heavy industries, and other branches of the national economy.

Table 3.5
Women's Employment in Handicraft Enterprises, 1975–1976

	Total	Female	% Female
Carpet weaving	72,600	67,065	92.4
Rug weaving	11,814	10,803	91.5
Felt rugs	1,589	751	47.3
Flat-weave cotton rugs	3,699	42	1.1
Sheepskin coats and vests	3,117	114	3.7
Embroidery	27,685	27,524	99.4
Knife making	456	—	—
Pottery	531	113	21.3
Shawl weaving	1,952	72	3.7
Canvas weaving	6,051	1,847	30.5
Cap making	1,990	1,595	80.2
Bag and sack making	5,057	4,377	86.6
Total	136,541	114,303	83.7

Source: Pamela Hunte, Women in the Development Process in Afghanistan, 1978, project for the
U.S. Agency for International Development (USAID) (USAID, 1978), p. 40.

Men and women were paid roughly equal wages and salaries in all departments within the state apparatus, but this gender equity was mostly transparent because women were virtually without exception kept in the lower-paid echelon with no real opportunities for promotion. Women were underpaid in private enterprises and similarly had no avenues for advancement. Although most privately owned industries adhered to the principle of equal employment opportunity, in practice they did not treat women equally to men. For instance, in the Spinzar Company in Qunduz, "women pottery workers with four years' experience of doing the delicate trimming operations on the unfired teapots and jugs . . . earn only about two-thirds of the pay of men doing a similar job."[51] Women were paid less than men by the private sector because they are generally less educated than men, and this factor made them unqualified for many jobs as well as for advancement. Most women also accepted low-paying jobs with more flexible hours so that they would be able to take care of their children. Table 3.7 shows female employment in various professions in urban areas in 1972–1973. Women in the workplace had to wear clothing suitable for work, a situation that caused them to discard their traditional veil.

Table 3.6
Women's Employment in Rural Areas, 1972–1973

	State Sector	Public Sector	Self-Employed	Family Workers	Total
Technical	725	—	—	—	725
Administration	—	49	166	481	696
Clerical	163	—	—	—	163
Sales	—	—	—	109	109
Services	—	2,957	—	1,475	4,432
Agriculture	—	1,433	—	17,643	19,076
Production and related works	76	5,678	210	108,196	114,160

Source: Pamela Hunte, *Women in the Development Process in Afghanistan, 1978,* project for the U.S. Agency for International Development (USAID) (USAID, 1978), p. 36.

Table 3.7
Women's Employment in Urban Areas, 1972–1973

	State Sector	Public Sector	Self-Employed	Family Workers	Total
Technical and professional	6,056	184	23	34	6,297
Administration	294	—	12	—	306
Clerical	1,559	146	—	—	1,705
Sales	—	80	—	191	271
Services	451	4,697	—	975	6,123
Agriculture	—	198	105	761	1,064
Production	289	1,259	80	13,682	15,310

Source: Pamela Hunte, *Women in the Development Process in Afghanistan, 1978,* project the for U.S. Agency for International Development (USAID) (USAID, 1978), p. 35.

WOMEN IN THE POLITICAL ARENA

In the political arena, growth in women's education and employment opportunities have had very little impact on women's accession to high government posts. Only a few educated women of upper-class families and of other influential families have participated in state politics. Their active participation in the political arena began after the promulgation of the 1964 constitution. In 1963, King Zahir appointed a committee to draft a new constitution and called for elections of a Loya Jirgah to endorse the constitution. In mid-August 1964 elections were held, and of the total 452 delegates, 176 were elected by popular votes. The king also appointed four women to the Loya Jirgah; two were principals in girls' schools, one was an archivist at the Ministry of Foreign Affairs, and one was director of the publicity department of the Red Crescent Society. Another two women, Masuma Esmati and Kubra Noorzayi, were included in the constitutional advisory commission. The Loya Jirgah was convened in September 1964 in Kabul. Even the highest officials, while vocally supporting participation of women in the public sphere, belittled what they saw as a weakness of women that interfered with their ability to serve. For example, one of the female delegates "had a baby during the *Loya Jirgah,* so she was unable to participate in all sessions, leading to unofficial comments by several religious leaders on the superiority of men in legislative matters, even while admitting to the biological superiority of women."[52]

The constitution contained 128 articles defining the rights of individual citizens, members of the king's immediate family, and the government. The political system, in theory, was based on a separation of powers—executive, judiciary, and legislative—but in reality it proved otherwise. The constitution called all ethnic communities by the name "Afghan." Article 1 of the constitution stated:

Afghanistan is a constitutional monarchy; an independent, unitary and indivisible state. Sovereignty in Afghanistan belongs to the nation. The Afghan nation is composed of all those individuals who possess the citizenship of the state of Afghanistan in accordance with the provisions of the law. The word "Afghan" shall apply to each such individual.[53]

Women were not specifically mentioned in the constitution, but the word "Afghan" was considered to apply to men and women equally. During deliberations on the constitution by the Loya Jirgah, female delegates protested the content of the article and insisted that the article must be changed so that women were specifically mentioned. Many non-Pushtun delegates also disputed the language of the article on the grounds that the term "Afghan" referred only to the Pushtuns, not to all nationalities of the country. However, the Loya Jirgah refused to introduce any changes, and the constitution was endorsed in 1964.

The constitution was mainly a reconciliation of traditional and modern civil codes and legally prohibited, in theory at least, members of the king's family from holding top administrative posts in the bureaucracy, the usual system in the past. However, in practice, top government positions remained the exclusive monopoly of the king's family and intellectuals associated with them. Article 89 of the constitution stated:

The government shall be formed by the person designated as Prime Minister by the king. The members and policy of the government are presented by the Prime Minister to the *Wolesi Jirgah,* House of the People, which, after debate, resolves on a vote of confidence in the government. When the vote of confidence is given, the King issues a royal decree appointing the Head and members of the Government. Afterwards the Prime Minister acquaints the *Meshrano Jirgah,* House of the Elders, with the policy of the government.[54]

The constitution granted freedoms of association, the press, and formation of independent political parties. According to Article 31, freedom of expression was inviolable and every citizen of the country possessed it. In reality, newspapers were subject to state censorship after publication. Article 32 provided the basis for political activity and stated:

Afghan citizens have the right to assemble unarmed, without prior permission of the State, for the achievement of legitimate and peaceful purposes, in accordance with the provisions of the law. Afghan citizens have the right to establish, in accordance with the provisions of the law, associations for the realization of material or spiritual purposes. Afghan citizens have the right to form political parties, in accordance with the terms of the law.[55]

Soon after the promulgation of the constitution several private papers were published and political parties were formed. Both the private and state-owned papers hailed the constitution as a progressive national document that protected women's liberties and granted them equal rights with men. One of the privately owned publications, *Wahdat,* Unity, stated that the constitution treated men and women equally with regards to civil and political rights. Stating that the woman was now equal to the man in all walks of life, *Wahdat* promised to campaign for the amendment or replacement of all discriminatory or undemocratic laws and regulations that did not serve the interests of all the people.[56] Another privately owned paper, *Parwana,* Moth, expressed its approval of the constitution, saying that the primary theme of their publication concerned equal rights for women. They supported the campaign to give women equal rights in all areas of life, and promised also to campaign for the abolition of all laws that contradicted the democratic values of the new constitution, and that were not conducive to social justice and human dignity.[57]

On the basis of the new constitution women began to participate in politics. A number of women of upper- and middle-class backgrounds were appointed to cabinet posts. From 1965 to 1972, two women served as ministers in the government. Kubra Noorzayi served as minister of public health under Mohammad Hashim Maiwandwal from 1965 to 1967, and again under Noor Ahmad Etemadi from 1967 to 1969. Shafiqa Ziaye served as political adviser to Abdul Zahir in 1971–1972. However, the government of Mohammad Musa Shafiq, 1972–1973, who was regarded by the leftists as one of the leading figures of the Islamic fundamentalists, had no women ministers.[58]

Ruling-class family background, wealth, and association with a political-economic organization or the state were considered necessary factors in order for women to run for a seat in the House of the People, Parliament, and the House of the Elders, the Senate. During a 1965 election several women of upper-class backgrounds competed for seats in the House of the People. There were two women candidates from Kabul, one from Herat and one from Qandahar province. They were Anahita Ratibzad, Khadija Ahrari, Ruqia Abubakr, and Masuma Esmati. All four were elected as *wakil*, representatives to the House of the People. There were also two women in the Senate, Homaira Saljuqi and Aziza Gardizi.[59] Although most voters were male, a few women in urban and in rural areas voted. Table 3.8 shows the proportion of men and women in the cabinet, Senate, and Parliament in the period 1965–1972.

Participation of working-class women in elections began on a very limited scale. No women in the villages went to the polls except in the Doshi district of Baghlan province, where Nasir Naderi, a chieftain of the Isma'ili community, contested the parliamentary elections in 1965. He encouraged his female followers to vote for him so that he would be able to secure a seat for himself in Parliament and was elected *wakil* from one of the districts of Baghlan province for the period of 1965–1969.[60]

Table 3.8
Women in the Cabinet, Parliament, and Senate, 1965–1972

	Male	Female
Members of cabinet	20	2
Representatives in Shura-e-Milli	216	4
Senators	56	2
Total	292	8

Source: Marvin G. Weinbaum, "Afghanistan: Non-Party Parliamentary Democracy," *The Journal of Developing Areas* 7:1 (October 1972): 68.

During the 1969 parliamentary elections no woman was elected. Esmati, the incumbent *wakil* from one of the districts of Qandahar who won the 1965 elections due to the last-minute decision by the two contestants to withdraw from the race in her favor, was defeated, as was Zuleikha, a candidate from the Badakhshan center.[61] During the 1969 elections female participants were mainly from Kabul. A significant number of women, mostly wives of bureaucratic officials and government employees in the big cities, participated in the elections and went to the polls to cast their votes.

Politics and participation in public affairs were considered the exclusive domain of men in rural areas. Tribal chiefs and landowners are local arbiters and always act as spokespersons of their respective village and community. Although there are a few influential women in some families who play an important role in providing guidance and counseling to men concerning social issues related to the community, they did not participate directly in politics or act as spokespersons of their communities. It was rare to see a woman occupy the position of *Arbab,* arbiter, in rural areas, but a few cases have been documented. For instance, Agha Narg was a prominent woman in the village of Tagaw Barg in Panjaw, Bamiyan, in the 1950s and 1960s. She was chosen for the position of *Arbab* by the community to succeed her father, Mohammad Baig. Agha Narg received elementary education at home and served the people of Nargis, Gargar, and Tagaw Barg. She was considered a dedicated and passionate woman and people always sought her advice and judgment over that of government officials. She died at the age of sixty in the late 1960s.[62]

Another prominent woman in the public service in the late 1970s was Khadija, daughter of Murad Ali Karbalaye. She was chosen *Arbab* of the Anda and Shatu villages in Bamiyan province. Although her father had two sons, neither of them was a suitable candidate for the position. People respectfully addressed her by the title *Arbab* Khadija. During cold winters, when people had to cross the Shatu pass on their way to another village or back home, they could always stay over at Khadija's house; she looked after them and provided them with food. She traveled long distances even into the interior of the province, for meetings with local government officials to settle community-related issues. It was generally agreed that she was best suited to serve as the local arbiter and spokesperson to the government, and she would be responsible for all decisionmaking with regard to village matters.[63] Her reputation as a successful community leader drew the envy of men of similar stature.

During the decade of constitutional experiment, 1964–1973, a number of women of upper- and middle-class families also held leading positions within academic institutions, law schools, and the legal system. Of twenty-three professors in Islamic law and thirty-two in the law and political science departments, there were two female professors in the Law School at

Kabul University and one female judge in the High Central Court of Appeals in Kabul. Several other women received appointments to lower statutory tribunals and a number of other women served as defense attorneys in Kabul.[64] In the 1970s women also were employed in law enforcement agencies. Jamila Naim was among the first group of graduates of the Police Academy in 1970 who served as anti-smuggling squad officers, and others were commissioned at various departments.[65] Women's appointments to such positions helped to combat male stereotypes that a woman's role was in the domestic arena only, rearing children and performing other domestic chores.

NOTES

1. Lowell Thomas, *Beyond Khyber Pass: Into Forbidden Afghanistan* (New York: Grosset and Dunlap, 1925), pp. 181–182.

2. *Nizamnamah-ye-Asasi-e-Dawlat-e-Aliyah-e-Afghanistan, 20 Hamal 1302* [Constitution of Afghanistan, April 9, 1923]. For English text, see Leon B. Poullada, *Reform and Rebellion in Afghanistan, 1919–1929: King Amanullah's Failure to Modernize a Tribal Society* (Ithaca, N.Y.: Cornell University Press, 1973), pp. 278–279.

3. Hasan Kakar, *Government and Society in Afghanistan: The Reign of Amir Abd al-Rahman Khan* (Austin: University of Texas Press, 1979), pp. 175–176.

4. Mir Ghulam Mohammad Ghubar, *Afghanistan dar Masir-e-Tarikh* [Afghanistan in the Path of History], vol. 1 (Qum, Iran: Payam-e-Muhajir, 1359/1980), p. 794.

5. Thomas, *Beyond Khyber Pass*, p. 212.

6. Vartan Gregorian. *The Emergence of Modern Afghanistan: Politics of Reform and Modernization, 1880–1946* (Stanford, Calif.: Stanford University Press, 1969), p. 242.

7. Fahima Rahimi, *Women in Afghanistan* (Liestal: Stiftung Foundation, Stiftung Bibliotheca Afghanica, 1986), p. 44.

8. Gregorian, *Emergence of Modern Afghanistan*, p. 244.

9. *Anis*, quoted in Ministry of Information and Culture, *Progress Report* (1977), p. 9. Cited in Nancy H. Dupree, "Revolutionary Rhetoric and Afghan Women," in *Revolutions and Rebellions in Afghanistan*, M. Nazif Shahrani and Robert L. Canfield (eds.) (Berkeley: University of California Press, 1984), p. 307.

10. Poullada, *Reform and Rebellion in Afghanistan*, p. 40.

11. Helena Malikyar, "Development of Family Law in Afghanistan: The Roles of the Hanafi Madhhab, Customary Practices, and Power Politics," *Central Asian Survey* 16:3 (1997): 393.

12. *Anis*, p. 9. Cited in Dupree, "Revolutionary Rhetoric," p. 308.

13. Rahimi, *Women in Afghanistan*, p. 46.

14. Ghubar, *Afghanistan dar Masir-e-Tarikh*, p. 798.

15. Cited in Gregorian, *Emergence of Modern Afghanistan*, p. 259.

16. Ghubar, *Afghanistan dar Masir-e-Tarikh*, vol. 1, pp. 812–813.

17. Poullada, *Reform and Rebellion in Afghanistan*, p. 85.

18. Mohammad Alam Fayzzad, *Jirgaha-e-Bozurg-e-Milli Afghanistan, Loya Jirgahs, wa Jirgaha-e-Namnihad wa Tahti Tasalut-e-Kamunistha wa Rus-ha* [Grand

National Assemblies of Afghanistan, Loya Jirgahs, and So-Called Jirgahs Held Under Communists and Russians] (Islamabad, Pakistan: Author, 1368/1989), p. 123.

19. Poullada, *Reform and Rebellion in Afghanistan*, p. 77.

20. Gregorian, *Emergence of Modern Afghanistan*, p. 244.

21. Mir Mohammad Siddiq Farhang, *Afghanistan dar Panj Qarn-e-Akhir* [Afghanistan in the Last Five Centuries], vol. 2 (Peshawar, Pakistan: Author, 1373/1994), p. 533.

22. Poullada, *Reform and Rebellion in Afghanistan*, p. 130.

23. Amir Habibullah, *My Life: From Brigand to King, Autobiography of Amir Habibullah* (London: Octagon Press, 1990), pp. 96–98.

24. Surkha [Sazman-e-Rahaye-e-Bakhshi Khalqha-e-Afghanistan, or Organization for Liberation of the People of Afghanistan], *Chegunagi-e-Paidayish wa Rushdi Bourgeoisie dar Afghanistan* [The Process and Development of the Bourgeoisie in Afghanistan] (Berlin: Ayendagan Press, 1981), p. 30.

25. Hafizullah Emadi, "State, Modernization, and Women's Movement in Afghanistan," *Review of Radical Political Economics* 23:3–4 (Fall–Winter 1991): 228.

26. Mustafa Chokaiev, "The Situation in Afghanistan," *Asiatic Review* 26:86 (April 1930): 329.

27. Mir Ghulam Mohammad Ghubar, *Afghanistan dar Masir-e-Tarikh*, vol. 2 (Herndon, Va.: Hishmat Khalil Ghubar, 1999), p. 48.

28. Gregorian, *Emergence of Modern Afghanistan*, p. 294.

29. Fayzzad, *Jirgaha-e-Bozurg-e-Milli Afghanistan*, pp. 170–172.

30. Cited in Gregorian, *Emergence of Modern Afghanistan*, p. 306.

31. Ghubar, *Afghanistan dar Masir-e-Tarikh*, vol. 2, p. 43.

32. A. Hakim Ziai, "General Development of Afghanistan up to 1957," *Afghanistan* 16:3 (July–September 1961): 48.

33. Sondra Howell Bechhoefer, "Education and the Advancement of Women in Afghanistan" (M.A. thesis, University of Maryland, 1975), p. 74.

34. Arthur Bonner, *Among the Afghans* (Durham, N.C.: Duke University Press, 1987), p. 23.

35. Gregorian, *Emergence of Modern Afghanistan*, p. 350.

36. Rahimi, *Women in Afghanistan*, pp. 89–92. Note: Mohammad Rahim Ziyai, known as Shiwan Kabuli, was king Abd al-Rahman's grandson. He married Bibikuh, daughter of an influential chief of Badakhshan. Their first daughter, Khadijah, began a career as a singer at Radio Station under an assumed name, Mirman-e-Afghan, and later as Parwin. Cited in Wali Ahmad Noori. "Shiwan Kabuli." Unpublished paper, Paris: October 1994, 18 pp.

37. Bechhoefer, "Education and the Advancement of Women," p. 166. There were some discrepancies in spelling of names. I verified them by consulting Tawab Assifi, former minister of mines and industries.

38. Rahimi, *Women in Afghanistan*, p. 74.

39. *The Kabul Times Annual* (Kabul: Government Press, 1967), p. 13.

40. Andrew Wilson, "Inside Afghanistan: A Background to Recent Troubles," *Royal Central Asian Journal* 47:3–4 (July–October 1960): 287–288.

41. Akhgar [Sazmani Mubariza Bara-e-Azadi Tabaqa-e-Kargar dar Afghanistan, or Organization for Liberation of Working Class of Afghanistan], *Chand Sanand Wa Maqala Dar Mawridi Awza-e-Eqtisadi, Siyasi Wa Ejtima-e-Afghanistan*

[Documents and Articles on Economic, Political, and Social Conditions in Afghanistan] (Tehran: Published by revolutionary students, n.d.), p. 66.

42. Jan Goodwin, *Price of Honor: Muslim Women Lift the Veil of Silence on the Islamic World* (Boston: Little, Brown, 1994), p. 89.

43. Wali M. Rahimi, *Status of Women: Afghanistan* (Bangkok: UNESCO, Principal Regional Office for Asia and the Pacific, 1991), pp. 17, 60.

44. Louis Dupree, "An Informal Talk with Prime Minister Daoud," *AUFS Reports* 3:3 (September 1959): 2–4.

45. Bechhoefer, "Education and the Advancement of Women," p. 78.

46. *Afghanistan Industrial Development Projects,* Checchi and Co. Final Report, Washington, D.C., and Kabul, September 1974.

47. Bechhoefer, "Education and the Advancement of Women," p. 93.

48. Ibid., p. 100.

49. Beatrice Dupont, *Unequal Education: A Study of Sex Differences in Secondary-School Curricula* (Paris: UNESCO, 1981), p. 40.

50. Sayed Bahaouddin Majrooh and Sayed Mohammad Yusuf Elmi, *The Sovietization of Afghanistan* (Peshawar, Pakistan: Afghan Information Center, 1986), p. 125.

51. John C. Griffiths, *Afghanistan: Key to a Continent* (Boulder, Colo.: Westview Press, 1981), p. 100.

52. Louis Dupree, "Constitutional Development and Cultural Change, Part III: The 1964 Afghan Constitution (Articles 1–56)," *AUFS Reports* 9:3 (September 1965): 2.

53. *Constitution of Afghanistan,* 9 Mizan 1343 [October 1, 1964], in *The Kabul Times Annual,* Nour M. Rahimi (ed.) (Kabul: Matbaa-e-Dawlati, 1967), p. vii.

54. Ibid., pp. xvii–xviii.

55. Ibid., p. xi.

56. G. Shindandi, "Matboat-e-azad dar Afghanistan bad az infazi qanun-e-assasi jadid" [Free Press in Afghanistan After the Promulgation of the New Constitution] (B.A. thesis, Kabul University, Faculty of Law and Political Science, 1348/1969), p. 7. Cited in Mohammad Hashim Kamali, *Law in Afghanistan: A Study of the Constitutions, Matrimonial Law, and the Judiciary* (Leiden: E. J. Brill, 1985), pp. 155–156.

57. Shindandi, "Matboat-e-azad dar Afghanistan," p. 63. Cited in Kamali, *Law in Afghanistan,* p. 156.

58. Erika Knabe, "Afghan Women: Does Their Role Change?" in *Afghanistan in the 1970s,* Louis Dupree and Linette Albert (eds.) (New York: Praeger, 1974), p. 160.

59. Ibid., p. 160.

60. Author's personal account of developments in Afghanistan.

61. Louis Dupree, "Afghanistan Continues Its Experiment in Democracy: The Thirteenth Parliament Is Elected," *AUFS Reports* 15:3 (July 1971): 6.

62. Hafizullah Emadi, "Breaking the Shackles: Political Participation of Hazara Women in Afghanistan," *Asian Journal of Women's Studies* 6:1 (2000): 153.

63. For details, see ibid., p. 154.

64. Marvin G. Weinbaum, "Legal Elites in Afghan Society," *International Journal of Middle East Studies* 12:1 (August 1980): 47.

65. Rahimi, *Women in Afghanistan,* p. 104.

4

Political Mobilization: Women's Struggle for Equality

Modernization and capitalist development in Afghanistan in the post–World War II period led not only to women's greater employment in various industrial and manufacturing enterprises but also to increased enrollment of women in schools, vocational and technical colleges, and universities. Work outside the home significantly contributed to the development of women's social and political consciousness, made them aware that their society denies them equal rights with men, and motivated them to fight not only for radical social and political changes, but also for their own liberation.

POLITICS OF CLASS STRUGGLE

Women's clubs, societies, associations, and organizations, so prolific in Western societies and elsewhere, were alien to Afghanistan's politics until recent times. Although the struggle of individual women against social injustice and inequality started in the early 1950s, it did not result in any significant changes regarding women's status because it lacked both a coherent strategy for women's emancipation and an organization to coordinate their activities. Women's organized movements and resistance to societal injustices began after the promulgation of the 1964 constitution. There were two types of women's organizations: liberals and leftists.

The liberals, whose rank and file came from upper- and middle-class families, were represented by the state-sponsored Muassisa-e-Khayria-e-Zanan, Women's Welfare Association (WWA). The association was founded in 1946 under the Ministry of Finance and later was administered by the Ministry of Education. Zainab Enayat Seraj, a member of a ruling family, was appointed head of the association.[1] The WWA had several members and volunteers, including ex-king Amanullah's sister, Bibi Jan, age eighty-two, who also was of one of the founding members of the association. In exile in Peshawar, Pakistan, Bibi Jan reflected on the association's activities:

I liked working with families, especially women. We greeted women who were just sitting at home, and we gave them jobs with a salary. We started sewing projects and clinics and kindergartens and literacy classes. The women who were involved in these projects were very happy because it was the beginnings of a new life for them. . . . We had a very large vocational high school for women in Kabul. . . . At that time many women wore the *burqa* and we tried to get women to feel comfortable not wearing it. That was one of our major campaigns.[2]

In 1975 the WWA became an independent institution called Muassisa-e-Zanan, the Women's Institute. It gradually grew and expanded its activities by establishing branch offices in Parwan, Nangarhar, Balkh, Ghazni, Herat, Maimana, Badghis, Baghlan, Paktiya, Qunduz, Takhar, Qandahar, Kapisa, Bamiyan, and Badakhshan provinces and had 8,000 members. The association claimed it represented the interests of women irrespective of their class background or ideological position. It advocated gender equality, elimination of sex discrimination in employment, and increased participation of women in the state apparatus. Article 1 of its charter articulated that the society's goals were to "further extend the women's movement by increasing the participation of women in the progress and modernization of the community . . . through the increase in training and education of women . . . and the improvement of their social and political status."[3] Through the association's monthly journal, *Merman,* Woman, which was founded in 1953, the liberals made a concerted effort to propagate policies concerning the improvement of women's status in the country. Articles published in *Merman* criticized the patriarchal tradition, supported women's education, and glorified mothers who despite economic hardship and poverty managed to raise healthy children.[4]

One of the significant achievements of the liberal groups was the establishment in 1957 of Sahna-e-Tamsil-e-Niswan, a women's center for the performing arts that later was called Sinama-e-Zainab, named after one of its founding members, Zainab Enayat Seraj.[5] The Women's Institute also promoted fashion shows, and local models were encouraged to participate in the pageant shows displaying classic and new clothing styles worn by women of different tribes of the country. In Kabul there were several beauty parlors and seamstress shops creating modern dresses for women.

Fashion shows were organized once or twice a year in Kabul and a number of locals and foreigners were invited.

Other achievements by the liberals included the creation of women's volunteer groups in 1964 to combat illiteracy and the founding of Anjuman-e-Rahnuma-e-Khanawada-e-Afghan, or the Afghan Family Guidance Association (AFGA), on July 22, 1968, which was headed by Nazifa Nawaz, daughter of former prime minister Shah Mahmood.[6] By 1973 the AFGA had six clinics in Kabul and thirteen branches in major towns in the provinces. The liberals regarded high fertility rates as the prime cause of women's suffering. To alleviate women's suffering they supported family planning measures and the use of contraceptives and abortion, but they were not yet in a position to propagate the use of contraceptives through the mass media. They feared that publicizing such programs might provoke opposition by clerics and the conservative social strata. In order not to antagonize these social forces they adopted a very conservative approach in informing women about family planning and the use of contraceptives. Female personnel of the AFGA had to go door to door and personally inform the female population regarding this matter.

The health policies advocated by the liberals had no significant appeal among the majority of women because social tradition and Islamic laws, which prohibit premarital sexual relations, and the extremely cloistered daily lives of most girls, effectively curtailed premarital pregnancy; because having many children serves to enhance a woman's social prestige and influence; and because religious institutions and the general community dealt very severely with those who violated laws or rules of traditional conduct. Fear of reprisals at the discovery of an abortion or even an attempt to induce an abortion discouraged most women from considering it as an option. Women who wanted to use family planning measures were forbidden to do so by their fathers and husbands. The men did not allow their women to go to family clinics, considering the use of contraceptives to be against their religious beliefs. The majority of women in rural areas, as well as many women in urban areas, did not approve of the use of contraceptives for a variety of reasons. Many women believed that having children is God's will and that interference with God's will is a sin. Only a small percentage of women who did not wish to have more children and those who had to avoid the embarrassment and severe social punishment for secret sexual relations used contraceptives. Although sanitary products and modern methods of family planning (e.g., the pill, IUDs, diaphragms, condoms, and contraceptive jellies) were available in stores, women of poor families could not afford them and did not know how to use them. Children bought condoms from stores to play with as balloons. Table 4.1 shows the number of women who took advantage of services performed by AFGA clinics in 1976.

Table 4.1
Women Who Received Services Performed by AFGA Clinics,
1976

	New Visitors	Repeat Visitors
Pill	8,853	34,333
IUD	1,181	3,781
Diaphragm	24	47
Condom	5,160	18,624
Depo provera	71	586
Total	15,289	—

Source: Pamela Hunte, *Women in the Development Process in Afghanistan,*
  1978, project for the U.S. Agency for International Development
  (USAID, 1978), p. 21.

The percentage of women who used family planning measures was considerably higher in urban areas both because of the existence of a number of family clinics and because those who used these facilities were mostly educated women of upper middle classes.

Another achievement by the liberals during this period was the establishment of a Girl Scouts organization in 1957. Kamela Wayezi was the first woman who chose scouting as a career, and she participated in scouting activities in the United States, Germany, Pakistan, India, and Iran, and in the International Women's Congress in Moscow.[7] The organization enlisted school and college students both in Kabul and in provinces, but the majority of the scouts were in Kabul. Girl Scouts at Kabul University were relatively active in organizing scouting activities and participating in such activities outside the country. Although the liberals had initiated various social programs for women, they could neither establish their influence on women in rural areas nor formulate a successful political strategy to counterbalance the increasing influence of revolutionary and anti-establishment organizations that were engaged in organizational work among women in schools and in private and public sectors in urban areas. The liberals failed because they did not concentrate their work among blue-collar workers in various industrial and manufacturing enterprises that could have been organized to support their policies concerning women's liberation, and because their political work was limited to celebrating Mother's Day on June 14 each year throughout the country by organizing official meetings and publishing articles on the role of women in the upbringing of children, polygamy, and so forth.

The leftists postulated a revolutionary transformation of the socio-economic system and its ideology and politics as the only means of achieving gender equality. They were ideologically and politically divided in their support of the Hizb-e-Demokratik-e-Khalq-e-Afghanistan, the People's Democratic Party of Afghanistan (PDPA) and Sazman-e-Jawanan-e-Mutaraqi, the Progressive Youth Organization (PYO). The PDPA was founded on January 1, 1965, and advocated an evolutionary and peaceful transition to socialism. Although the party supported class struggle in words, it remained reformist in practice. A few years later the party split into two factions: Khalq (Masses) and Parcham (Banner). Soon afterward the Parcham faction formed Sazman-e-Demokratik-e-Zanan-e-Afghanistan, the Women's Democratic Organization of Afghanistan (WDOA), which was headed by Anahita Ratibzad (Ratibzad was born in 1931, studied nursing in the United States, and attended the medical school at Kabul University in 1957–1963). The WDOA's main goal was to expand the social base of Parcham among women in both government and private institutions.

Sazman-e-Jawanan-e-Mutaraqi, also referred to as Sazman-e-Demokratik-e-Nawin, the Neo-Democratic Organization of Afghanistan (NDOA), was also founded in 1965. The organization stressed class struggle and revolutionary armed uprising as a means of ending class oppression and building a socialist society. A great number of women of both white- and blue-collar backgrounds supported the organization, and some even became active members. These women identified with the goals of this organization and saw their methods as providing more immediate results. Supporters of the organization participated in political, ideological, and organizational activities among blue-collar workers and took part in workers' strikes and protest demonstrations for higher wages and better living conditions.

One of the major political works of the leftists was the celebration of Women's Day on March 8 every year, which coincided with the International Women's Solidarity Day (IWSD). Both the WDOA and the PYO sponsored rallies and meetings on that day and marched through the streets in downtown Kabul with placards and red banners inscribed with political slogans of women's liberation and solidarity with the women's movement internationally. Conservatives regarded the women's movement as anti-religious and began opposing it. Women organized a rally on July 22, 1968, when conservative deputies in Parliament proposed to authorities at Kabul University to modify the university's constitution to prohibit women from studying abroad. Opposition to the women's movement escalated and during a women's protest demonstration in Kabul in April 1970, "young religious fanatics threw acid on the women, some of whom wore miniskirts, inflicting painful and sometimes serious burns. Over twenty were hospitalized."[8] Security forces intervened and arrested several suspects, who later were sentenced to several years in prison. In

October a bicycle-riding man from Herat province, Gul Mohammad, assaulted schoolgirls and inflicted severe injuries on several of them. When he was arrested and sentenced to eighteen years in prison, he said that he would do it again if he were released. The incident provoked more than 5,000 women to demonstrate in front of the Prime Ministry, the Ministry of Interior, and the Ministry of Education, shouting, "Give him back to us!"[9]

During the constitutional period, 1964–1973, the country's economy was in shambles. Agricultural productivity was declining yearly. For example, wheat production declined from 2,282,000 metric tons in 1965–1966 to 2,033,000 tons in 1966–1967, and to 2,000,000 in 1967–1968.[10] Skyrocketing prices, inflation, and unemployment forced a great number of laborers and agricultural workers to migrate to neighboring countries in search of employment. Two consecutive drought years, 1970–1972, also contributed to the country's economic problems. The impact of the drought on poor farmers in several regions of the country was so severe that workers in villages had nothing to eat and many were compelled to sell their young daughters to landowners, rich people, and government employees in exchange for bread. The drought claimed the lives of an estimated 80,000 people, mostly women and children.[11] The decade of constitutional monarchy riddled with corruption was characterized as follows:

Favoritism and nepotism, corollaries of a tribal system superimposed on a government and long rampant in Afghanistan, remain widespread. Some collateral members of the royal family have never completely accepted the democracy-e-naw [new democracy] and look on its structure as simply a personal inconvenience. They ask official favors of cabinet ministers and other high ranking officials, and, if rebuffed, they usually manage to have their requests approved somewhere in the middle-range bureaucratic levels, in return for reciprocities, present or anticipated. Many tribal leaders go to the royal family with petitions, which are then transmitted to acquiescent middle-range bureaucrats in the ministries concerned. . . . Of course, such motives and actions exist in varying degree in all states, democratic and non-democratic alike.[12]

Polarization to overthrow the monarchy was increasing rapidly. Various political groups were organizing themselves intending to overthrow the monarchy, and there were also rumors of a coup by Abdul Wali, son-in-law of the king, and former prime ministers Mohammad Daoud, Mohammad Hashim Maiwandwal, and Mohammad Musa Shafiq. It was during this time that Daoud, who was supported by the Parcham faction of the PDPA, staged a coup and seized power on July 17, 1973. Pro-Soviet forces heralded the change as the beginning of a new era while common people viewed it simply as yet another change in the old guard. Shah Wali, uncle of the ousted king, thought that it was his son, Abdul Wali, who spearheaded the change. Din Mohammad, an attendant at Shah Wali's residence in Paghman, in describing Shah Wali's reaction to the coup, said that the first question Shah Wali asked was, "Has Abdul staged the revolution? The police had not told the Marshal that he was being arrested, only that he was being summoned to Kabul for important consultations. When he was told that it was Daoud who had brought about the revolution, he is reported to have said, 'After all, he too is our son.'"[13]

WOMEN DURING THE REPUBLICAN ORDER, 1973–1978

Daoud, who earlier supported the unveiling of women in 1953–1963, did not vigorously pursue measures to eliminate gender inequality during his rule in 1973–1978. Daoud declared that soon he would promulgate a new constitution, but did not do so until a year after he formed a new political party, Hizb-e-Enqilab-e-Milli, the National Revolution Party, in 1975. He appointed a committee of forty-one persons including two women, Alia Hafeez and Fatima Kayfi, to draft a new constitution.[14] The constitution contained 136 articles. Article 20 declared Afghanistan a republic and Article 23 recognized Persian and Pushtu as two official languages from among other languages. The constitution also declared equality of men and women before law. According to Article 27, "all the people of Afghanistan, both women and men, without discrimination and privilege, have equal rights and obligations before the law." Article 29 stated that "every Afghan who attains the age of eighteen has the right to vote in accordance with the provision of the law."[15]

The constitution restricted political activities to just one party, Hizb-e-Enqilab-e-Milli, and recognized the institution of Milli Jirgah, the National Assembly (formerly known as Loya Jirgah) as the only body with the authority to amend the constitution and elect or accept the resignation of the head of the state or remove him from his office if he was found guilty of wrongdoing. Article 76 stated that the Milli Jirgah, with a two-thirds majority vote of its members, would elect the president to a six-year term after his nomination by the political party. Daoud designed the system in such a manner that by manipulating the Milli Jirgah, he could easily re-elect himself for additional terms.

During the Milli Jirgah elections, conducted under the watchful eyes of the state, 219 desirable representatives were elected, including four women: Kubra Noorzai, director of the Women's Institute from Kabul City; Aziza Amani, principal of a high school from Qunduz; Najiba Siir, principal of Mahasty High School from Khulm, Samangan; and Najiba, principal of the Malika-e-Jalali High School from Herat. Another eight women were appointed by Daoud: Humaira Hamidi, Khalida Ghaus, Khadija, Zainab Amin, Mahbooba, Aziza Ehsan Omar, Suraya Khadim, and Zakia.[16] All these women were college graduates under thirty-five years of age. In February 1977 the Milli Jirgah was convened in Kabul, debated the constitution, and eventually approved it and elected Daoud president of the country.

Daoud had no women in his cabinet but his administration involved a number of women in junior-level positions within the state apparatus, which included fifty-four women in the Presidential Secretariat, ninety-one in the Office of the Minister of the State, and three at the Ministry of Foreign Affairs.[17] Daoud's social development programs for women included the introduction of a civil code in 1977 that contained several articles concerning relations between men and women. The civil code defined a minimum marriage age (sixteen for females and eighteen for males), allowed men and women to freely choose their marriage partners, permitted a couple to marry despite family opposition, and set rules for divorce. Although the law gave the exclusive right of divorce to men, women were allowed to submit an application for divorce under certain conditions, for instance if the husband had or should contract an incurable illness or if he refused or was unable to support his wife financially. In addition, if he was imprisoned for a long period of time, she could file for divorce anytime after the first five years.[18] Furthermore, Article 183 of the civil code permitted a wife to demand a divorce whether or not she could prove the existence of prejudice or harm if arbitration failed to bring a reasonable compromise between her and her husband. Similarly, Article 88 of the civil code required a wife to stipulate in writing, when registering for marriage, her right to divorce if her husband married a second wife. According to Article 89, a wife was also permitted to file a divorce application if her husband had hidden from her a marriage to another woman.[19]

The law also stipulated rules concerning child custody. After divorce a mother could get custody of a boy up to age seven and a girl up to age nine. The period could be extended for another two years provided that the court deemed it necessary for the child's best interests. If a mother remarried or was found to have behaved in an improper manner she was barred from seeking child custody. Although legally a woman could request a divorce, in practice it was still very difficult for her to do so because a woman was entirely dependent on a man in terms of economic support; there were not many opportunities for a woman to obtain employment and support herself, and a divorce was considered a social stigma and a dishonor to families. For this reason many women refused to seek a divorce even if their husbands abused them or married second wives.

To improve women's status, Daoud instructed the Ministry of Education to provide educational programs for women. Kumita-e-Ensijam-e-Zanan, the Women's Coordinating Committee, was established to promote the cause of women and encourage their participation in public affairs. The committee sponsored a series of educational programs via Radio

Afghanistan, which included programs on family affairs, short dramas, discussions of family issues, and the like. The government-owned media published feature articles and progress reports about women's activities and their role in socioeconomic development projects. During the annual celebration of Mother's Day on June 14, 1977, Daoud initiated a program to honor the most outstanding women, those who were widowed or abandoned and who without education or outside support managed to rear and educate several sons and daughters.[20]

Daoud's policies of promoting freedom for women also included establishing a family court in Kabul. Soraya Parwiz, who graduated from the Faculty of Law, Kabul University, in 1967, was appointed head of this court to resolve family-related issues. Similar courts were established in several other provinces such as Herat, Qandahar, and Qunduz. The state also recruited a limited number of women into the police and armed forces. There were seven women in junior positions at the Ministry of Defense and eight women at the Ministry of the Interior. In 1978 the government also introduced legislation designed to provide family health plans aimed at helping the mother and child. This legislation granted a husband a tax exemption for a wife, for each of his first five children, and for his unemployed parents.

Daoud, however, was preoccupied with consolidating his rule. The liberals had expected that Daoud would encourage increased participation of women in the state apparatus. They were disappointed when Daoud neither appointed a woman to his cabinet nor promoted women to key administrative positions. Although members of the WDOA and a number of the liberals criticized the leadership for not advancing the cause of women, they did not take any practical action to make their voice heard among women. Members and supporters of Jamiat-e-Enqilabi-e-Zanan-e-Afghanistan, the Revolutionary Association of Women of Afghanistan (RAWA), which was founded and headed by Meena in 1977, advocated and supported the cause of women's equality. However, they and other revolutionary women were not so concerned with the degree of women's participation in the state apparatus as they were with a revolutionary transformation of the system. Daoud was overthrown in a coup staged by members of the PDPA army officers on April 27, 1978, and Afghanistan was declared a "democratic" republic.

KHALQ AND PARCHAM RHETORIC OF WOMEN'S LIBERATION

Leaders of the PDPA who were arrested earlier by Daoud were released from jail. Noor Mohammad Taraki, head of the Khalq faction of the PDPA, became president, prime minister, and chairman of the Revolutionary

Council, and Babrak Karmal, head of the Parcham faction, became vice chairman and deputy prime minister. One of the socioeconomic reforms of the new regime concerned itself with the emancipation of women. The regime declared the equality of women and men in all social, economic, political, cultural, and civil aspects and appointed a female member of the party, Anahita Ratibzad, as minister of social affairs. A few months later political differences soured relations between the leadership of Khalq and Parcham and a decision was made to remove prominent Parcham leaders from sensitive posts and send them to diplomatic posts abroad. In June 1978 Mahmood Baryali, Karmal's half-brother, was sent to the Afghanistan embassy in Pakistan and soon afterward Karmal was appointed ambassador to Czechoslovakia, Ratibzad to Yugoslavia, Noor Ahmad Noor to the United States, and Abdul Wakil to England. Karmal and Ratibzad left their posts and went to Moscow, where they remained until the Soviet invasion of Afghanistan in December 1979.

Taraki dissolved the Ministry of Social Affairs on the grounds that it was no longer needed. The state renamed the WDOA Sazman-e-Khalqi-e-Zanan-e-Afghanistan, the Khalq Organization of Afghanistan Women (KOAW), and appointed the former principal of Amina-e-Fidawi High School, Delara Mahak, president of the organization. After a few months she was replaced by Aziza Azizi. The KOAW organized meetings and rallies and forced women to attend them in support of government policies. The organization employed approximately 510 teachers and 60 supervisors and declared that it would use their officers to train 6,000 army soldiers to read and write within a year.[21]

To win women's support, the state also issued Decree no. 7 concerning the emancipation of women. The decree contained six articles that stipulated marriage practices and ceremonies. According to the decree, no one could marry a girl in *nikah,* marriage, in exchange for cash money or commodities, nor could any one force a bridegroom to pay in cash or commodity the *toyana,* marriage expenses, at the time of the marriage. The decree further stated that the bridegroom and his family cannot be compelled to give holiday clothing or presents to the bride and her family for occasions such as religious festivities and the New Year, which traditionally demand such gift-giving. The decree limited to Afs. 300 (U.S.$6 in 1978) the amount in cash or kind a girl and her family could legally accept for *mahr*. Engagements and marriages would take place only with the full consent of both parties. A widow could no longer be forced into marriage to one of her husband's male relatives. Also, no one could prevent a legal marriage from taking place in order to collect engagement expenses. The decree enforced the minimum marriageable age of sixteen years for women and eighteen years for men. Those who violated the provisions of this decree were subject to imprisonment for six months to three years, and any money or commodities accepted illegally were confiscated.[22]

The state claimed that these laws had brought a new equality to women throughout the country, but many other issues such as child custody and the right to divorce remained unchanged. Decree no. 7 did not abolish the rights of men to marry up to four wives; it did not grant women the right to seek divorce; and it failed to stipulate what kind of punishment a man would be subject to if he physically abused his wife. Furthermore, the decree failed to protect the future of women seeking divorce. The Afs. 300 *mahr* (bride price) that a woman was entitled to upon divorce would not ensure a future for her if she had been divorced or expelled from the house by her husband. The decree was not based on democratic principles, nor did it contradict the Islamic Sharia law, yet feudal landowners and conservatives considered it to be anti-Islamic. Thus state policies of women's liberation provided feudal landowners and conservatives with the opportunity to oppose the regime's social reforms.

Although the regime passed a law forbidding arranged marriages, many top male officials in the party did not abide by it. An example can be found at the highest levels of the government, in the case of Premier Hafizullah Amin's eldest daughter, Ghaurgati. Amin arranged for her to marry Asadullah Amin, son of his brother, Abdullah Amin. In exchange, Abdullah's daughter was to be married to Hafizullah Amin's eldest son, Abdul Rahman Amin. Ghaurgati was in love with a young Kabuli non-Pushtun named Rafiq and was not interested in this marriage. However, she eventually bowed to tremendous familial pressure to fulfill the contract and married Asadullah Amin.[23]

Junior party officials also used the new marriage law for their own interests. Some took second wives by coercing young women into marriage, claiming that the marriage was based on love and mutual consent. In practice, female members of the ruling party still could not choose their marriage partner. They were obliged to follow tradition and let their parents decide for them whom to marry. Sohaila Shirzai, an economics major from Kabul University and member of the WDOA who went to the Soviet Union for further training and participated at the UN Decade for Women World Conference in Nairobi, admitted that she could not marry the person she liked because of her parents' objections.[24] She explained that while she was in college she met a number of men who wanted to marry her. Her favorite, Wahid, worked in the Ministry of Foreign Affairs and was a friend of her brother. But her father forbade her relationship with Wahid and threatened to disown her if she continued it.[25]

To further expand its social base of support among the female population, the regime launched a campaign against illiteracy and opened night schools. The literacy classes were intended as a means to promote political indoctrination. Although basic textbooks were used in the classes, teachers in charge of these classes emphasized political rhetoric in their instruction. These literacy centers thus became political centers. Members of the KOAW were sent to villages to conduct literacy courses. The government forced men to send their wives and daughters to the literacy centers. When conservatives opposed sending their women to these centers, young party members ordered accompanying guards to forcibly bring them. Some party members also abused their power and sexually molested their female students. Taraki did not hold members of his own ruling party responsible but instead attributed the crimes to hooligans, bandits, and thieves. He said that "there has occurred only one event after the revolution in which a few thieves broke into a house and molested the family. So far we have not reached any agreement on what kind of severe punishment should be meted out to those thieves."[26]

In 1979 the Kabul regime declared that since its seizure of power more than 18,000 women had received a basic education.[27] The number of female employees in various branches of manufacturing and industrial enterprises also increased during this period, as most young men left the country or joined the resistance groups. Table 4.2 shows the number of women employed in different economic sectors in 1979.

Although the Kabul regime signed into law policies concerning women's rights that no previous government had even discussed, its

Table 4.2
Structure of Economically Active Population, 1979

	Total	Percentage	Males	Females
Agriculture	2,369,481	60.1	2,358,821	10,660
Mining and quarrying	59,339	1.5	57,492	1,847
Manufacturing	423,373	10.7	170,908	252,465
Electricity and water	11,356	0.3	11,078	278
Construction	51,086	1.3	50,670	416
Wholesale trade, restaurants, hotels	137,860	3.5	135,242	2,618
Transportation	66,243	1.6	65,376	867
Major divisions[a]	749,345	19.0	716,511	32,834
Seeking better jobs	77,510	2.0	66,057	11,453
Total	3,945,593	100.0	3,632,155	313,438

Note: a. Refers to business services and community, social, and personal services.

Source: International Labor Organization (ILO), Yearbook of Labour Statistics (Geneva: ILO, 1982), p. 52.

social and political reforms intended to boost social developments failed because the method that the regime used to implement them was repressive and autocratic. This resulted in generating public disenchantment and subsequently provoked bitter opposition against the regime, with people declaring its policies regarding women's education as having a negative influence upon their wives' morals and perceptions.

One of the regime's policies of promoting the cause of women's liberation involved the appointment of women to high government positions. Prominent women holding key positions in the state apparatus in 1978–1979 included Sultana Umayd, director of the Kabul Girls School; Ruhafza Kamyar, principal of the Vocational High School; and Firoza, director of the Red Crescent Society. The government also supported female singers who could sing songs composed by the regime. Many veteran female singers of Radio Afghanistan, like Qamar Gul and Gulshan, and new singers like Parisa Mursal and Setara, known as the Girl of Herat, were called to work for the new regime. The state rehabilitated these stage performers and called them "revolutionary" women of Afghanistan.[28]

In addition to the campaign against illiteracy and support of women's liberation, the state forced government employees to participate in various development projects on weekends and holidays. Those who did not participate or who disagreed with government policies were called "counter-revolutionaries" and subsequently were imprisoned, tortured, and even executed. The state's repressive strategies of development and the systematic torture and execution of innocent civilians were intended to build a society in which there was no opposition, and all were members of the Khalq. Sayed Abdullah, the notorious commander of the Pol-e-Charkhi Prison, stated that "a million Afghans are all that should remain alive—a million communists. The rest, we don't need. We'll get rid of all of them."[29] Many prisoners were murdered and thrown into a common graveyard. Although men were the main victims of repression, the mothers, wives, sisters, daughters, and grandmothers of prisoners were also victimized. They were the first to mobilize against the regime. Their political invisibility and marginality in public activities provided them an opportunity to become major players during the Khalq's rule, whose terror tactics made it extremely difficult for men to engage in public political or organizational activities.

REPRESSION AND WOMEN'S RESISTANCE

Women's resistance against the state's repressive strategies of modernization emerged gradually in informal gatherings of small groups of women. These women used the traditional female activities, such as knitting, sewing, and tea parties, to camouflage their meetings and discussions. They exchanged information about the whereabouts of their loved ones and supported each other. These women often encountered each other outside prisons and government intelligence centers while seeking information about their missing and imprisoned relatives. They met other women facing similar problems and began to develop a mutual trust. When they failed to obtain any information on the whereabouts of their loved ones, they gradually realized that their individual efforts were not yielding any significant results and that they needed to unite in their struggle against the Kabul regime. In October 1978 they staged a protest demonstration in front of the Ministry of the Interior, demanding information on the whereabouts of their husbands, daughters, and sons. To bring the situation under control the state ordered the police to disperse the crowd and fire on those who resisted.[30]

Although the state dispersed the women demonstrators and imprisoned several women to intimidate future protesters, the women would not give up their struggle for freedom. In November 1978 the women once again assembled in front of the Ministry of the Interior to demand that the ministry release the names of those who had died or who had been executed. On November 16, 1979, the ministry released a list of as many as 12,000 who had died in Kabul jails after the 1978 April coup. The dead included professors, teachers, students, civil servants, religious leaders, merchants, and shopkeepers.[31] The release of a document containing so many names outraged the women to the extent that as they left the ministry, they chanted anti-government slogans and called upon people to overthrow the regime.

Women's opposition and resistance to the pro-Soviet government grew and spread throughout the country as the state's repressive policies for building a "democratic" society affected the country's population. Women members of several nationalist and revolutionary organizations participated in the anti-government resistance. Malalay, a member of Sazman-e-Mubariza Bara-e-Azadi Tabaqa-e-Kargar dar Afghanistan, the Organization for Liberation of the Working Class (Akhgar), was an active participant in the anti-government resistance in Kabul. She was arrested by the government security forces and was tortured for carrying and distributing anti-state literature. In order to force Malalay to reveal her organization's policies and its activities, government security agents subjected her to various types of torture that included skinning her hands, sprinkling salt on her wounds, shutting the door on her fingers, tying her hair to the ceiling and clubbing her with electric sticks, sticking needles in her body and connecting electric wires to her fingers, and raping her. When these methods of torture failed to produce the desired result, the security agents resorted to a different method. They sent two disguised women members of the ruling party to prison in order to make friends with her and obtain information from Malalay about her activities. But Malalay recognized this ploy and remained uncooperative to the end. During interrogation and torture she neither revealed her organizational secrets nor divulged the names of other members of the organization.[32]

Opposition to the Kabul regime was escalating daily throughout the country. Political differences between Taraki and his deputy, Amin, exacerbated their already strained relationship. In September 1979 Taraki visited Moscow and met with then Soviet leader Leonid Brezhnev and Karmal, head of the Parcham faction of the PDPA, and a decision was made to unite the Khalq and Parcham factions, involve nonparty members in the government, and dismiss Amin, who was considered to be the main reason for the party's disunity and political repression. When Taraki returned home, he tried to convince Amin to step down from his position. Amin refused to resign, a fight broke out, and Taraki was killed. Soon afterward Amin convened the party's central committee and was elected president and prime minister.

To consolidate his power base Amin dismissed a number of individuals still loyal to Taraki from their position in the state apparatus. He also tried to exonerate himself from the crimes the ruling party had committed by blaming Taraki and his men for the killing of thousands of political prisoners and declared that legality, justice, and security would be the cornerstones of his domestic policies. Amin did not have any women in the cabinet but had appointed four women to a committee to draft a new constitution. They were Aziza Azizi, president of the Khalq Organization of Afghanistan Women, KOAW; Fawzia Shahsawari, vice president of the KOAW; Shirin Afzal, president of the Reformatory Schools; and Alamat Tolqun, president of Kindergartens.

In his foreign-policy orientation, Amin tried to normalize relations with Pakistan and the West, with the expectation that these countries would then cease their support to the Islamic parties fighting to overthrow him. The Soviet Union was not pleased with the new developments in Afghanistan, could not tolerate seeing the country draw away from its spheres of influence, and decided to intervene. They convinced Amin to agree to the deployment of a small contingent of the Soviet armed forces to Afghanistan to repress the insurgency. Amin acquiesced and did not suspect the Soviets would later turn on him. The Soviet Union deployed a small contingent of the Red Army to Afghanistan, not only to maintain its imperial domination of the country but also to install a new puppet leader. It is argued that Ratibzad, a female party member, volunteered to take part in the operation in order to identify Amin to the Soviet soldiers. On December 27, 1979, the Soviet army stormed Amin's residence, killed him and some of his die-hard supporters, and installed Karmal to power.

THE SOVIET INVASION AND OCCUPATION

Once in power, Karmal released political prisoners, declared general amnesty, and embarked upon new policies aimed at expanding the party's base of support. To attract women's support, Karmal appointed Ratibzad as a member of both the so-called Revolutionary Council and the PDPA's Central Committee. He also appointed two more women to the Revolutionary Council, Karmal's cousin, Soraya, president of the WDOA, and Jamila Palwashah. The government condemned Amin for torturing and executing innocent men and women. In an editorial, the state's official newspaper, *Haqiqat-e-Enqilab-e-Saur,* Truth of the Saur [April] Revolution, compared Amin to Hitler and Mussolini. A section of the editorial was translated into English and published in the state's English daily, the *Kabul New Times:*

A version of Hitlerites, Mussolinis, and Ganghis Khans. . . . More murderous and cruel than all the hangmen and murderers of history. His reign of terror will form the most bloody pages in our history. . . . He was not a cultured man. He repeatedly insulted and humiliated women who sought their husbands from him.[33]

On March 8, 1980, the regime celebrated the anniversary of Women's Day at the Gymnasium of Polytechnic Institute in Kabul. A great number of women, both party members and loyalists, gathered and spoke on the role of women in society and passed a resolution condemning external interference in Afghanistan's internal affairs and expressed their readiness to defend the country and the gains of the "revolution."[34] The government-controlled press and media presented special programs and articles on the subject of women and their role in the country's development. In order not to antagonize public opinion, the *Kabul New Times* praised Islam for granting women the right to education:

One important criterion of a progressive regime is the efforts it makes to ensure equality between male and females. . . . It was not religion that stood against women's progress. . . . For Islam made learning incumbent upon both men and women . . . but men used women as second-rate citizens and did not allow them to acquire knowledge and therefore women are not aware of their rights.[35]

To expand the party's base of support among women, Karmal appointed a number of women to key government offices and to positions in the army and the police department. The KOAW, renamed as the Women's Democratic Organization of Afghanistan (WDOA), was the only women's organization that supported the Soviet invasion and worked to rally women in support of the Kabul regime. In 1984 the WDOA maintained that the organization had succeeded in uniting approximately 30,000 women in 669 primary organizations throughout the country and had "mobilized more than 80,000 countrywomen in social production of whom 17,000 were trade union members."[36] The Kabul regime suffered enormous casualties in the battle with the Islamic parties supported by Pakistan, the United States, and other conservative Middle Eastern countries. To win support of families whose sons had died in the war, the Kabul regime established the Association of Mothers and Wives of Martyrs of Revolution (AMWMR) in April 1986 and appointed Bibi Marjan as its president.[37] The state also changed the name of the WDOA to the All Afghanistan Women's Council (AAWC), and Shafiqa Razmenda was appointed vice president of the organization. In June 1987 the AAWC was renamed the Afghanistan Women Council (AWC), and Masuma Esmati became its chair. Article 1 of the AWC charter stated the organization's goals as follows:

[It] is a mass social organization, which unites, in its ranks, on a voluntary basis, the women of different classes and strata of the society, all nationalities, tribes and ethnic groups residing in the country for realizing the requirements of the socio-economic development of women. The [AWC] shall carry its activities under the leadership of the PDPA and under the National Front of the DRA [Democratic Republic of Afghanistan]. It is the active executor of the policy of the revolutionary state in solving the problems of women, and functions in all-embracing manner, for attracting the women to the process of work and the new life.[38]

The AWC stated that it had 94,816 members, 1,490 workers, 3,334 peasants, 1,087 artisans, 22,306 intellectuals, 2,476 students, 20,539 teachers and 20,445 housewives.[39] Other women in key government positions included Soraya, director of the Women's Club in Kabul (fourteen such clubs existed in Kabul and thirty in other provinces); and Sohaila Siddique, chief surgeon of the 400-bed Military Hospital in Kabul. Sohaila was born in 1938, studied medicine in Moscow in 1967–1976, and was promoted to the rank of major-general in December 1986.[40] Karmal also founded a center called Parwarishga-e-Watan, the National Nursery, to provide for the needs of children born out of wedlock or those abandoned by their parents and to indoctrinate them with the ideology of the ruling party. The state also established new cultural centers and used them as vehicles for political indoctrination. Youths were encouraged to participate in cultural activities and other programs organized by these centers. Young male and female party members often socialized in such centers, but the public reviled these institutions as enterprises that promoted cultural degeneracy, as described by one critic:

Moral corruption and degradation was at its height after the so called *Saur* Revolution. An important meeting place of the young *Parchamis*–boys and girls–was the outhouses of the *Bagh-e-Bala*, Kabul. The *Parchamis* used to take pride in such corrupt practices and boasted to be belonging to an advanced society.[41]

Although the Soviet occupation and the continuation of armed struggle for national liberation resulted in the shutdown of most educational centers in the countryside, in 1984 the state claimed that it had made great progress in combating illiteracy. It stated that an estimated 1,048,000 persons learned to read and write since April 1978. The state also claimed that it had established 2,300 reading and writing classes within the armed forces and 1,131 similar literacy centers in the police forces, and had provided special radio-television programs for literacy classes.[42]

Continued Soviet involvement in Afghanistan's politics further eroded Karmal's already tarnished image as a puppet ruler. Karmal was replaced as general secretary of the party on May 4, 1986, relieved of his remaining posts in November 1986, and sent into exile in the USSR in May 1987. The Soviets most favored man, Najibullah, was elected general secretary of the party on May 4, 1986, and president of Afghanistan in September 1987. To project a different image of the party, Najibullah initiated some cosmetic reforms in the political arena allowing formation of civic and political parties that remained supportive of the regime. He appointed two women to cabinet posts in May 1990. Masuma Esmati became minister of education and training and Saleha Farooq Etemadi became minister of social security. Najibullah's policies of involving women in top government posts did not prove effective to garner women's support because these women were not elected representatives and a vast majority of women in both rural and urban areas could not relate to well-known female party members, personally or socially. They also despised some young female party members for immorality and socialization with men.

THE WOMEN'S MOVEMENT

Women of other political and ideological orientations (nationalists, Islamists, and revolutionaries) opposed the Soviet occupation, and active participation of women in the resistance movement began a few months after the Soviet invasion as schools entered winter recess. The women's movement was limited to Kabul and other big cities because the overwhelming majority of intelligentsia, students, and blue-collar women lived in these cities. Jamiat-e-Enqilabi-e-Zanan-e-Afghanistan, the Revolutionary Association of Women of Afghanistan (RAWA) is one of the revolutionary groups that opposed the Soviet invasion. RAWA's prime objective was to mobilize and organize women and girls in support of the war of national liberation. Members of the association began their political work among high school students and factory workers at industrial plants.

Although several revolutionary organizations such as Akhgar, Sazman-e-Watanparastan-e-Waqiei, the Organization of True Patriots (SAWO), Sazman-e-Azadi Bakhsh-e-Mardum-e-Afghanistan, the Organization for

Liberation of People of Afghanistan (SAMA), and others disagree with RAWA on issues related to the strategy of transformation in Afghanistan's politics, RAWA is the only active organization that continues to fight for women's rights and equality. RAWA regards the politics of the Islamic parties as reactionary, and supported the establishment of an Islamic republic in the post-Soviet era. RAWA articulated its political strategy of development in Afghanistan in these words:

It is our mission, men and women, to unite and fight for the independence of our beloved country, to establish an Islamic republic, and to build a society in which oppression, torture, execution and injustices must be replaced by democracy and social justice. We will not be able to achieve these objectives until people and all political forces unite and form a united national front. . . . RAWA, which is comprised of progressive women, fights for women's equality, and maintains that the liberation of the oppressed women is inseparable from the liberation of our oppressed nation. . . . RAWA will continue its principled struggle for women's rights and liberation after the restoration of the country's independence and freedom from the superpowers and other imperialist powers.[43]

To achieve its objectives, RAWA defined the responsibilities of its rank and file. Some of the most important points of RAWA's political platform included the organization and mobilization of women for a continuous fight for national liberation, and opposition to reactionary trends regarding women's roles in society. Another aim was to expose the Kabul regime's hollow rhetoric and its oppression of women. RAWA also had a goal to support the people's armed struggle for liberation. RAWA expressed solidarity with the strikes of shopkeepers, students, teachers, workers, and government employees. It supported the fight against imperialist culture, particularly that supported by the Kabul regime, and joined in the struggle to revive Afghanistan's national and cultural heritage.[44]

A major anti-Soviet protest took place on April 21, 1980, when the Kabul regime held an official ceremony for replacing the red flag of the Khalq era with a new one having traditional black, red, and green colors. During this protest demonstration students shouted slogans such as "Long Live Liberty" and "Soviets Leave Afghanistan." Student rallies continued for several days, and during a rally on April 25 armed party members fired on the crowds, claiming the lives of four students of Omar Shahid High School and one of Habibiya High School. Another anti-Soviet protest demonstration in Kabul occurred on the second anniversary of the regime's seizure of power on April 27, 1980, when girls of Soriya High School marched on Kabul University. They were joined by hundreds of students from other schools in the neighboring areas. Security forces were called in to disperse the crowd and to bring the situation under control. Party members within the security forces tried to persuade the students to return to their classes. Students were shouting slogans like "Liberty or Death," "Russians Leave Afghanistan," and "Death to Babrak Karmal."

Students were planning to leave the university campus and march toward downtown Kabul. The security forces tried to prevent further escalation of this student protest by not allowing the protesters to leave the university compound. A party member with a loudspeaker warned students to disperse, telling them, "You are being manipulated by the enemies of the revolution. They are the ones who have misled you." The demonstrators continued to shout, "Liberty or Death." During this expression of anti-Sovietism, Nahid, a junior of Rabia-e-Balkhi High School, stepped forward and shouted, "You are the ones who have been manipulated by the Russians." She then shouted, "Liberty or Death." The security forces tried to arrest her and other key leaders of the protest demonstration. Clashes broke out. Soviet helicopters hovering overhead began firing on the crowd and killed scores of students.[45]Among the dead were two young activists, Nahid and Wajhia. Although both girls were not members of any political or religious organization, nationalists, liberals, conservatives, and revolutionaries alike praised them for giving their lives to the cause of freedom.

On the same day female students elsewhere in Kabul also marched on the streets in defiance of the Soviet occupation of the country. When they passed local soldiers, they threw their headscarves at army officers, telling them, "These scarves are for you. You are not men. With your machine guns you oppose your sisters armed only with books." They scolded army officers, telling them to stay home and let them fight for the liberation of the country. To disperse the crowd, party members of the army ordered soldiers to fire on the demonstrators. As a result, three girls were killed and many others wounded.[46]

This incident provoked a huge anti-Soviet demonstration in Kabul the next day. Students again marched several miles through the streets of Kabul chanting anti-Soviet slogans. Although government security forces accompanied the demonstrators, this time they did not intervene. Students told the soldiers that they were all one people and had one common enemy, the Russians, and that they should be like brothers and sisters fighting for national independence. When the security forces refused to open fire on the students, armed party members were called in to disperse the demonstrators. As soon as they arrived they began firing on the crowds, and several students were killed and many others injured. Hundreds more were arrested and taken to police stations, army posts, and Pol-e-Charkhi Prison.[47] After a few days the government released most of the students and claimed that it had been deceived by the "counter-revolutionaries" and declared its readiness to work for the cause of the "revolution." The students were not in a position to immediately dispute these claims out of fear for their safety. Student protests continued and on May 22–23, 1980, the regime suppressed a student protest at Kabul University. One of the surprising incidents that unfolded in Kabul during the second week of June 1980 was the poisoning of female students of Soriya High School and a number of other schools in Kabul, as well as of a number of employees of the government printing press. An estimated 500 students were hospitalized but no fatalities were reported and the government denounced the Islamic groups for this act.

In order to maintain stability, the Kabul regime imposed a curfew from late in the evening to early dawn and prohibited social gatherings and meetings of any kind. This situation posed problems for the opposition parties that were trying to organize and mobilize people for the war of national liberation. The opposition parties distributed *shabnamas*, underground letters, to carry their message to the people. In November 1980 RAWA distributed a *shabnama* denouncing the kidnapping of two school girls by Soviet soldiers. RAWA publicized this incident to mobilize the public in support of the war of national liberation. The *shabnama* appealed to the religious beliefs, national pride, and honor of a wide spectrum of the populace. A portion of the *shabnama* read as follows:

RAWA informs our noble sisters and patriotic brothers that the time of impartiality, neutrality, and of seeking the trivialities of life have passed. It is a time in which our honor, pride and country are at stake. If you do not do anything you will drown in the river of blood created by the deaths of your compatriots and those who are still fighting and dying in the resistance fronts in towns and villages. RAWA asks all Mujahidin, resistance fighters in cities, and sisters and brothers in exile to transform every place they live into a fighting front. . . . Two paths exist today—that of submission to the Soviets and that of becoming their gravediggers. The nation has chosen the second path. . . . Let us unite. Let our hands become familiar with the trigger of machine guns. The enemy must envision the Malay's spirit in each of us.[48]

In September 1981 schoolgirls in Kabul organized a massive protest demonstration to denounce the Soviet occupation and the government's policy of enlisting youth in the army. In downtown Kabul the government and Soviet forces confronted the demonstrators and ordered them to disperse. Students did not obey the order issued by the Soviet troops. According to an eyewitness report, a voice coming from inside a tank was amplified through loudspeakers, announcing, "Stop the demonstration, don't go ahead, go back to your classes, otherwise you will be shot." The girls continued to protest and to shout anti-Russian epithets. In order to disperse the crowd, the Soviet troops fired on them, killing six girls.[49] During the same day Khedamat-e-Itilaat-e-Dawlat, the State Information Services (KHAD) conducted house-to-house searches for suspected individuals and anti-government activists. KHAD often arrested family members for the purpose of obtaining information about another member of the family. For example, in June 1983 Shahnaz, Natila, and eleven members of their family were taken to the KHAD interrogation center in the Sadarat, the former official residence of the prime minister, in Kabul. They were questioned about the activities and whereabouts of a family member, Khozhman Ulumi, because he was reputed to be a leader of Sazman-e-Rahaye, a revolutionary group active in the resistance to the government of Karmal.[50]

As the struggle against the Soviet occupation of the country continued, many more men and women were arrested, interrogated, and tortured in various detention centers in Kabul. Most arrests were made at night, with the security forces surrounding the houses of those suspected to be anti-government. Students suspected of being members of underground political parties and of distributing *shabnamas* were among those arrested. Anti-Soviet protest demonstrations continued, and in mid-January 1983 an estimated 400 women congregated at the Mourning Hall of the Shahr-e-Naw Pavilion, in Kabul, and demanded the return of dead bodies of their sons and husbands lost in the war and the release of their imprisoned loved ones. Security forces fired tear gas into the crowds to disperse them.[51]

Women members of underground political parties usually participated in distributing anti-government *shabnamas*. Although these women did not approve of the tradition of wearing veils in public, they wore them to hide their identities and also to be able to safely carry a considerable quantity of *shabnamas* under their veils. During the first week of November 1984 the security agents arrested approximately fifteen female students of Kabul University for carrying and distributing *shabnamas*.[52] The KHAD agency directed its efforts mainly toward eliminating members of the urban-based guerrilla movement who belonged to a variety of revolutionary political organizations, such as Akhgar, Rahaye, SAWO, SAMA, and RAWA. Farida Ahmadi, one of RAWA's leading supporters, was arrested for distributing anti-Soviet tracts and subjected to several months of interrogation and torture. She stated that six female party members, all roughly her own age, had carried out most of the interrogation. Her experiences included beatings, electric shocks, being forced to stand for two weeks without moving, and being forced to watch other victims as they were tortured. She said that other inmates sometimes had their fingers, hands, and arms crudely amputated. When the women members of the ruling party could not make her confess, male torturers, including a Russian, were brought in. One of them, in order to frighten her, made her watch him gouge out the eyes of another victim.[53]

There was a separate prison block for women in Kabul's main prison, Pol-e-Charkhi. Conditions varied from one block to another. Tobah Hamid, a former inmate, described the women's section of Pol-e-Charkhi. Cells were empty save for a single constantly burning light bulb. Some of the more fortunate inmates had blankets brought by family members, who were only rarely permitted visits to the prison. Washing was not allowed, and almost all the women suffered from lice and body sores. Most of them were sick, and all had been tortured with varying degrees of severity. They were not allowed to talk to each other, nor were they let out of their cells except twice daily to visit the toilet facilities.[54]

The torture of women inmates in Kabul's central prison was graphically depicted by Fahima Nassery, a school teacher who was arrested twice, in 1981 and 1984. She was beaten, and her hair was pulled out during her interrogation. She was then taken to a room with other women; all were told to sleep on the floor. After three nights they came for Nassery again. They continued to ask questions about her activities and her associates, but this time the interrogation was accompanied by repeated electric shocks from an instrument with a number of wires attached to an iron collar around her neck. After four nights of this treatment, she was taken to another room, where she was slapped and beaten and her hair was pulled for hours at a time for another thirteen nights. She was also forced to view a bloodied room containing a corpse and a number of severed limbs and fingers scattered around. After four months of interrogation she was sentenced to one year of imprisonment and a half year of parole.[55]

Women's role in the national liberation struggle was not restricted to rallies, protest demonstrations, noncooperation, and the like. Women participated in organized struggles, such as the abduction and assassination of supporters of the government and the Soviets. A large number of the disappearances and assassinations of Soviet soldiers and personnel of the government in Kabul have been attributed to women's works and initiatives. Tajwar Kakar, also known as Tajwar Sultan, was a leading woman fighter who actively participated in the struggle and organized other women in the resistance. Kakar was a schoolteacher in Qunduz province and was transferred to a school in Kabul. On December 28, 1982, Kakar was arrested on charges of anti-state political agitation and activities. In prison she experienced all kinds of beatings and torture. She was given repeated electric shocks during the interrogation. She was accused of committing a variety of crimes, and when she denied the charges her torturers brought in people she knew to "confirm" that she was guilty. A Soviet official also took part in the interrogation. Kakar said that the Soviet officials did not have any right to question a citizen of Afghanistan in his or her home country. This outburst further angered her tormentors, and they tied her hands, burned her lips with cigarettes, and gave her electric shocks until she fell unconscious. She was also bound and forced to stand buried up to her neck in snow for several hours. The interrogation and torture continued, with needles and electric shocks. After finally being forced to sign a written confession, Kakar was released.[56] She fled to

Peshawar, Pakistan, hoping that she would be able to work with refugees. The authorities in charge of refugee affairs did not allow her to engage in politics and continuously threatened her with death if she did not stay at home.

Another woman fighter, Nadia, lured the enemy into ambushes and executed them. She was responsible for at least fifteen successful operations against the Soviet occupation forces.[57] In Herat province, Razia was a well-known freedom fighter. She joined the resistance when both her father and her brother were killed on the battlefield. Razia pursued her father and brother's mission and established an independent group of women fighters in Herat in 1983.[58] In the Khost region of Paktiya province, Bibi Mukhta was known for her participation in the armed struggle against the occupation forces. She joined the guerrillas following the deaths, on the front, of her son and brother.[59]

Women's participation in the national liberation struggle in Qandahar province dates as far back as the second Anglo-Afghanistan war in 1880, the battle of Maiwand, exemplified in the role of seventeen-year-old Malalay. On the battlefield Malalay picked up a standard from a dying soldier and, to boost soldiers' morale, sung these words: "I shall make a beauty spot of my beloved's blood, which will put to shame the roses in my garden. Young love, if you do not fall in the battle of Maiwand, By God, someone is saving you for a token of shame."[60] Women's participation in the resistance against the Soviet occupation forces in Qandahar started after 1981. Young women worked with the resistance fighters behind the front lines, carrying arms, ammunition, and intelligence communications hidden under their veils. Some undertook the dangerous task of luring Russians and Kabul agents into ambushes prepared by the resistance fighters. The older women did their part by looking after the homes and young children.[61]

Another woman in the liberation struggle was twenty-five-year-old Nur Bibi of Paghman, Kabul, who is credited with killing several Russians. "Nur Bibi had to watch as her whole family was killed. In her despair she grabbed a pistol and shot at three completely surprised Soviets. None of them survived. But Nur Bibi, too, was seriously injured. She was left for dead on the grounds." A group of men took her to a hospital across the border to Pakistan, where she received medical treatment. While in the hospital she expressed her determination to return and participate in the war of national liberation when she was cured.[62] Women played a major role in the liberation struggle, often risking their lives and those of their families. The notion that they were women and must stay home never prevented them from taking bold action to demonstrate that men must not underestimate their resolve. A woman who participated in the war of national liberation described her role in these words:

I was right there in the war front, where *Mujahidin* fought against the Russians. . . . We took an active part in the resistance. . . . There were three of us women who cooked for six hundred men. We washed clothes for six hundred men. During the night, we carried a gun and took our turn at standing watch. . . . My husband died twelve years ago. My daughter was three months old at that time. He [the husband] was arrested in Pakistan. Gulbuddin's party arrested him and took him to [an]other prison in the Shamshatoo refugee camp because he was against them. I never heard from him again.[63]

There is no precise figure for civilians who died of war-related injuries between 1978 and 1987. Various government agencies and individual scholars in the West claim that 1.3–1.5 million people were killed during this period. Anthony Arnold, who was affiliated with the CIA in Afghanistan during the early 1970s, quoting a German volunteer agency working with refugees, wrote that "in 1986 about one million civilians and 80,000 Mujahidin had been killed. In addition, some 45,000 others were missing and presumed dead, and a further 100,000 had been executed by the DRA. Some 65,000 were thought to be imprisoned."[64] It is extremely difficult to ascertain the validity of these figures. Influenced by their own emotional and psychological affiliation with the suffering of their compatriots, many scholars and researchers from Afghanistan who reside in Pakistan and in the West exaggerate the number of casualties. Government agencies in the United States also may have exaggerated the figures for political reasons in order to publicly discredit their adversary, the Soviet Union, and to equate communism with brutality. Table 4.3 shows war-related deaths of the female population in the country in 1978–1987.

Table 4.3
War-Related Deaths, 1978–1987 (per 1,000)

Age	Males	Females
0–10	31	28
11–20	59	36
21–30	173	33
31–40	224	21
41–50	220	68
51–60	207	46
60+	173	70
All ages	134	38

Source: Marek Sliwinski, "Afghanistan: The Decimation of a People," *Orbis* 33:1 (Winter 1989): 43.

A great percentage of female casualties during the war is attributed to aerial bombings and artillery shelling of civilian residential areas, suspected as hideouts and shelters for resistance fighters, by the Soviet troops. The intensity of aerial bombings compelled people to abandon their homes and migrate to Pakistan and Iran. Mines and booby traps hidden in the fields by the Soviet troops in rural areas to incapacitate the resistance forces also accounted for a high proportion of the casualties of women and children fleeing the country. A small percentage of female casualties was also due to lack of medical treatment and infections caused during their travel to neighboring countries—travel that under unusual conditions normally takes a week at most on foot from Afghanistan to the closest towns in Pakistan. Despite tremendous pressure and violent actions against them, women continued to fight their battles small and large with hostile forces, sometimes including members of their own families arrayed against them. They continue their struggle without benefit of aid from the international community.

NOTES

1. Mohammad Nasir Gharghasht, *Rahnuma-e-Kabul* [Kabul's Guide] (Kabul: Government Press, 1345/1966), p. 252.

2. Deborah Ellis, *Women of the Afghan War* (Westport, Conn.: Praeger, 2000), p. 165.

3. Cited in Pamela A. Hunte, *Women in the Development Process in Afghanistan, 1978*, project for the U.S. Agency for International Development (USAID) (USAID, 1978), p. 87.

4. Ibid., pp. 89–90.

5. Gharghasht, *Rahnuma-e-Kabul*, p. 173.

6. Louis Dupree, "Population Dynamics in Afghanistan," *AUFS Reports* 14:7 (April 1970): 5.

7. Fahima Rahimi, *Women in Afghanistan* (Liestal: Stiftung Foundation, Stiftung Bibliotheca Afghanica, 1986), p. 82.

8. Louis Dupree, "A Note on Afghanistan: 1971," *AUFS Reports* 15:2 (July 1971): 17.

9. Ibid.

10. Ministry of Planning, *Majmua-e-Aisayawi-e-Sali, 1350* [Statistical Dictionary, 1971] (Kabul: Matbaa-e-Dawlati, 1971), p. 16.

11. "Afghanistan King Overthrown, a Republic Is Proclaimed," *The New York Times*, July 18, 1973, p. 8.

12. Louis Dupree, *Afghanistan* (Princeton: Princeton University Press, 1973), pp. 657–658.

13. Raja Anwar, *The Tragedy of Afghanistan: A First-Hand Account*, translated from the Urdu by Khalid Hasan (New York: Verso, 1988), p. 260.

14. Mir Mohammad Siddiq Farhang, *Afghanistan dar Panj Qarn-e-Akhir*

[Afghanistan in the Last Five Centuries], vol. 3 (Peshawar, Pakistan: Author, 1373/1994), p. 40.

15. [English translation of] The Constitution of the Republican State of Afghanistan (Kabul: Kabul Times, 1976).

16. Rahimi, *Women in Afghanistan,* pp. 96–98.

17. Ibid., p. 72.

18. Mohammad Hashim Kamali, *Law in Afghanistan: A Study of the Constitutions, Matrimonial Law, and the Judiciary* (Leiden: E. J. Brill, 1985), pp. 153–154.

19. Ibid.

20. *The Kabul Times,* June 14, 1977.

21. Anwar, *Tragedy of Afghanistan,* p. 146.

22. Ministry of Information and Culture, *Democratic Republic of Afghanistan Annual, Saur 7, 1358* (Kabul: Kabul Times Publishing Agency, Government Printing House, 1979), pp. 86–87.

23. Anwar, *Tragedy of Afghanistan,* pp. 144–145. There may be an error concerning Amin's daughter's name. Her name may be spelled as "Gul Ghotai," because that is closer to a common spelling in Pushtu.

24. Jan Goodwin, *Caught in the Crossfire* (New York: E. P. Dutton, 1987), pp. 114–115.

25. Ibid., p. 144.

26. Ministry of Information and Culture. *Democratic Republic of Afghanistan,* p. 258.

27. *Afghanistan Today* 1:3 (January–February 1986): 14.

28. General Union of Democratic Students and Patriotic Afghans (GUDSPA), *Afghanistan-e-Azad* [Independent Afghanistan] (October 3, 1980): 3.

29. Edward R. Girardet, *Afghanistan: The Soviet War* (New York: St. Martin's Press, 1985), p. 107.

30. Author's personal observation of events in Afghanistan.

31. Amnesty International, *Amnesty International Reports* (London: Amnesty International, 1980), p. 177.

32. GUDSPA, *Afghanistan-e-Azad* (October 3, 1980): 2–6.

33. *Kabul New Times,* January 5, 1980. Cited in Nancy H. Dupree, "Revolutionary Rhetoric and Afghan Women," in *Revolutions and Rebellions in Afghanistan,* M. Nazif Shahrani and Robert L. Canfield (eds.) (Berkeley: University of California Press, 1984), p. 328.

34. *Kabul New Times,* March 9, 1980. Cited in Dupree, "Revolutionary Rhetoric," p. 329.

35. *Kabul New Times,* March 16, 1980. Cited in Dupree, "Revolutionary Rhetoric," p. 329.

36. Ministry of Foreign Affairs, *Achievements of the April Revolution in Afghanistan* (Kabul: Ministry of Foreign Affairs, 1984), pp. 61–62.

37. S. Fida Yunas, *Afghanistan: Organization of the People's Democratic Party of Afghanistan/Watan Party, Governments, and Bibliographical Sketches, 1982–1998,* vol. 1 (Peshawar, Pakistan: S. Fida Yunas, 1998), pp. 237–238.

38. Ibid., p. 397.

39. Ibid., p. 243.

40. Ibid., vol. 2, pp. 923–924.

41. Ibid., p. 930.

42. Ministry of Foreign Affairs, *Achievements of the April Revolution,* p. 42.

43. RAWA, *Barnama, Wazayif wa Asasnama-e-Jamiat-e-Enqilabi-e-Zanan-e-Afghanistan* [Policy, Responsibility, and Platforms of the Revolutionary Association of the Women of Afghanistan, RAWA], Tabistan 1359 [Summer 1980], n.p.

44. Ibid.

45. Girardet, *Afghanistan,* p. 178. Other sources indicate the death tolls to be seventy persons. See Dupree, "Revolutionary Rhetoric," p. 332. GUDSPA says the death toll was fifty persons. See GUDSPA, *Afghanistan-e-Azad* (September 2, 1980): 8. The day Nahid was killed was not positively confirmed due to conflicting reports of the actual date. A few sources wrote that she was killed on April 27; another source maintained the date was April 29; still another claimed she was killed in May 1980.

46. Ibid., p. 178.

47. Ibid., p. 179.

48. *Shabnamaha-e-Jamiat-e-Enqilabi-e-Zanan-e-Afghanistan* [Underground Letters of Revolutionary Association of Women of Afghanistan, RAWA] (Bonn: Published by supporters of RAWA who live abroad, Fall 1981). RAWA refers to the woman whose name is spelled "Malalay," who participated in the battle of Maiwand during the second Anglo-Afghanistan war in 1880, encouraging men to fight the enemy.

49. Helsinki Watch Committee, *Tears, Blood, and Cries: Human Rights in Afghanistan Since the Invasion, 1979–1984* (New York: Helsinki Watch Committee, December 1984), pp. 97–98.

50. Ibid., pp. 127–128. A common name, "Khuzman," may also be spelled as "Osman."

51. Afghan Information Center, Peshawar, Pakistan, *Monthly Bulletin* no. 23 (February 1983): 9.

52. Afghan Information Center, *Monthly Bulletin* nos. 44–45 (November–December 1984): 14.

53. Girardet, *Afghanistan,* p. 126.

54. Helsinki Watch Committee, *Tears, Blood, and Cries,* p. 152.

55. Helsinki Watch and Asia Watch Committees, *To Die in Afghanistan: A Supplement to Tears, Blood, and Cries: Human Rights in Afghanistan Since the Invasion, 1979 to 1984* (New York: Helsinki Watch and Asia Watch Committees, December 1985), pp. 60–61.

56. Amnesty International, *Afghanistan: Torture of Political Prisoners* (New York: Amnesty International, 1986), pp. 37–38.

57. Doris Lessing, *The Wind Blows Away Our Words, and Other Documents Relating to the Afghan Resistance* (New York: Vintage Books, 1987), p. 148.

58. Ibid., p. 149.

59. Hakim K. Taniwal, "The Impact of Pushtunwali on Afghan Jihad," *WUFA* (Writers' Union of Free Afghanistan) 2:1 (January–March 1987): 12–13.

60. Rahimi, *Women in Afghanistan,* p. 32.

61. Lessing, *Wind Blows Away Our Words,* p. 149.

62. Wilhelm Dietl, *Bridgehead Afghanistan* (New Delhi: Lancer International, 1986), pp. 262–263.

63. Ellis, *Women of the Afghan War,* pp. 47–48.

64. Anthony Arnold, "Afghanistan," in *The New Insurgencies: Anti-Communist Guerrillas in the Third World,* Michael Radu (ed.) (New Brunswick, N.J.: Transaction, 1990), p. 244.

5

Politics of Regression: Women in the Post-Soviet Era

Development and modernization programs initiated by the ruling party, Hizb-e-Demokratik-e-Khalq-e-Afghanistan, the People's Democratic Party of Afghanistan (PDPA) only brought about a limited number of cosmetic reforms. The party's coercive approach to building a new society based on the Soviet model of socialism antagonized conservatives and opposition political groups. As opposition to the regime mounted, the PDPA relied on the Soviet Union for support and intervention. The Soviet occupation of Afghanistan not only compelled nationalists, revolutionaries, and Islamic groups to fight for liberation of the country but also spurred the rejuvenation of religious-oriented policies as an alternative strategy of development. It also led to increased U.S. financial and military support to Islamic parties in their struggle against the Soviet occupation forces.

THE STATE AND POLITICS OF RECONCILIATION

The Russians failed to subjugate the people of Afghanistan during their nine years of occupation, suffering an estimated 13,310 dead and 35,478 injured, and the Kremlin leadership finally decided to cut its losses and withdraw its troops, considering the war in Afghanistan as a bleeding wound in the Soviet empire. Prior to its troop withdrawal Soviet leader Mikhail Gorbachev summoned the ruler of Kabul, Najibullah, to Tashkent in July 1987 and informed him of the Soviet decision to pull out its troops.

Five months later the Soviet leadership announced its readiness to pull out its troops from Afghanistan within a twelve-month period. Washington and Moscow endorsed the UN-sponsored Geneva Peace Accord, which was signed by Afghanistan and Pakistan, as international guarantors on April 14, 1988. Soon after the signing of the Geneva Accord the Soviet Union began to pull out its troops from Afghanistan and the withdrawal was completed on February 15, 1989.

The Kabul regime began a series of attempts to consolidate its power base after Soviet troops left the country. One of its major initiatives included active encouragement of the formation of civic and political groups supportive of the Kabul government, albeit only to simulate their complete independence. Several political parties, such as Sazman-e-Azadi-Bakhshi Zahmatkashan-e-Afghanistan, the Revolutionary Organization of Toilers of Afghanistan (SAZA), Sazman-e-Pishahangi Zahmatkashan-e-Afghanistan, the Organization of Avant-Garde Toilers of Afghanistan (SPAZA), and several others were formed. The regime also revoked some of the state's earlier reforms and amended land reform bills so that feudal landowners cooperating with the state could keep their land as an incentive to support the regime. It also declared that it was ready to share power with opposition groups. The ruling party changed its name to Hizb-e-Watan, Party of the Homeland, during a meeting on June 27–28, 1990. In so doing it sought to win the support of nationalists and progressive forces.

To win women's support the Kabul regime initiated new legislation that supported women's rights to employment. Article 10 of the 1987 labor law stipulated equal pay for equal work and other articles entitled pregnant women to ninety days leave with all rights and privileges and the possibility of additional fifteen days of extension in case of health complications. Article 146 prohibited agencies from rejecting women's right to work on the basis of gender, and from reducing their pay because of pregnancy or childbirth.[1] The Kabul regime also involved women in the party, the government, and the army and used them also to enlist the support of other women for the regime. Some female members of the PDPA had also participated in a few combat operations. Najiba Arash, a Pushtun woman, was appointed as alternate member and secretary of the PDPA from the eleventh precinct, Kabul, and representative to Parliament. Senzila Ana of Khost in Paktiya province became a member of Sazman-e-Demokratik-e-Zanan-e-Afghanistan, the Women's Democratic Organization of Afghanistan (WDOA), a member of the Loya Jirgah in April 1985, a member of the High Jirgah of Frontier Tribes in September 1985, and commander of the Women's Defense Groups in the Khost army division. Ruhafza Kargar, who had completed only the seventh grade at the literacy center, was appointed a member of the Self-Defense Group Complex, a member of the commission to draft a new constitution in February 1986, and an alternate member of the PDPA's Central Committee in 1986.[2] Similarly, Nazar Khal, daughter of Jora from Jawzjan, was appointed commander of the Revolutionary Defense Group in Misar Abad area and became a member of the state's Revolutionary Council in 1986.[3]

From Chak-e-Wardak, Feroza Fedaie became a member of the Women's Defense Group in Kabul in 1981, a member of the National Fatherland Front in 1982, a member of the Loya Jirgah in 1985, and president of the All Afghanistan Women's Council (AAWC) on August 6, 1986.[4] A widow who lost one of her six sons during Taraki-Amin's rule claimed to have participated in combat battles in 1980 and 1981. While she was displaying the folding commando-style AK-47s and Soviet Papasha machine guns, she stated that "we are breaking traditions just by having these women's defense groups; we must move slowly."[5] Another woman who participated in the battle in defense of the regime was Bibi Marjan of Chil Dukhtaran village of Char Asyab district, Kabul. She became a member of the WDOA in 1982, commander of the Women Defenders of Revolution Group (WDRG) in 1983 (ten members), and commander of the WDRG in Char Asyab in 1984 (fifty-two members). She also became president of the Association of Wives and Mothers of Martyrs of Revolution in 1986 and chair of the AAWC's Central Committee in 1990. It is reported that she participated in 150 battles against the Islamic parties.[6]

In the post-Soviet era the Kabul regime tried to secure its position. For this reason it withdrew some of its military units from peripheral areas and concentrated them in major cities. The Kabul regime also called upon opposition leaders to participate in the national reconciliation government and declared its readiness to permit opposition forces to administer the daily affairs of regions that it occupied during the war or those that the government forces abandoned for political and strategic reasons. In regions where Islamic groups had established their rules, they dismantled the state's socioeconomic reforms and imposed strict Sharia rules and regulations. They opened some local schools to teach the Quran and restored feudal relations of production. A report on the Taliqan district stated that peasants again labored as sharecroppers for landlords on the plots they once briefly owned. Women were again told to stay in the home, and it was a common sight in the city to have a car equipped with loudspeakers patrolling the neighborhood, blaring the teachings of the local mullah and calling upon people to abstain from playing music.[7] The Kabul regime's policies of reconciliation failed to broaden its power base and the Islamic parties continued their struggle to topple the Kabul government and establish an Islamic regime in its place. Although a small number of refugees returned home, the overwhelming majority remained in refugee camps in Pakistan and Iran.

THE ISLAMIC REGIME AND CIVIL WAR

Although the Kabul regime introduced some cosmetic reforms, convened Loya Jirgahs, and co-opted nonparty members to the state apparatus to give the regime an aura of legitimation, armed struggle by the Islamic parties and internal clashes between the Parcham and Khalq factions of the ruling party continued unabated. There were several coup attempts by the Khalq to overthrow Najibullah, but all failed. The UN's efforts to find an acceptable formula for peaceful transfer of power led to Najibullah's resignation and his expected departure for India. On his way to the airport his opponents prevented him from leaving the country and Najibullah was forced to seek refuge at the UN office in Kabul.

In April 1992 the Kabul regime transferred power to a coalition of Islamic parties and Sebghatullah Mojaddadi, head of Jabha-e-Milli-e-Islami Afghanistan, the National Islamic Front of Afghanistan, who was interim president in exile, was sworn in as the new president. In August of that year Mojaddadi's term of office ended and Burhanuddin Rabbani, head of Jamiat-e-Islami Afghanistan, the Islamic Society of Afghanistan, became president. When Rabbani's term ended in December 1992, he maneuvered his way to a second term, which was opposed by rival Islamic parties. This factor, along with the unwillingness of rulers of Kabul, Rabbani, and Rabbani's defense minister, Ahmad Shah Masoud, to work toward forming a broad-based government, paved the road for a bloody war among the Islamic parties. The war destroyed 70 percent of Kabul City and forced thousands of people to leave Kabul for rural areas and the neighboring countries, mainly Pakistan and Iran.

Shortly after seizing power the Islamic regime began a series of programs intended to Islamicize an already Muslim society. Their policies adversely affected women's lives and liberties. For example, on August 27, 1993, the Government Office of Research and Decrees of the Supreme Court issued an order to government agencies and state functionaries to dismiss all female employees from their posts and issued further guidelines concerning women's societal obligations. The decree read:

Women need not leave their homes at all, unless absolutely necessary, in which case, they are to cover themselves completely; are not to wear attractive clothing and decorative accessories; do not wear perfume; their jewelry must not make any noise; they are not to walk gracefully or with pride and in the middle of the sidewalk; are not to talk to strangers; are not to speak loudly or laugh in public; and they must always ask their husbands' permission to leave home.[8]

As the Islamic parties fought one another for domination of the country, soldiers and armed men abducted men and women and molested and subsequently killed them. Raping women was used not only as a means of dishonoring an entire rival ethnic community but also as a method of intimidating the people not to oppose their rule. The warring factions treated abducted women as spoils of the war and used them to reward their soldiers and militias. International agencies and human rights groups working in Afghanistan reported atrocities committed against women in Kabul. One report stated:

Women are killed for being related to men wanted by various Islamic Mujahidin groups. Others are killed for resisting rape or abduction. Many young women are abducted to be wives of Mujahidin commanders. Some are sold into prostitution. Some are stoned to death. Some just disappeared. . . . Women who are working in professions or in government jobs, are assassinated because some Mujahidin groups consider their minds to have been poisoned. Many educated women are assaulted in their homes and offices.[9]

There was no security for women and most were also forced to stay home to avoid abduction by rival Mujahidin groups controlling different parts of Kabul City. Alima testified to the following incident that occurred in Kabul, in which armed men prevented a pregnant Pushtun woman from going to a hospital:

She was on her way to the hospital to give birth. They [the Mujahidin] said "we have seen everything, but we have not yet seen how a woman gives birth." They took her and her husband to an army post, took the woman's clothes off, and watched her have the baby. She died giving birth. The husband took the new baby and left, but came right back and said: "What life is this that you have left me with—you should kill me also." And they did. There was another woman who came to our apartment block from another building. Her husband had been killed by the Russians. A Mujahid came to the house and tried to rape her daughter. The girl resisted, so he killed her with eighteen strokes of the knife. He told the mother if she said anything, he would kill her too.[10]

Violence against women continued in the period between 1992 and 1996. Warring factions who spoke in defense of human rights often violated them, and their talk on respecting human rights was nothing but a smokescreen intended to legitimize their actions vis-à-vis their rival factions.

THE RISE AND CONSOLIDATION OF THE TALIBAN

The civil war not only destroyed the country's infrastructure but also claimed thousands of lives and generated despair among a wide spectrum of the population in both rural and urban areas. People prayed for an immediate end to the armed conflicts in order to rebuild their shattered lives. Amid the squabble for power and domination of Afghanistan a new force, the Taliban, whose name literally means "student of religious studies," was created. The Taliban's slogan of peace and stability and their declared intention to rid the country of warring factions was initially welcomed by war-weary residents of the country.

As early as 1994 the Taliban seized Qandahar, where they established their base. After consolidating their position the Taliban began a war of conquest toward the eastern and western parts of the county by employing both co-option and coercion approaches. By offering financial rewards and other privileges, the Taliban won the support and loyalty of some opposition commanders and launched a blitzkrieg attack on others who would not join them. The Taliban defeated well-known warlords like Ismail Khan in Herat, and Hajji Qadir in Nangarhar, and in late September 1996 it swiftly moved into Kabul. Rabbani and Masoud evacuated their forces and retreated to the northern parts of the country. The Taliban militias triumphantly marched into Kabul, entered the UN office, dragged Najibullah and his brother, Shahpoor Ahmadzai, outside, and killed them and hanged their mutilated bodies in a public square in Kabul. By 1998 the Taliban had defeated several other warlords in the northern and central regions of the country, such as Abdul Rashid Dostam, head of Junbish-e-Milli-e-Islami Afghanistan, the National Islamic Movement of Afghanistan, in Balkh; Mansoor Naderi, chief of the Isma'ili communities of Doshi, Pul-e-Khumri and Kayan in Baghlan; and Karim Khalili, head of Hizb-e-Wahdat, the Unity Party, in Bamiyan.

The Taliban's policy of building a highly regimented Islamic society severely affected the lives and liberties of women throughout the country. On September 28, 1996, Radio Sharia (formerly called Radio Afghanistan) announced that according to orders of the Amir al-Muminin, Commander of the Faithful Mullah Mohammad Omar, women were forbidden to work outside the home and girls were not allowed to go to school. When an estimated 250 women in Herat defied the Taliban's rule, they were beaten by Taliban security forces for not observing Islamic rules. The Taliban leadership defended their regressive polices concerning seclusion of women as evidenced in a speech by the governor of Herat, who stated:

It is a matter of pride for all Afghanistan that we have kept our women at home. . . . The *Sharia* has described everyone's way of conduct. I mean that the *Sharia* allows for a woman to see a male doctor when she becomes ill. The fact of the matter is that no other country has given women the rights we have given them. We have given women the rights that God and his Messenger have instructed, that is to stay in their homes and to gain religious instructions in *hijab* [seclusion].[11]

The Taliban's policy demanded that women cover their bodies from head to toe and not leave their homes unless for a reason in accordance with the Sharia, and if they did leave their homes they were to be accompanied by a male relative. Women also were forbidden to visit male tailor shops or wash clothes outside the home. The Taliban's Islamicization policies also required people to hang dark curtains over the windows so women would not be seen from outside. Men were ordered to refrain from playing music, singing songs, and sitting with women in the same room during wedding ceremonies. Local and expatriate women were barred from driving vehicles, as such actions were considered against Afghanistan's traditions. The Taliban ordered men to grow thick, untrimmed beards; to avoid Western hairstyling, watching television (the Taliban soon embarked upon a campaign to destroy all television sets), and playing kites and cards; to perform five daily prayers; and so on. Hindu residents of the country were forced to wear identifying labels (yellow patches) on their clothing to distinguish them from Muslims. The Taliban justice system dispensed severe punishment to those who violated such rules, which included amputation of a person's hand if he or she committed robbery, public flogging for sexual impropriety, and even stoning to death. To implement its strict version of Sharia laws the Taliban unleashed an army of enforcers throughout territories under its domination. Its supreme leader was reported to have defended the Taliban's rigid policy and violation of human rights in these words:

We do not accept something which somebody imposes on us under the name of human rights which is contradictory to the holy Quranic law. Anybody who talks to us should be within Islam's framework. The holy Quran cannot adjust itself to other people's requirements. People should adjust themselves to the requirements of the holy Quran.[12]

The Taliban's war of conquest led to the displacement of thousands of people and the migration of many others to neighboring countries. Table 5.1 shows the number of internally displaced persons (IDPs) between October 1, 1996, and August 1, 1997.

The Taliban imposed severe restrictions on UN staff and employees of nongovernmental organizations (NGOs) engaged in humanitarian works and limited their access to women. Fear of punishment by the Taliban prevented thousands of poor women from seeking an education, employment, and even excursion outside the home without a close male relative in attendance. Women who defied the Taliban's edicts

were taken to detention centers where they were humiliated or beaten by officials of the Department for the Promotion of Virtue and Prevention of Vice, DPVPV. On 17 June the DPVPV ordered the closure of all home schools [schools held secretly in individuals' houses, defying the ban on girl's education] and suspension of community-based vocational training programs for women in Kabul, further restricting women's movement. Scores of Hazara young women were taken by the Taliban as *kaniz,* servants, to be married off to Taliban militia deployed at war fronts.[13]

Displaced Persons (IDPs), October 1, 1996–August 1, 1997

In	From	No.
Badghis[a]	Badghis	Unknown
Herat[b]	Badghis	25,000
Kabul[c]	Shamali, north of Kabul	214,000
Panjshir Valley	Kabul, Shamali	24,000
Northern Provinces	Kabul, Parwan, Kapisa, etc.	48,000
Total		311,000

Notes: a. Registered camps exclude 3,000 IDPs who came in 1993–1994. b. Does not include IDPs who arrived in Kabul between October 1, 1996, and January 1, 1997. c. Based on the IRC's estimate of 4,000 families.

Source: Arafat Jamal, "Dark Side of the Moon," *Refugees* no. 108 (II-1997): 10.

WOMEN AND THE POLITICS OF ISLAMIC PARTIES

Conservatives, tribal chiefs, mullahs, and Islamic fundamentalists had always opposed women's rights to modern education and their participation in public, political, social, and cultural activities. Religious leaders of both the Shiite and the Sunni communities did not issue rigorous guidelines for the advancement of women. Although progressive Muslim scholars and a small number of enlightened clerics supported women's right to education, none of these leaders actively worked to eliminate gender discrimination. The only Muslim religious leader who boldly spoke against gender discrimination was Sultan Mohammad Shah, the Aga Khan III, forty-eighth imam of the Isma'ili community. He told a gathering of Muslims:

How can we expect prayers from the children of mothers who have never shared, or even seen, the free [intermingling] of modern mankind? This terrible cancer must either be cut out, or the body of Muslim society will be poisoned to death by the permanent waste of all the women of the nation.[14]

Aga Khan's followers often quote him regarding education, "if a father has two children, one a son and the other a daughter and if he can educate only one of them, such parents, if they were to consult me, I would advise them to educate the daughter first." Such a statement reflects the thinking that by educating a man one educates one individual and by educating a woman one educates a family.

The issue of women's equality with men did not occupy an important position in the political platform of the Islamic parties in Afghanistan since their emergence in the 1960s. When confronted with questions regarding women's rights and equality, individuals within and outside the movement often quoted verses from the Quran that contained references to the equality of men and women in the eyes of Allah to demonstrate gender equality. A verse from the Quran says that God created men "from a single cell and from it created its mate, and from the two of them dispersed men and women in multitudes (4:1)."[15]

An overwhelming majority of women in Afghanistan are illiterate and know little about the Islamic faith. They rely upon mullahs to interpret the religion and their role within it and within society. Most mullahs are themselves not well versed in Islamic philosophy and teachings and interpret the scriptures the way they understand them. The Islamic parties continue to disregard the contributions of women to societal development and seek to limit their role in society. Conservative clerics often call for the restoration of women's traditional role in society—that of domestic responsibility—and encourage and praise the roles of mother, wife, and sister. The primary objective of their teachings is to ensure the continued subordination of women to men and to perpetuate the concept of men as the guardians of women.

A large number of educated women who played an active role in Afghanistan's socioeconomic development prior to and during the Soviet occupation migrated to Pakistan. Some of these women believed that if they went to Pakistan they could still participate in one way or another in the liberation struggle. However, while in Pakistan they were confined to their homes and were compelled to wear the *chadar* when outside. A former teacher, Sameen, who lived in the Lakti Banda refugee camp in Peshawar, described her situation as follows:

I was not like this before the war. . . . I wore Western clothes, had my hair styled regularly. Now look at me. Today I live in Purdah. I cannot go out unless I am covered by a veil. . . . There are also many things I can no longer do. Last year, for example, I tried to start a school here. Our camp doesn't have one, and I wanted my children to be able to read and write. I also thought it would be a way to put my education to good use.[16]

Conservatives did not approve Sameen's proposal for opening a school for children. They considered her proposal to be anathema to tradition and culture. They ostracized her and her family for several months, not only to punish her but also to teach a lesson to other women who might think of doing the same thing. Conservatives did not allow women to leave the refugee camps. Beatrice Koekoek, a member of the French Medical Organization, described the situation of women in refugee camps in these words: "[W]e have to fight with the men to take women to a hospital when necessary. If they are lucky, their husbands let them go to the basic health units. . . . [T]o go to the doctor is their only chance to get out of the house."[17]

Although there are a few schools for refugees, girls are generally not allowed to continue schooling past the age of ten, at which young age they are forced to work. In refugee camps women and girls weave carpets and rugs and do embroidery. According to some conservatives, no matter how intelligent a girl is, at age ten or eleven she will have to leave school, learn to weave carpets, and start earning money.[18] According to 1983 data, there were approximately 5,000 girls in schools, representing a mere 2 percent of all school-aged girls in the refugee camps. Since women were not permitted to go to the market or to engage in transactions with men, they had to sell their goods through middlemen for prices far below their true market value. Conservatives and Islamic fundamentalists opposed women's involvement in self-supportive projects. They launched a campaign against such activities, which resulted in the destruction of a number of such projects for women in Pakistan:

In 1990, our projects in Nasir Bagh were completely destroyed. . . . At the request of the Social Welfare Division of UNHCR [UN High Commission for Refugees] we built a compound in the widows' section of the camp. This women's center had walls around it and a door in the wall that was guarded. No one was allowed in there. Inside was a sewing project, a vegetable garden, a children's play ground, a big kitchen where women could cook food together, a place for courses to be held, a place for women to do things together without men looking at them and judging them. Problems started very soon. Men threw stones and rocks over the walls. Gulbuddin's party operated a school and threatened to expel any student whose mother went to the women's center. Someone claimed to see women on a swing, and said it was a sin for women to do that. . . . During *Ramadan* Gulbuddin's party stirred more problems. . . . On the first day of the *Eid*, they preached in the mosque, and said if the men did not destroy the women's center, none of the prayers they said during *Ramadan* would be answered.[19]

Revolutionary and politically active women in Pakistan endured constant harassment and were sometimes even subject to assassination. Islamic fundamentalists not only forbade women to participate in social projects and the resistance movement but also prohibited their participation in politics following the Soviet withdrawal from Afghanistan. They did not support women's rights and did not recognize their equality with men. For example, Hizb-e-Islami-e-Afghanistan, the Islamic Party of Afghanistan, headed by Gulbuddin Hikmatyar, articulated its position regarding women's status as follows:

Chapter 1, Article 6: Laws and regulations that will curb at the earliest adultery, drunkenness, gambling, obscenity and moral corruption will be enacted. . . . Article 7: The issue of the veil by women, as dictated by the *Sharia,* will be totally observed throughout the country, and their *Sharia* and legal rights will be restored. Article 8: Necessary and essential rules and regulations will be laid down for the improvement of social life and establishment of healthy relationships among the people. . . . Chapter 3, Article 31: The present system of co-education, where girls and boys acquire education side by side, will be abolished altogether. . . . Chapter 5, Article 81: The system, under which men and women are working together, will be completely abolished and Islamic principles will be strictly observed in this respect.[20]

In a similar vein, Jamiat-e-Islami-e-Afghanistan, the Islamic Society of Afghanistan, headed by Burhanuddin Rabbani, stated its position regarding the future of Afghanistan and the position of women. The party's main political concern is the revival of Islamic culture. According to Jamiat-e-Islami, the party defends and protects the tenets of Islam. It supports the efforts of all religious schools to achieve a reputation for scientific and social development and to act as centers for the propagation of Islamic revolutionary teachings. Jamiat-e-Islami called for all radio programs, press, and other publications to be in the service of the public, to be used for training and guidance of the society as well as for the propagation of Afghanistan culture and values. In articulating its position on women, the party stated: "*Jamiat* wants the women to be able to utilize those rights and privileges given to them by Islamic eternal teachings. *Jamiat* also wants all women to get their proper status in the pure Islamic society."[21]

Other Islamic parties, such as Hizb-e-Islami-e-Afghanistan, the Islamic Party of Afghanistan (a breakaway faction of Hikmatyar's party), headed by Mohammad Yunus Khalis; Harakat-e-Enqilabi Islami-e-Afghanistan, the Islamic Revolutionary Movement, led by Mohammad Nabi Mohammadi; Jabha-e-Milli-e-Nijat-e-Afghanistan, the National Front for Liberation of Afghanistan, headed by Sebghatullah Mojaddadi; and Ittehadi Islami-e-Afghanistan, the Islamic Union of Afghanistan, led by Rasoul Sayyaf, do not specifically mention women in their political platforms but make general references to men and women and their legal rights in an Islamic society.

The political platform of Mahaz-e-Milli-e-Islami Afghanistan, the National Islamic Front of Afghanistan (NIFA) led by Sayed Ahmad Gilani, makes a general reference to women and their role in social development:

In the Field of Domestic Affairs: Article 5. The NIFA supports social, economic and political justice, and the participation of all the people, both women and men, in the task of development and progress of the country in accordance with the principles of the religion of Islam and acceptable national traditions [of Afghanistan] and opposes all kinds of discrimination, exploitation, despotism and oppression. . . . Article 7. The NIFA considers free education, with no discrimination whatsoever, as the legitimate and clear right of the people of Afghanistan, and actively supports overall and effective measures towards the popularization of literacy. Acquiring of knowledge is obligatory on all Muslims, men and women.[22]

Religious leaders do not approve of women studying in non-Muslim countries except when accompanied by a male escort. However, some have no objection to their own children doing so. Gilani's daughter, Fatima, went to study Persian literature at a university in Tehran in 1979 and moved to England when schools in Iran were closed soon after the 1979 revolution. Fatima was a student in a college in London in 1991, but a year later she left her studies and returned to Afghanistan. Fatima often acts as the spokesperson of the women of Afghanistan and expressed her opinion regarding polygamy:

How I feel may not be very popular with the Western women's liberation movements but under certain circumstances, such as exists in my country right now, where many women are war widows, I think polygamy should be a temporary law, encouraged even, to give these women some kind of protection. If a woman is a widow with young children and has no means to support herself, why should she not become a second, third, or fourth wife to a man?[23]

Fatima did not seek alternative solutions such as state-sponsored welfare for these women but prescribed a solution that supported polygamy. One wonders if she would endorse such a prescription for herself if she were in a similar situation. Prescriptions like these are regularly suggested for poor women but rarely considered by women of upper- and middle-class families.

Gilani's other daughter, Fatana, is head of the Pakistan-based Afghanistan Women Council (AWC), which was founded in 1993. The organization provides assistance in areas of education and health to refugee women and children. Although Fatana has nothing in common with women of the poor and underprivileged in terms of ideology and lifestyle, she sees herself as a representative of the interests of women of Afghanistan. She often travels internationally to solicit funds for the AWC and claims to have received numerous death threats from the fundamentalists who oppose women's work in the public arena.

Besides the AWC there are other organizations in Pakistan that provide services to refugees. One such organization is the Afghan Institute of Learning (AIL), which was founded in 1992 by Sakena Yacoobi. It is an apolitical NGO that provides support for education and technical training for women and children in Peshawar. Yacoobi, who was born in Herat, received her college education in the United States and taught at D-Etre

University in Detroit, Michigan. She was appointed coordinator for women's education programs at the International Rescue Committee in Peshawar.[24] Similarly, Khursheed Afrasyabi, head of the Muslim Women Society, is engaged in activities aimed at promoting women's causes on the basis of Islamic teachings.

WOMEN AND THE POLITICS OF REVOLUTIONARY MOVEMENTS

There has been no significant change or revision in the political platforms of most secular political movements regarding women's oppression and their liberation since the 1978 April coup and the Soviet occupation of the country, December 1979–February 1989. Prior to the Soviet occupation these movements did not view women's oppression as separate from overall social and political oppressions. Although a great number of educated women of middle- and upper-class families had been active participants in the movement for social and political change, they did not assume leading positions within these movements. Their roles were auxiliary to those of men and they followed instructions issued by men within the movement's hierarchy.

Women's organizations that had been formed by various political parties did not agitate in support of feminist issues or matters of immediate interest to women. Their main objective was to expand their respective party's social bases among women in schools and workplaces. In a society where women are secluded and social traditions inhibit them from talking to men other than immediate relatives, it is easier and more practical for female members of the party to establish contacts with other women. Female members of the progressive social movements did not engage in promoting the feminist cause per se, although they echoed the formal line of the party concerning women's liberation.

The secular and progressive movements' failure to address the question of women's oppression can be attributed to the urgent need for political democracy; lack of political experience; difficulty of establishing links with women other than those in schools and colleges; and the Soviet occupation and the resulting armed struggle for national liberation. These factors, which made it difficult to formulate policies and programs for women, largely inhibited progressive movements. The intensification of ideological, political, and armed struggle against the Soviet occupation forces led these movements to dedicate most of their efforts to organizing and mobilizing people for the cause of national liberation.

The progressive and secular movements recognized women as a revolutionary force and maintained that no social revolution could succeed without the active participation of women, who constituted half of the country's population. Sazman-e-Mubariza Bara-e-Azadi-e-Tabaqa-e-

Kargar dar Afghanistan, the Organization for Liberation of Working Class of Afghanistan (also known as Akhgar), articulated its position concerning the role of women in social and political development in Afghanistan as follows:

A universal franchise of the citizenry eighteen years old and over

An end to social and class privileges, and the safeguarding of equality regardless of sex, religious, national and ethnic affiliations

Support for women's emancipation and their complete equality with men in every walk of life

An end to women's work in economic sectors that are harmful to their health

Support of paid leave from work for women during pregnancy

Support for day-care centers and kindergartens for working families

An end to the employment of children under eighteen.[25]

Sazman-e-Azadi Bakhsh-e-Mardum-e-Afghanistan, the Organization for Liberation of People of Afghanistan (SAMA), which was founded in 1979 by Majid Kalakani, supports the rights of women and their equality with men. Kalakani was active in the struggle for freedom, democracy, and national liberation. He lived among the dispossessed and marginalized. Unlike other intellectuals who looked at people from above, Kalakani was much closer to them. His language and ideals were the language and ideals of the people. He was known by the name of Majid Agha by the people, but Western media portrayed him as Afghanistan's "Robin Hood." Kalakani was arrested by government security agents on February 27, 1980, and was executed on June 8 of the same year. SAMA's political platform concerning the rights of women included the following goals:

Full equality for women

Economic assistance for mother and child protection

Recreational centers for the people

An end to social and cultural degeneracy.[26]

Sazman-e-Rahaye-Afghanistan, the Afghanistan Liberation Organization (ALO), formerly known as Guruh-e-Enqilabi, Revolutionary Group, was founded in 1973 and supports women's rights and equality with men. According to the ALO the country's economic backwardness, domination of backward cultures, and exploitative policies of the ruling class deprived women of their rightful position in the society and their equal participation in income production as well as social and cultural life. The ALO maintains that no measures would lead to the elimination of gender inequality except those of women's social, political, and class awareness and their own relentless struggle for equality. The organization argues that when women are organized and participate in the anti-feudal, anti-imperialist, and revolutionary struggle under the leadership of the proletarian party, then they would be able to break off the shackles that keep them in bondage.[27] According to the ALO:

Equal rights of men and women can be realized and assured only with complete democratization of society. Struggling for women's rights is an integral part of the struggle for true democracy and none but the proletariat and its political party can be the true champions of true democracy. It was with staunch belief in this principle that the ALO from the very outset focused on women's revolutionary suffragist movement by undertaking to raise its Marxist awareness and assisting in its political organization. Under the circumstances, we can claim remarkable achievements.[28]

The ALO's leader, Faiz Ahmad, was abducted and murdered by supporters of Hikmatyar's Hizb-e-Islami on November 12, 1986. Although Ahmad's murder was a loss to the organization, it did not deprive it of leadership or compel it to abandon politics and its support of women's rights and equality.

In addition to supporting women's rights and equality, the revolutionary movements also made it their policy to glorify women who gave their lives in the liberation struggle. These women were depicted as "heroines" of those in Afghanistan who opposed the Soviet occupation and who gave their lives to advance the cause of the national liberation. They have since been idealized by the people and are perceived as role models for young women, an example to follow as they continue their fight for freedom and liberation of the country.

WOMEN'S STRUGGLE AGAINST OPPRESSION

Prior to and after the Soviet occupation of Afghanistan, the Revolutionary Association of Women of Afghanistan (RAWA) continued its struggle for national liberation. It sponsored rallies and meetings among refugee women in order to organize women in the struggle for a free and democratic Afghanistan. During the Soviet occupation era many revolutionaries were forced to leave the country and settle in Pakistan, India, and elsewhere, where they conducted political works among refugees and continued their fight for the country's liberation. In New Delhi, India, one such politically active woman was Adeena Niazi, daughter of a former governor of Maimana province. Adeena was a student of literature at Kabul University and in 1977 she went to India for higher studies. In New Delhi:

She knows how to move about everywhere, whether in a group of Islamic fundamentalists, or with the representative of SAMA . . . or in Delhi's pseudo-

Western enclaves. . . . She is the connecting links there for all the resistance groups of her community. She knows every functionary and is often the driving force behind demonstrations or propaganda actions like the distribution of pamphlets.[29]

Conservatives and Islamic fundamentalists despised women's participation in politics and pressured them to abandon political activity and even assassinated those who defied their orders. For example, Meena, head of RAWA, was assassinated on February 4, 1987, in Pakistan.[30] Meena and her supporters were active in the women's movement, trying to raise social and political awareness among women to fight for their rights as well as the country's independence. She was a paladin of women's rights who boldly stated:

> I am a woman who has awoken
> I have arisen and become a tempest through the ashes of my burnt children
> I have arisen from the rivulets of my brother's blood
> My nation's wrath has empowered me
> My ruined and burnt villages replete me with hatred against the enemy
> O' compatriot, no longer regard me weak and incapable
> My voice has mingled with thousands of arisen women
> My fists are clenched with fists of thousands compatriots
> To break together all these sufferings, all these fetters of slavery.
> I am the woman, who has awoken,
> I've found my path and will never return.[31]

Supporters of RAWA often exposed the policies of the Kabul regime and condemned the torture and execution of political prisoners and actively participated in the campaign to defend women's rights. For example, Farida Ahmadi was one of the active supporters of RAWA who was arrested in Quetta, Pakistan, on February 2, 1989, because of her political works. It is argued that "the Pakistani police arrested her under orders of Hikmatyar . . . and [she] was released by posting bail on 12 March 1989."[32] Harassment by conservatives and Pakistani security did not deter women's determination to continue their struggle for peace and women's rights. On December 27, 1989, RAWA organized a women's rally in Rawalpindi, Pakistan, to observe the tenth anniversary of the Soviet occupation of Afghanistan. It was estimated that over 300 women, many of them carrying their children, participated in the protest demonstration. The crowd carried flags, banners, and placards inscribed with political slogans expressing women's opposition to the Kabul regime as well as the Pakistan-based Afghanistan Interim Government (AIG).[33]

At the end of the rally, RAWA issued a resolution in which it called for the establishment of an independent government in Kabul by means of a free national election, and denounced the formation of the AIG on the

grounds that such a government had no legitimate mandate for its formation. The resolution condemned the policies of some of the Islamic
parties for the indiscriminate bombings of residential areas in Kabul and
other cities in Afghanistan. Some points of the resolution included:

Exposure of the brutal tactics of individual Wahabi Arabs who raped and mo-
    lested women when they captured towns and villages from the regular gov-
    ernment forces.

A call upon the government of Pakistan to bring to justice the person who as-
    sassinated Meena, leader of the RAWA organization.

Condemnation of the politics of the Iranian leadership concerning their rap-
    prochement with the government in Kabul and their restricted policies toward
    refugees living in various parts of Iran.

Denunciation of the apartheid politics in South Africa and expression of solidarity
    with the Palestinians in their struggle for liberation.

Security forces in Islamabad ordered the demonstrators to disperse.
Fakhria, a member of RAWA, described police action and behavior toward
refugee women: "The police contingent ordered them [the women] to
vacate the place immediately and while doing this, they laughed at them
and passed uncivilized remarks. The irony is that the police had no lady
police officers. Their tongue-lashes were worse than physical lashes."[34]
    Authorities in Pakistan not only did not defend women's rights against
abuses by the Islamic parties but also did not heed to their aspiration for
education. In August 1998 they ordered the closing of five universities for
refugees in the North-West Frontier Province (NWFP), especially the university for women, Ummatul Mominin in Hayatabad, Peshawar, which
was closed for six months.[35] The closing of educational institutions for
women compelled progressive women to seek alternative solutions. To
this end RAWA "has launched a challenge to the warring factions in its
devastated homeland. Convinced that neither the Taliban nor the Northern Alliance is willing to guarantee or is capable of guaranteeing a worth-
while future, the association has decided to establish its own university
and medical school in Pakistan."[36]
    RAWA also established a medical clinic named for Malalay in Quetta
in 1986. The clinic was closed in 1996 due to financial problems; however,
RAWA continues to provide healthcare to needy people through its mo-
bile clinics. In appreciation of RAWA's struggle to promote women's rights
and welfare, Jean Berthault, in-charge for Afghanistan affairs at the French
embassy in Islamabad, Pakistan, presented RAWA with the "French
Republic's Liberty, Equality, Fraternity, and Human Rights Prize" on April
15, 2000, during an official ceremony in Islamabad. The French ambassador, Yannick Gerard, as well as journalists and many RAWA supporters,
attended the ceremony.[37]

In addition to RAWA, individual women also participated in the politics of enlightenment and engaged in projects intended to empower women. One such individual is Sima Samar. Samar was born in 1957 in Ghazni and after she graduated from a high school in Lashkargah she studied medicine at Kabul University and received her M.D. in 1984. When Samar's husband was executed by the PDPA when it seized power in April 1978, she was forced to leave Kabul for the safety of her hometown, Jaghori, and later sought refuge in Quetta, Pakistan. She was an active supporter of RAWA, but later she left the organization as she developed a different perspective regarding the revolutionary movement, particularly the role of women in the liberation struggle. Samar maintained that RAWA did not pay enough attention to ethnic questions and did not tackle the problems and issues that women of minority ethnic communities had encountered both in Afghanistan and in exile.

In 1989 Samar established the Shuhada (martyred) clinic in Quetta. She and her aides administered some fifty schools in both Afghanistan and Pakistan. Although Hizb-e-Wahdat's policy toward women does not significantly differ from the regressive policies of other Islamic parties, Samar nonetheless joined Hizb-e-Wahdat and became a member of the party's central committee and participated in conferences and meetings on behalf of the party.[38] On June 5, 2001, the Women's Commission for Refugee Women and Children, which was founded under the aegis of the International Rescue Committee to protect the rights of women and children in refugee situations, awarded Samar recognition for her part in such endeavors.[39]

The Afghan Women's Resource Center (AWRC) is another nonpolitical organization, established in October 1989 in Pakistan. The center's main objective has been to promote the interests of refugee women by providing vocational education and training to enable women to become self-supportive through its programs, such as literacy, sewing, and knitting. The center has a library and a daycare center for children.[40]

REFUGEES AND PROBLEMS OF ADJUSTMENT

The first group of people to enter Pakistan a few months after the 1978 April coup were officials of the previous governments and families of middle- and upper-class backgrounds. The number of refugees in Pakistan increased when the regime in Kabul tried to suppress opposition social forces. By the end of 1979 there were 400,000 refugees in Pakistan and 200,000 in Iran, and the number of refugees in Iran and Pakistan reached 6.2 million in 1990.[41]

In May 1979, Noor Mohammad Taraki vehemently denounced those who sought refuge in Pakistan and called them, using the standard political epithets, "bowl lickers" of *farangis* (foreigners), "reactionaries," and so forth. In October 1979 Taraki's successor, Hafizullah Amin, in a speech to the elders of the Torai, Mangal, and Waziri tribes in Kabul, called upon the refugees to return. He asked leaders of these tribes to "tell your countrymen that their fathers and forefathers were proud and high-headed. They were not looking to the black hands of foreigners to throw a loaf of bread in their mouths."[42]

The number of refugees in Pakistan substantially increased from an estimated 1 million in 1980 to an estimated 2.8 million by 1986, and the number of refugees in Iran during this period was estimated to be 1.9 million.[43] The majority of the refugees were poor peasants, laborers, and farmers. They lived in squalid refugee camps and received food rations provided by international organizations. The Soviet-installed ruler Babrak Karmal (December 1979–May 1986) had consistently denied the presence of the large number of refugees in Pakistan and instead depicted them as nomads who traditionally cross the borders between Afghanistan and Pakistan. Anahita Ratibzad, a member of the Central Committee of the ruling party and a cabinet member during Karmal's rule, expressed her opinion concerning the presence of refugees in Pakistan in these words:

The majority of Afghans in Pakistan are nomads, 2.5 million of them. The remaining one million are mostly aristocrats who lost their comfortable lifestyles in the revolution, which is why they left Afghanistan. Just a few are deceived peasants. But Zia [Pakistan's late president, General Mohammad Zia ul Haq] likes to keep all these people and call them refugees. This way, he receives international funding, which he then passes on to the leaders of the counter-revolutionary groups.[44]

The majority of refugees (approximately 70 percent) were settled in the NWFP. Other areas with heavy concentration of refugees included Peshawar, Kurram, Mardan, Bajaur, North Waziristan, Kohat, Abbottabad, and Chitral. It is estimated that over 25 percent of the refugees lived in Quetta, capital of Baluchistan, and 5 percent lived in Punjab province; however, a small number of refugees were scattered throughout Pakistan. The greatest concentration of refugees was in the districts of Pishin, Chagai, and Quetta. According to a report published by the UNHCR in 1983, children composed 55 percent of the refugees in Baluchistan and a little over 48 percent in the NWFP. Adult males and adult females composed 20 and 24 percent in Baluchistan and 24 and 28 percent respectively in the NWFP.[45]

Most of these refugees were peasants who had lost their homes and property during the Soviet occupation of Afghanistan. The better-off families within this category constructed permanent mud-brick houses while poorer families lived in tents. The mud-brick houses usually consisted of several rooms including a kitchen, a storage area, living and dining rooms, and perhaps a guest room. The guest room, as the place of honor, was usually the only room decorated with elaborately embroidered cloths created by the wife.[46]

In refugee camps women generally engaged in traditional female-oriented activities. A UNHCR report stated that refugee women were primarily engaged in activities such as childcare, fetching wood and water, and washing clothes, often assisted by their children. They were also engaged in sewing, knitting, and making garments. Usually the women were also called upon to repair or even construct necessary household items such as stoves and storage bins. In addition to cooking food, they were responsible for looking after the poultry, sheep, and goats in the compound and for tending the kitchen gardens. "Although seldom resulting in much cash income, these activities made a vital contribution to family maintenance and welfare."[47]

Leadership was the exclusive domain of men in every refugee camp. *Maliks*, tribal chiefs, had the absolute right of representation of their tribes and communities. Their wives often had leading roles among refugee women. According to UNHCR reports, a *malik*'s wife, with his consent, could play a critical part in organizing women for the various stages of distribution of assistance, as well as facilitating smooth communication in other areas of refugee life. Older women in the community often had a special role because they were respected by the younger women and sought out for their experience and wisdom in areas such as childbirth, which still occurred for the most part at home using traditional methods.[48]

Refugees can be classified into four distinct economic groups: middle class, intellectuals, skilled and semi-skilled laborers, and laborers.

The Middle Class

This group of refugees made up a small portion of the refugee population in Pakistan. They left the country after the Soviet invasion in December 1979 and brought their movable properties and financial resources to Pakistan. Some of these families established their own businesses in various cities in Pakistan. Male family members engaged in business, while female members were involved in indoor activities such as cooking, cleaning, and rearing children. Some middle-class families also hired other refugee women to do some of the cooking, cleaning, and other menial jobs.[49]

Intellectuals

This group of refugees consisted of educated people who had previously worked in public and state enterprises in Afghanistan. After the Soviet invasion they left the country and settled in various urban areas in Pakistan. Some of these intellectuals advocated various political orientations such as feminism, socialism, and nationalism.[50] They believed that they could best contribute to the struggle for national liberation while in exile. However, conservative social forces that enjoyed the support of Pakistan, conservative regimes in the Middle East and the West, suppressed women who engaged in politics. The plight of educated refugee women in Pakistan was characterized as follows:

For eight years, urban, middle-class women have suffered from the strengthening of ultra-conservative Afghan attitudes, exacerbated by conservative Pakistani attitudes, denying them education and career opportunities. Emerging secondary education programs for these women have been heartening developments, for it seems the abruptly halted pre-1978 evolutionary emancipation movement might again be moving forward, albeit slowly. Still, a whole generation of professional women is in danger of being lost.[51]

This situation made life even more difficult for women than what they had encountered back home and compelled a number of them and their families to emigrate to Western Europe, North America, and elsewhere. But a number of women espousing revolutionary and progressive ideologies stayed in Pakistan and continued to fight for women's liberation as well as for their country's independence. Some taught refugee children while others worked as medical doctors and nurses in the few health centers established for refugees in Pakistan.

Skilled and Semi-Skilled Laborers

This group of refugees consisted of women who used to work in manufacturing and other light industrial enterprises in Afghanistan prior to their migration to Pakistan. In Pakistan they wove carpets and rugs, and did embroidery. A number of women worked in projects that were established in Peshawar by international agencies, and the majority of them worked at home. For instance, in Peshawar in the poorest refugee camp of Kababian, which had a population of 19,000, the British volunteer agency Lobsand and Yangchen Yeshi established a quilt-making industry in August 1985. The industry employed approximately 125 families, who carded cotton and sewed quilts. When the work was completed a male member of the family took the product to the market. These refugees earned their living through their own labor and did not have to rely much on food rations provided by international agencies.[52]

Laborers

The overwhelming majority of refugees were laborers. They were illiterate and did not have skills to easily enable them to gain employment and support themselves. Included in this category of refugees was a large number of widows, orphans, and young women of childbearing age. The condition of these women, who composed approximately 22 percent of the refugee population, was distressing. The birth rate was alarmingly high, with 418 live births per 1,000 women. These women had subsisted on unbalanced diets. They did not space their pregnancies, nor did they receive the medical and nutritional treatments pregnant and nursing mothers require. Thus they were increasingly prone to giving birth prematurely, and even full-term babies were usually born underweight. These children were particularly susceptible to a variety of health, mental, and developmental problems.[53]

These people were entirely dependent on international agencies for material assistance. Corruption was pervasive in refugee camps, and many officials in charge of refugee assistance appropriated the bulk of aid for themselves and gave only a small fraction of it to refugee families. This situation compelled these refugees to seek menial jobs outside the camp. Some of the women worked as tailors and some others engaged in the cloth trade as itinerant traders, occasionally conducting sidewalk vending in the bazaars.[54] Others went from house to house working as servants for Pakistanis and middle-class refugee families. Table 5.2 shows the number of women refugees in Pakistan in 1990.

In exile, refugee women encountered various hardships. Most women interviewed by UN refugee officials in Pakistan expressed their dismay concerning their situation in the camps. The tents were not secure, leaving refugees exposed to the elements. In hot weather the tent could be stifling, even suffocating. In cold weather everyone endured freezing temperatures. The women claimed they were told that the camps would be safer than their homes and that well-stocked villages had been set up es-

Table 5.2
Refugees in Pakistan, 1990

	Male	Female	Children Under 15 Years	Total
NWFP	526,148	594,764	1,118,378	2,239,290
Baluchistan	193,652	227,330	420,982	841,964
Punjab	29,133	40,510	110,001	179,644
Sind	5,868	5,229	8,964	20,061
Total	754,801	867,833	1,658,325	3,280,959

Source: Badruddin Zahidi, "Relief Assistance to Refugees and Displaced Women and Children in Pakistan," paper submitted to Expert Group Meeting on Refugee and Displaced Women and Children, Vienna, July 2–6, 1990.

pecially for them in Pakistan. Instead they found themselves languishing in squalid conditions, waiting for a change in their situation that they were no longer sure would ever happen. They were provided with some vegetables, but fruits and meat were in short supply. Families were broken up and scattered in their flight from the villages. Women in the camps who were alone or widowed, some quite young, faced many dangers. "'If a brother or a cousin of the fiancé finds them, they could marry. If not, what would become of them?' said one young girl. 'I hope our cousins won't find us,' she blurted out defiantly. 'I certainly don't want to get married.'"[55] Many refugees suffered from depression, insomnia, anxiety, and post-traumatic stress disorder. Many used drugs and opium to treat physical and psychological problems. Lack of income also forced a significant number of poor refugee women into prostitution to support their family.

A great number of refugees in Pakistan were young people aged ten to twenty. The majority of these young people worked in various manufacturing and construction projects for wages far below those paid to local Pakistani workers. Most of these young refugees could not afford to go to school. They left school in order to get a job to be able to buy food for their families. In March 1983 there were approximately 60 schools for refugee children in Baluchistan and 249 primary schools in the NWFP. A small number of students primarily from affluent families attended Pakistani colleges and universities.[56] The UNHCR had provided a substantial amount of educational aid to refugees in Pakistan and several NGOs had also provided advisory support as well as teaching materials. The Islamic parties also had established several private schools in the NWFP, and admitted students of families affiliated with any of the parties. In 1990 there were approximately 128,143 students and 3,637 teachers. Females constituted 6 percent of the enrollment in these schools. The Islamic parties imposed strict discipline on both pupils and instructors and "compiled text books heavily oriented toward Islamic ideology, 60 percent religion and 40 percent science."[57]

The UNHCR also established a few schools for refugees in Peshawar. The curriculum of these schools was based on the Pakistani model of the educational system, with much emphasis on Islamic ideology. In both systems of schools in Pakistan, most instructors were nonprofessional and were recruited on the basis of political and ideological affiliation with the Islamic parties and the Pakistani authorities in charge of refugee affairs, respectively. Table 5.3 shows the number of schools, teachers, and students in refugee camps in the NWFP and Baluchistan and Punjab provinces, Pakistan, in 1990.

A significant number of refugees returned home soon after the Soviet troop withdrawal from Afghanistan. New refugees arrived in Pakistan when the Islamic parties seized power in Kabul in 1992 and fought each other for domination of the country. The conquest of Kabul and other

Table 5.3
Schools, Teachers, and Students in Refugee Camps in Pakistan, 1990

	NWFP		Baluchistan		Punjab		Total
	Male	Female	Male	Female	Male	Female	
Schools							
Primary	403	77	88	12	7	1	588
Middle	141	4	45	—	1	—	191
High	15	—	—	—	—	—	15
Total	559	81	133	12	8	1	794
Teachers							
Primary	1,457	177	267	24	36	3	1,964
Middle	1,403	23	180	—	3	—	1,609
High	64	—	—	—	—	—	64
Total	2,924	200	447	24	39	3	3,637
Students							
Primary	58,522	7,627	8,059	666	1,780	128	76,782
Middle	43,681	633	5,927	—	21	—	50,262
High	1,069	—	—	—	—	—	1,069
Total	103,272	8,260	13,986	666	1,801	128	128,113

Source: Badruddin Zahidi, "Relief Assistance to Refugees and Displaced Women and Children in Pakistan," paper submitted to Expert Group Meeting on Refugee and Displaced Women and Children, Vienna, July 2–6, 1990.

regions by the Taliban in 1996–1998 forced many more people to seek refuge in Pakistan. On March 20, 1999, the number of refugees in Pakistan was estimated to be 1,119,168 in the NWFP, 331,908 in Baluchistan, 132,058 in Punjab, and 56,219 in Islamabad.[58] The newly arrived refugees were mainly non-Pushtuns who were forced by the Taliban's invading militias to leave their homes. Lack of employment opportunities and reduction of aid by the international community forced many women into prostitution and beggary. A refugee woman described her living conditions in Pakistan in these words:

I came to Peshwar from Kabul. There are eight people in my family and we all came together. We lost everything in the bombing. Our house was destroyed and everything in it was destroyed or stolen. We were just women and girls in the house. My son and husband were murdered by rockets. . . . Now we live in Nasir Bagh camp. The girls are very young, 8, 9, and 10. They do not go to school. Usually I come to beg in this spot. Sometimes I go to other places. From early morning until late at night, I get ten, maybe twelve Rupees, often young boys will come and hit me. It would be better to die than to keep doing this.[59]

Living conditions in refugee camps such as Jalozai, Aza Khel, and Akora Khattak in the NWFP was distressing. The Jalozai camp was called "plastic camp" because refugees covered the tents with flimsy plastic sheets. Many children died of cold in the camp, "where grimy plastic sheets strung over wooden poles provide the only protection against freezing temperatures."[60] Poverty often forced families to sell their daughters to men in other countries, particularly in the Middle East and the West, with the hope of a better future. It is often the case that a girl who marries such a person is resold again to another wealthy man, who pays the husband more than the dowry he had paid when married. A married woman who left for Dubai wrote to her family that "my husband sold me here and now I am in a place that every night I am dancing, and I have been raped a lot and the people I am living with, they are taking money from me."[61]

The plight of refugees in Iran is not entirely dissimilar from those in Pakistan. In 1987 the number of refugees in Iran was estimated to be between 2 and 2.5 million. Most of the refugees settled in Tehran, Khurasan, Mashhad, Kirman, and other provinces.[62] The majority of these refugees were seasonal laborers, exploited by Iranian private firms and enterprises for their cheap labor; they could barely make ends meet. An estimated 20,000 of the poorest refugees lived in *urdugah*s, refugee camps. Unlike the refugees in Pakistan of the 1980s, refugees in Iran did not receive much international attention and even less support either from their host country or from the international community. While Iran in the 1980s provided minimal support to refugees, which included subsidized state food, health, and education,[63] refugee women found it virtually impossible to find any kind of employment. Refugees were routinely deprived of basic human rights, their movement from one city to another was restricted, and they experienced frequent abuse by the host country.

Iran's position toward refugees gradually changed and the government began to refuse to issue them refugee cards, particularly to those who left Afghanistan after the outbreak of the civil war in 1992. Iranian leadership regards these refugees as little more than illegal immigrants and blamed them for taking away jobs from Iranian laborers. Iran prohibited refugees from seeking employment and announced that private enterprises hiring refugees would face severe penalties. As a result of such a policy an estimated 615,000 refugees were repatriated to Afghanistan between 1992 and May 2000 and many others were forced to leave for Pakistan and other places. Iranian officials defended their position, maintaining that repatriation of refugees occurs on a voluntary basis;[64] however, refugees have no other alternatives but to leave Iran. It is estimated that 1.4 million refugees still remain in Iran, and Iranian authorities continue to force them to return home.

NOTES

1. Wali M. Rahimi, *Status of Women: Afghanistan* (Bangkok: UNESCO Principal Regional Office for Asia and the Pacific, 1991), p. 55.

2. S. Fida Yunas, *Afghanistan: Organization of the Peoples' Democratic Party of Afghanistan/Watan Party, Governments, and Bibliographical Sketches, 1982–1998*, vol. 2 (Peshawar, Pakistan: S. Fida Yunas, 1998), pp. 920–921.

3. Ibid., p. 917.

4. Ibid., pp. 889–890.

5. Jan Goodwin, *Caught in the Crossfire* (New York: E. P. Dutton, 1987), pp. 139–140.

6. Yunas, *Afghanistan,* p. 884.

7. Steve Le Vine, "The War Within the War: Rebel Infighting Gives Relief to the Afghan Regime," *Newsweek,* January 22, 1990, p. 41.

8. "Fitwai-e-Sharia-e-Satr wa Hijab," Kabul, August 27, 1993. Cited in Helena Malikyar, "Development of Family Law in Afghanistan: The Roles of the Hanafi Madhhab, Customary Practices, and Power Politics," *Central Asian Survey* 16:3 (1997): 396.

9. Edward Girardet and Jonathan Walter (eds.), *Afghanistan: Essential Field Guides to Humanitarian and Conflict Zones* (Geneva: Crosslines Communications, 1998), p. 58.

10. Deborah Ellis, *Women of the Afghan War* (Westport, Conn.: Praeger, 2000), pp. 48–49.

11. Peter Marsden, *The Taliban: War, Religion, and the New Order in Afghanistan* (Karachi, Lahore, Islamabad: Oxford University Press; London and New York: Zed Books, 1998), p. 98.

12. Amnesty International, *Women in Afghanistan: Pawns in Men's Power Struggles* (London: Amnesty International Secretariat, November 1999), p. 6.

13. *Amnesty International Report 1999* (London: Amnesty International, 1999), p. 69.

14. Part of the Aga Khan's speech cited in Anne Edwards, *Throne of Gold: The Lives of the Aga Khans* (New York: William Morrow, 1995), pp. 83–84.

15. *Al-Qu'ran,* a commentary translation by Ahmed Ali (Princeton: Princeton University Press, 1984), p. 73.

16. Goodwin, *Caught in the Crossfire,* p. 145.

17. Women's International Network, *News* no. 2 (Spring 1988): 58.

18. Ibid., p. 58.

19. Ellis, *Women of the Afghan War,* p. 45.

20. "Charter of *Hizbi Islami* Afghanistan," *Afghan Jehad* 1:3 (January–March 1988): 60–68.

21. "Aims and Goals of *Jamiat-e-Islami* Afghanistan," *Mirror of Jehad: The Voice of Afghan Mujahideen* 1:1(January–February 1982): 11–12.

22. "Charter of *Mahazi Melli-e-Islami-e-Afghanistan,*" *Afghan Jehad* 1:3 (January–March 1988): 56–57.

23. Jan Goodwin, *Price of Honor: Muslim Women Lift the Veil of Silence on the Islamic World* (Boston: Little, Brown, 1994), p. 85.

24. Courtney W. Howland (ed.), *Religious Fundamentalism and the Human Rights of Women* (New York: St. Martin's Press, 1999).

25. Akhgar (Sazmani Mubariza Bara-e-Azadi Tabaqa-e-Kargar dar Afghanistan, or Organization for Liberation of the Working Class of Afghanistan], *Dar Sangari Mubariza wa Barnama-e-Ma Barai-e-Enqilabi Milli-Demokratik* [In the Battlefield and Our Policy for National-Democratic Revolution] (Kabul: 1361/1982).

26. Nida-e-Enqilab [Voice of Revolution], Organ-e-Tiyurik-Siyasi Kamunistha-e-Afghanistan [Theoretical-Political Organ of Revolutionary Cells of Afghanistan's Communists], vols. 4–5 (1365/1986), pp. 25–33.

27. "Standpoints of the Afghanistan Liberation Organization on a Number of Key Issues," www.geocities.com/tokyo/ginza/3231. Accessed at various dates in early 2001.

28. Ibid.

29. Wilhelm Dietl, *Bridgehead Afghanistan* (New Delhi: Lancer International, 1986), pp. 262–264.

30. Revolutionary Association of Women of Afghanistan (RAWA), *Payam-e-Zan* [The Message of Women] 2:1 (December 1989): 45.

31. Translation of a part of a poem by Meena, *Payam-e-Zan* no. 1 (1981).

32. Asia Watch Committee, *Afghanistan: The Forgotten War, Human Rights Abuses and Violations of the Laws of War Since the Soviet Withdrawal* (New York: Human Rights Watch, 1991), pp. 83–84, 118–119.

33. "Afghan RAWA Holds Protest Rally," *The Pakistan Times,* December 28, 1989.

34. "Afghan Refugees with No Future in Sight," *Pakistan Observer,* December 28, 1989.

35. The five universities closed included Ummatul Mominin, Sayed Jamal al-Din Afghani, Ahmad Shah Abdali, Hewad, and Islami Pohantoon. See Nasreen

Ghufran, "Afghan Refugee Women in Pakistan" (Paper presented at the International Conference on "Refugees, Internally Displaced Persons, and Stateless People: The Humanitarian Challenge," Hanns Seidel Foundation, Germany, April 12–13, 1999), p. 6.

36. Bernard Leeman, "The Education of the Exiled," *The Times Higher Education Supplement*, April 27, 2001, Section Worldview, no. 1484, p. 9.

37. http://www.rawa.org, accessed on various dates in January and March 2001.

38. For details, see Hafizullah Emadi, "Breaking the Shackles: Political Participation of Hazara Women in Afghanistan," *Asian Journal of Women's Studies* 6:1 (2000): 157–158.

39. Robert McMahon, Radio Free Europe/Radio Liberty, New York, June 5, 2001.

40. Ghufran, "Afghan Refugee Women in Pakistan," p. 11.

41. Rupert Colville, "The Biggest Caseload in the World," *Refugees* no. 108 (II-1997): 3–4.

42. *Kabul Times*, October 23, 1979.

43. "Pakistan and Iran," *Refugees* no. 36 (December 1986): 27.

44. Goodwin, *Caught in the Crossfire*, p. 150.

45. International Labor Organization (ILO) and UN High Commissioner for Refugees (UNHCR), *Tradition and Dynamism Among Afghan Refugees: Report of an ILO Mission to Pakistan (November 1982) on Income-Generating Activities for Afghan Refugees* (Geneva: ILO, 1983), p. 13.

46. Ibid., p. 17.

47. Ibid., p. 36.

48. Ibid., pp. 25–26.

49. Kathleen Howard-Merriam, "Afghan Refugee Women and Their Struggle for Survival," in *Afghan Resistance: The Politics of Survival*, Grant M. Farr and John G. Merriam (eds.) (Boulder, Colo.: Westview Press, 1987), p. 115.

50. Hafizullah Emadi, "Resettlement Pattern: The Afghan Refugees in Pakistan," *Cultural Survival Quarterly* 12:4 (Fall 1988): 22.

51. Louis Dupree and Nancy Hatch Dupree, "Afghan Refugees in Pakistan," in *World Refugee Survey: 1987 in Review*, 13th-anniversary issue (Washington, D.C.: U.S. Committee for Refugees, 1988), p. 19.

52. "Ockenden Venture Projects for Afghan Refugee Women," *Refugees* no. 31 (July 1986): 40.

53. Emadi, "Resettlement Pattern," p. 19.

54. ILO/UNHCR, *Tradition and Dynamism*, p. 20.

55. Annick Roulet-Billard, "First Person Feminine," *Refugees* no. 70 (November 1989): 24–26.

56. ILO/UNHCR, *Tradition and Dynamism*, p. 30.

57. Batinshah Safi, "Afghan Education During the War," in *The Tragedy of Afghanistan: The Social, Cultural, and Political Impact of the Soviet Invasion*, Bo Huldt and Erland Jansson (eds.) (London: Croom Helm, 1988), pp. 117–118.

58. Ghufran, "Afghan Refugee Women in Pakistan," p. 1.

59. Ellis, *Women of the Afghan War*, p. 170.

60. Kathy Gannon, "Fleeing Afghans Overwhelming Pakistan Camps," Associated Press, *The Seattle Times*, January 10, 2001, p. A-7.

61. Ellis, *Women of the Afghan War*, p. 145.

62. Anneliese Hollmann, "Islamic Republic of Iran: Host to over Two Million Afghan Refugees," *Refugees* no. 38 (February 1987): 10–11.

63. Colville, "Biggest Caseload," p. 4.

64. Field Survey of refugees in Tehran, Mashhad, Kirman, and Baluchistan, Iran, and discussions with Iranian officials in Tehran, Iran, June 2000.

6

Women's Empowerment: Prospects for the Future

As humankind enters the new millennium, strategies must be devised to raise the status of women and enable their progress toward participation in the reconstruction of the country. The word *empowerment,* which gained popular usage in development literature in the last few decades of the twentieth century, to a great extent focused on creating mechanisms that enabled women to break their economic dependency on men. However, such a strategy did not reflect much on women's empowerment in the social and political arenas and did not discuss women's active role in the process. Empowerment of women requires an examination and identification of multifaceted social, cultural, political, and economic factors that deprived women of their right to became equal participants in the development process and confined their activities to the domestic arena in their homes. Empowerment also entails active participation of women in the struggle for their liberation and elimination of gender disparity.

WOMEN IN THE STATE DEVELOPMENT PROGRAMS

The study of Afghanistan's political economy reveals that modernization and economic growth did not develop evenly throughout the country. Capitalist development did not transform the country's precapitalist mode of production except in those sectors that suited the interests of core societies. This trend of development and modernization benefited a small segment of the population but led to increasing marginalization of middle- and low-income social classes in both urban and rural areas. Contradictions between towns and villages and rich and poor were mounting daily. Oppression inevitably breeds opposition and there is no basis to believe that men and women will continue for long to be the victims of social injustices and class oppression.

This trend of development is also reflected in uneven development in social, cultural, and educational arenas among various social classes. Higher education and employment opportunities outside the home contributed to greater social and political awareness among women of upper- and middle-class backgrounds, enabling them to reflect upon women's strategic needs, for example, gender equality and empowerment. Women from low-income families who had difficulties even in fulfilling their immediate practical needs, such as food, clothing, and shelter, could not reflect on women's strategic needs. Thus women of the privileged social classes have spearheaded the struggle for gender equality.

Since the early 1960s women of upper- and middle-class families have actively participated in the struggle, not only agitating for socioeconomic changes but also promoting women's liberation. To advance their cause, they formed women's organizations and associations and encouraged women to participate in their activities and support their policies and struggle for political, social, and economic change and gender equality. Their struggle was not entirely successful due to lack of political unity within women's movements and regime changes in the early 1970s, including the Soviet occupation of the country in December 1979.

The Soviet occupation deflected the women's movements from the struggle for their rights and equality with men to that of either supporting or opposing the Soviet occupation. Women members and sympathizers of the People's Democratic Party of Afghanistan supported the Soviet occupation, maintaining that its backing of the regime in Afghanistan would ensure a better life for women. Jamiat-e-Enqilabi-e-Zanan-e-Afghanistan, the Revolutionary Association of Women of Afghanistan (RAWA), and women members of other revolutionary, nationalist, and Islamic organizations vehemently opposed the Soviet occupation of the country. Revolutionary women participated in the fight against the Soviet occupation forces because they were patriotic, but as women they were also determined to free themselves from the restrictions imposed by centuries of cultural and social traditions.

The nine-year armed struggle of the people compelled the Soviet leadership to withdraw its troops from Afghanistan. The last Soviet troops left the country on February 15, 1989, but the Soviet-installed regime's hold on power continued. In April 1992 the Kabul regime collapsed and the Islamic parties seized power and declared Afghanistan an Islamic state. The first interim president, Sebghatullah Mojaddadi, expressed his views concerning women's role and leadership in Afghanistan. During a public speech he urged the people to unite and elect a qualified person as their leader. Mojaddadi recommended that the nation not elect a woman as their leader. He said: "[T]he weakest nations in the world are those that had a woman as a leader. It doesn't mean that Islam is against women. On the contrary, it respects them and says they are equal to men. But [history shows] that weak nations are led by women."[1] Such views, expressed by the highest political and religious leaders in Afghanistan, indicate that women's struggle will not cease in the immediate future.

In August 1992 Mojaddadi's short term ended and Burhanuddin Rabbani, head of Jamiat-e-Islami, succeeded him. In December 1992 Rabbani convened a controversial council in an attempt to extend his tenure and was rebuffed by rival parties. The opposition groups condemned Rabbani and his defense minister, Ahmad Shah Masoud, for their heavy-handed policies and reluctance to work toward forming a broad-based government. This situation paved the way for armed confrontation among the Islamic parties, each trying to establish its own domination of the country's politics. The war not only destroyed the country's infrastructure and claimed the lives of thousands of innocent men, women, and children but also forced thousands of people to leave the country and seek refuge in neighboring countries, mainly Iran and Pakistan. The war also led to the displacement of thousands of others who abandoned their homes and villages and sought refuge in the safety of other regions throughout the country.

Women were victimized during the war. When a warring faction could not militarily defeat its opponent, it took men and women of the rival political party and ethnic group hostage, molested the women, and subsequently murdered most of their captives. In so doing the perpetrators' main intention was to belittle their opponents and also to intimidate civilians not to rebel against them, lest they face a similar fate. Scores of women were killed and many others simply disappeared and were sold to rich individuals abroad. Schools and colleges remained closed for the most part in the early 1990s as armed militias belonging to a variety of Islamic groups tried to implement their versions of an Islamic society. Their policies concerning a return to the Islamic way of life did not go beyond mandating women's seclusion, ordering them to cover their bodies from head to toe by wearing the *chadari*, veil, and forcing men to grow beards.

The policy of building an Islamic society by reliance on lethal modern weaponry rather than public consent also affected women in the rural areas. Rural women did not wear veils when they went to work on the farm or visited relatives in other villages and towns. Although they remained obedient to men and walked behind them without uttering any words in the public, they still enjoyed some degree of freedom in their village communities. Islamic orthodoxy and orthopraxy also led to the closure of schools for girls and restricted women's access to international aid agencies, as Islamic parties regard outsiders' involvement and help as having a contaminating influence on their women. Such measures have adversely affected the lives of the internally displaced women, depriving them of the opportunity to develop the capacity necessary for rebuilding their lives.

The rise and consolidation of the Taliban in the 1990s and its war of conquest of other areas of the country further curtailed women's activities in the public arena and compelled a significant number of educated women to leave the country. Similarly, the rising tempo of Islamic orthodoxy adversely affected the lives of women in exile, restricting their movement outside refugee camps. Although the Taliban's abuse of human rights and women's rights generated public outcry at the international level and condemnation for the practice of gender apartheid, it also provided an opportunity for the ousted rulers of Kabul and their allies to polish their own tarnished images and even worse record of human rights abuses. While in a defensive position the ousted rulers portrayed themselves as "humanists" and "champions" of human rights and women's rights, which they brazenly abused when they were in power in Kabul. A journalist who had interviewed Ahmad Shah Masoud (assassinated in early September 2001) characterized his attitudes toward women's rights in these words:

As the Taliban grew internationally notorious, banning television, sheathing women head-to-toe and amputating the hands of thieves, Masoud presented himself to the West as a reasonable Muslim. "I am for the rights of women," he said. "Women can work. Women can go to school." But once asked if his own wife wore the head-to-toe *burqa*, he smiled sheepishly and replied, "Yes, this is the custom."[2]

ALTERNATIVE APPROACHES TO WOMEN'S EMPOWERMENT

Afghanistan is one of the less developed societies in Asia. Numerous political groups and individuals aspired to transform their backward society into a modern one, but their ideas and strategies were based on modalities of the past without any relevance to the lives and requirements of the present era. Modernization policies imposed from the top by the state apparatus without actual participation of members of civil society did not alter the very fabric of the backward social formation and its corresponding ideology, politics, and culture. The ruling class within the state apparatus, whose function was nothing but the custodian of tribal interests, was only concerned in supporting modernization programs that served its interests and that did not pose a threat to the status quo. As the world was experiencing change, conservative leaders tried to insulate the country from the influence of change—a policy that sharpened struggle between the old, defenders of the status quo which was in the process of decay, and the new, agitating for radical social transformation. Such a policy deprived the ruling class of its cohesion and hegemony to lead the society into a new era, paving the road for greater struggle between them.

Although Afghanistan is a multiethnic and multilingual society, the culture of pluralism and diversity as a source of strength is absent in the process of building a nation-state. The country is divided on the basis of ethnic, regional, linguistic, and sectarian lines. Pushtuns wielded political power and suppressed non-Pushtuns, which provoked the latter to fight for autonomy and political equality. Policies of building a nation-state without giving an equal role and recognition to other ethnic communities by the ruling class backfired as they tried to forcibly unite ethnic groups under the umbrella of Afghan (Pushtun) nationalism. Today the Islamic parties follow a similar policy by replacing old concepts of national unity with new concepts such as *Millat-e-Mujahid,* Mujahid nation; *Millat-e-Islam,* Islamic nation; and so on. These concepts that have been presented by the Islamic parties as the only road to peace are nothing but hollow rhetoric that negates the very existence of national communities. Building a nation-state is only possible when a country's constituent national communities are treated on an equal basis and when women, who constitute half of the population, are involved in the process of rebuilding a new society.

Proponents of these ideas vehemently condemn any arguments on equality of national communities as a menace to Islamic unity. Their reluctance to adopt new strategies for rebuilding a new society have largely contributed to the widening of lacunae among national communities and the perpetuation of civil war, whose main objective had been the deconstruction of existing political inequality among national communities. Their policies failed to produce a comprehensive resolution of the existing social and political antagonisms among national communities and negatively impacted the status and role of women in the process of reconstruction of Afghanistan. They oppose women's empowerment and opportunities for them to develop their abilities and play a role in the public domain.

To improve the status of women and make them effective contributors in the rebuilding of Afghanistan it is essential to provide women with educational opportunities enabling them to learn new skills and update their knowledge regarding the reconstruction process. Without modern education and women's involvement in the development process it will be difficult and impractical to rebuild a modern society, because women are its critical ingredients. International agencies could play a major role in helping women in rural and urban areas to build their capacity as important partners in the rebuilding of Afghanistan—if they were to adopt a new and flexible approach in their programs of accessing women in a conservative milieu rather than linking the provision of development aid to having unfettered access to women. Given the realities in Afghanistan, such a measure and even political pressure by the international community have failed to convince conservative leaders to allow them access to women. Women's emancipation and the elimination of gender differences do not come about as a result of good intentions and external pressures. It takes time and culturally sound measures to promote activities that ensure life-sustenance for men and women and to design development strategies within the cultural context that necessitates women's involvement in community-based rehabilitation programs.

A significant reason that the international community failed to aid women was the fact that expatriate officials, managers, and executives lacked the cultural awareness that was needed to understand the mindset of the conservative leadership. Because of this they were ineffective at the delicate negotiations necessary to convince them of the need to promote gender awareness and education for women. If families were convinced of the benefits of modern education they would be willing to support women's education, and aid agencies working to involve women in community-based projects would also be more successful in their efforts. The international community's main agenda in Afghanistan has been education and health. They have not explored other arenas such as sponsoring small-income-generating projects, small business, and the like, that would effectively induce voluntary participation of women in such projects. If the international community does not adopt a new strategy to convince families of the benefits of education and vocational and technical training, its future policies are doomed to failure.

Policies of aid agencies at present are based on the "quick fix" and rendering emergency assistance on a short-term basis. Such an approach is flawed with complications and it cannot help women individually or collectively to build their capacity as critical participants in community-based development projects. Policies must be designed with the conditions that they promote long-term sustainable community projects and help women build upon their capacity as active participants in the planning and implementation of development projects in both rural and urban settings.

Development and rehabilitation policies must not exclusively focus on total participation based on Western concepts of development, but rather efforts must be implemented in a manner aimed at improving the material and social well-being of dispossessed men and women. Women's participation in the rehabilitation programs so far has been limited to their attendance at such meetings, but they are regarded as passive rather than active participants. Efforts must be made to involve women in the decisionmaking, planning, and implementation of development projects. Planning with women and for women must constitute an important aspect of development in the twenty-first century. Most development planners are males who readily ignore women's vital interests. Involving women in planning will help them learn, improve their skills, and make decisions that are relevant to their conditions within their own cultural context. Policies must be designed to train a cadre of women, in consultation with local leadership, to actively work among women in an environment where access is restricted and most often denied to local as well as expatriate men working with aid agencies.

The international community must work to design policies and create mechanisms to facilitate a meaningful involvement of women in the process of development in a culturally sensitive environment. One effective strategy that could facilitate women's involvement would be the creation of village committees organized and led by women. It would be appropriate to involve prominent women to head such village committees, because such women wield considerable influence among other women in their villages and their involvement would facilitate women's greater participation in the development programs.[3]

These measures alone do not necessarily lead to a change. Women's struggle to attain their rights is of critical importance and the new government that emerges and wishes to establish stability must recognize the potential role of women in the rebuilding and reconstruction of the country. If it continues to impose restrictions on the role of women in the process of development and undermine their aspirations for leadership, the country's liberation will be incomplete. Women constitute half of Afghanistan's population; if they are not equal participants in the making of a new society, the march to modernity will be hampered by women's continuous struggle for gender equality in the future. Women must fight for their rights and equality, and their increasing participation in the struggle will contribute to the eventual achievement of their rights and secure their position in the future of Afghanistan. Women's liberation, empowerment, and equality with men require women to take an active part in the struggle and break the chains that keep them in bondage.

Break the Silence

O women and men why are you silent
why do you look for an imaginary world
having illusions about your might
Forget not that you are the makers of history.
Be not occupied in day-dreaming
burn in your burning wrath
the invisible chain
which cunning hucksters spun around you.
You were the one who destroyed
the foundation of slavery and feudalism
smashed the foundation of Fascism,
threw the reign of terror into the dustbin of history

and built a new world on their ruins.
Like the early Red morning Sun
You have fertilized the earth with your blood
And hoisted high the lofty banner of peace and freedom.
Come and swim in the depth of the stormy seas
struggle against hardships
because the essence of life is continuous battle.
Sitting with folded-hand brings you no good
lamenting on the day's of yore brings you no prosperity
struggle makes you a great human being
it will record your name in the archives of history
because you are the makers of history.[4]

NOTES

1. Cited in *Newsweek,* May 11, 1992, p. 23.
2. Barry Bearak, "Taliban Opposition Confirms Death of Its Battle Commander," *The New York Times,* September 16, 2001, p. 26.
3. For details, see Hafizullah Emadi, "Rebuilding Afghanistan," *Contemporary Review* 278:1623 (April 2001): 200–208.
4. Hafizullah Emadi, "Break the Silence," *Horizons* 1:1 (1996): 37.

Appendix:
Bilateral Agreement Between the Republic of Afghanistan and the Islamic Republic of Pakistan on the Voluntary Return of Refugees

The Republic of Afghanistan and the Islamic Republic of Pakistan, hereinafter referred to as the High Contracting parties,

Desiring to normalize relations and promote good neighborliness and cooperation as well as to strengthen international peace and security in the region,

Convinced that voluntary and unimpeded repatriation constitutes the most appropriate solution for the problem of Afghan refugees present in the Islamic Republic of Pakistan and having ascertained that the arrangements for the return of the Afghan refugees are satisfactory to them,

Have agreed as follows:

Article I

All Afghan refugees temporarily present in the territory of the Islamic Republic of Pakistan shall be given the opportunity to return voluntarily to their homeland in accordance with the arrangements and conditions set out in the present Agreement.

Article II

The Government of the Republic of Afghanistan shall take all necessary measures to ensure the following conditions for the voluntary return of Afghan refugees to their homeland:

(a) All refugees shall be allowed to return in freedom to their home-
    land;

(b) All returnees shall enjoy the free choice of domicile and freedom
    of movement within the Republic of Afghanistan;

(c) All returnees shall enjoy the right to work, to adequate living con-
    ditions and to share in the welfare of the state;

(d) All returnees shall enjoy the right to participate on an equal basis
    in the civic affairs of the Republic of Afghanistan. They shall be
    ensured equal benefits from the solution of the land question on
    the basis of the Land and Water Reform;

(e) All returnees shall enjoy the same rights and privileges, including
    freedom of religion, and have the same obligations and responsi-
    bilities as any other citizen of the Republic of Afghanistan without
    discrimination.

The Government of the Republic of Afghanistan undertakes to implement
these measures and to provide, within its possibilities, all necessary assistance in the process of repatriation.

Article III

The Government of the Islamic Republic of Pakistan shall facilitate the
voluntary, orderly and peaceful repatriation of all Afghan refugees staying within its territory and undertakes to provide, within its possibilities,
all necessary assistance in the process of repatriation.

Article IV

For the purpose of organizing, coordinating and supervising the operations which should effect the voluntary, orderly and peaceful repatriation
of Afghan refugees, there shall be set up mixed commissions in accordance
with the established international practice. For the performance of their
functions the members of the commissions and their staff shall be ac-
corded the necessary facilities, and have access to the relevant areas within
the territories of the High Contracting Parties.

Article V

With a view to the orderly movement of the returnees, the commissions
shall determine frontier crossing points and establish necessary transit
centers. They shall also establish all other modalities for the phased return of refugees, including registration and communication to the country
of return of the names of refugees who express the wish to return.

Article VI

At the request of the Governments concerned, the United Nations High Commissioner for Refugees will cooperate and provide assistance in the process of voluntary repatriation of refugees in accordance with the present Agreement. Special agreements may be concluded for this purpose between UNHCR and the High Contracting parties.

Article VII

The present Agreement shall enter into force on 15 May 1988. At that time the mixed commissions provided in Article IV shall be established and the operations for the voluntary return of refugees under this Agreement shall commence.

The arrangements set out in Article IV and V above shall remain in effect for a period of eighteen months. After that period the High Contracting Parties shall review the results of the repatriation and, if necessary, consider any further arrangements that may be called for.

Article VIII

This Agreement is drawn up in the English, Pushtu and Urdu languages, all texts being equally authentic. In case of any divergence of interpretation, the English text shall prevail.

Done in five original copies at Geneva this fourteenth day of April 1988.
[Signed by Afghanistan and Pakistan]

Source: Refugees no. 53 (May 1988): 12.

A village family in Shibar, Bamiyan, 1975. Author and family.

Queen Soraya, Amanullah's wife, 1920s. *Courtesy of the Late Louis Dupree.*

A woman in traditional dress in Shibar, Bamiyan. Sayed Begum, author's mother, 1975.

Under the veil: women in Afghanistan. *Courtesy of RAWA, 2001.*

Meena, Leader of RAWA assassinated on 4 February 1987 in Quetta, Pakistan. *Courtesy of RAWA.*

Supporters of RAWA at a rally in Islamabad, Pakistan, December 2000. *Courtesy of RAWA.*

Bibliography

Afghan Demographic Studies. *National Demographic and Family Guidance Survey of the Settled Population of Afghanistan.* Vol. 1. *Demography and Knowledge, Attitudes and Practices of Family Guidance.* Buffalo: State University of New York Press, 1975.

Afghan Information Center, Peshawar, Pakistan. *Monthly Bulletin* no. 23 (February 1983), nos. 44–45 (November–December 1984).

"Afghan RAWA Holds Protest Rally." *The Pakistan Times,* December 28, 1989.

"Afghan Refugees with No Future in Sight." *Pakistan Observer,* December 28, 1989.

Afghanistan Government Agencies. *Afghanistan Industrial Development Projects.* Checchi and Co. Final Report. Washington, D.C. and Kabul, September 1974.

———. Central Statistics Office (CSO). *Preliminary Results of the First Afghan Population Census.* Publication no. 1. Kabul: CSO, 1981.

———. Central Statistics Office (CSO). *Statistical Yearbook.* Kabul: CSO, 1975–1976.

———. Ministry of Education. *Educational Statistics 1350* [1971]. Kabul: Matbaa-e-Dawlati, 1971.

———. Ministry of Foreign Affairs. *Achievements of the April Revolution in Afghanistan.* Kabul: Ministry of Foreign Affairs, 1984.

———. Ministry of Information and Culture. *Afghanistan Republic Annual 1975, 1976, 1978.* Kabul: Government Printing House, 1975, 1976, 1978.

———. Ministry of Information and Culture. *Democratic Republic of Afghanistan Annual, Saur 7, 1358* [1979]. Kabul: Kabul Times Publishing Agency, Government Printing House, 1979.

———. Ministry of Planning. *Afghan Agriculture in Figures.* Qaus 1357/[1978]. Kabul: Government Printing House, 1978.

————. Ministry of Planning. *Majmua-e-Aisayawi-e-Sali, 1350* [Statistical Dictionary, 1971]. Kabul: Matbaa-e-Dawlati, 1971.

————. Ministry of Planning. *Survey of Progress Reports, 1967–1968.* Kabul: Matbaa-e-Dawlati, 1968.

————. *Social, Economic, and Development Plan: Republic of Afghanistan, 1354* [1975]. Translated and edited by the UN Development Program (UNDP). Kabul: UNDP, November 3, 1975.

"Afghanistan King Overthrown, a Republic Is Proclaimed." *The New York Times,* July 18, 1973.

Ahmad, Jamal-ud-Din, and Muhammad Abdul Aziz. *Afghanistan: A Brief Survey.* London: Longmans, Green, 1936.

"Aims and Goals of Jamiat-e-Islami Afghanistan." *Mirror of Jehad: The Voice of Afghan Mujahidin* 1:1 (January–February 1982): 8–13.

Akhgar [Sazmani Mubariza Bara-e-Azadi Tabaqa-e-Kargar dar Afghanistan, or Organization for Liberation of the Working Class of Afghanistan]. *Chand Sanad Wa Maqala Dar Mawridi Awza-e-Eqtisadi, Siyasi Wa Ejtima-e-Afghanistan* [Documents and Articles on Economic, Political, and Social Conditions in Afghanistan]. Tehran: Published by revolutionary students, n.d.

————. *Dar Sangari Mubariza wa Barnama-e-Ma Barai-e-Enqilabi Milli-Demokratik* [In the Battlefield and Our Policy for National-Democratic Revolution]. Kabul: s.n., 1361/1982.

Al-Qu'ran. A commentary translation by Ahmed Ali. Princeton: Princeton University Press, 1984.

Ali, Mohammed. *The Afghans.* 3rd ed. Kabul: Kabul University, 1969.

————. *Afghanistan: Land of Glorious Past and Bright Future.* Kabul: Franklin Book Programs, Education Press, 1969.

Aman-e-Afghan (Kabul). October 10, 1928; January 8, 1929; January 10, 1929.

Amin, Samir. *Imperialism and Unequal Development.* New York: Monthly Review Press, 1977.

Amnesty International. *Amnesty International Report 1999.* London: Amnesty International, 1999.

————. *Amnesty International Reports.* London: Amnesty International, 1980.

————. *Afghanistan: International Responsibility for Human Rights Disaster.* New York: Amnesty International, 1995.

————. *Afghanistan: Torture of Political Prisoners.* New York: Amnesty International, 1986.

————. *Women in Afghanistan: Pawns in Men's Power Struggles.* London: Amnesty International Secretariat, November 1999.

Anwar, Raja. *The Tragedy of Afghanistan: A First-Hand Account.* Translated from the Urdu by Khalid Hasan. London: Verso, 1988.

Arnold, Anthony. "Afghanistan." In *The New Insurgencies: Anti-Communist Guerrillas in the Third World,* Michael Radu (ed.), pp. 233–258. New Brunswick, N.J.: Transaction, 1990.

————. *Afghanistan's Two-Party Communism: Parcham and Khalq.* Stanford, Calif.: Hoover Institution Press, 1983.

Asia Watch Committee. *Afghanistan: The Forgotten War, Human Rights Abuses, and Violations of the Laws of War Since the Soviet Withdrawal.* New York: Human Rights Watch, 1991.

Astarabadi, Bibi Khanum. *Ma'ayib al-rijal: Dar Pasikh ba Ta'dib al-Nisvan* [Vices of Men: In Response to Disciplining Women]. Edited with an introduction by Afsaneh Najmabadi. Chicago: Midland, 1992.

Bearak, Barry. "Taliban Opposition Confirms Death of Its Battle Commander." *The New York Times,* September 16, 2001.

Bechhoefer, Sondra Howell. "Education and the Advancement of Women in Afghanistan." M.A. thesis, University of Maryland, 1975.

Bhaneja, Balwant. *Afghanistan: Political Modernization of a Mountain-Kingdom.* New Delhi: Spectra, 1973.

Black, Richard, and Khalid Koser (eds.). *The End of Refugee Cycle: Refugee Repatriation and Reconstruction.* New York: Berghahn Books, 1999.

Boesen, Inger W. "What Happens to Honour in Exile? Continuity and Change Among Afghan Refugees." In *The Tragedy of Afghanistan: The Social, Cultural, and Political Impact of the Soviet Invasion,* Bo Huldt and Erland Jansson (eds.), pp. 219–239. London: Croom Helm, 1988.

———. "Women, Honour, and Love: Some Aspects of the Pushtun Woman's Life in Eastern Afghanistan." *Afghanistan Journal* 7:2 (1980): 50–59.

Bonner, Arthur. *Among the Afghans.* Durham, N.C.: Duke University Press, 1987.

Bowen, Donna Lee, and Evelyn A. Early (eds.). *Everyday Life in the Muslim Middle East.* Bloomington: Indiana University Press, 1993.

Canfield, Robert L. *Faction and Conversion in a Plural Society: Religious Alignments in the Hindu Kush.* Ann Arbor: University of Michigan Press, 1973.

"Character of Hizbi Islami Afghanistan." *Afghan Jehad* 1:3 (January–March 1988): 59–70.

"Character of Mahazi Melli-e-Islami Afghanistan." *Afghan Jehad* 1:3 (January–March 1988): 55–59.

Charpentier, C. J. "One Year After the Saur Revolution." *Afghanistan Journal* 6:4 (1979): 117–120.

Chatty, Dawn, and Annika Rabo (eds.). *Organizing Women: Formal and Informal Women's Groups in the Middle East.* Oxford: Berg, 1997.

Chokaiev, Mustafa. "The Situation in Afghanistan." *Asiatic Review* 26:86 (April 1930): 324–330.

Colville, Rupert. "The Biggest Caseload in the World." *Refugees* no. 108 (II-1997): 3–9.

"Constitution of Afghanistan, 9 Mizan 1343 [1 October 1964]." In The Kabul Times Annual. Nour M. Rahimi (ed.) Kabul: The Kabul Times Publishing Agency, Matbaa-e-Dawlati, 1967.

Constitution of the Republican State of Afghanistan [1976]. Kabul: The Kabul Times Publishing Agency, Matbaa-e-Dawlati, 1976.

Dariz, G. M. "Family Law in Afghanistan." In *Lawasia: Family Law Series,* vol. 1, Judith E. Sihombing and H. A. Finlay (eds.), pp. 13–22. Singapore: Singapore University Press for the Law Association for Asia and the Western Pacific, 1979.

Dietl, Wilhelm. *Bridgehead Afghanistan.* New Delhi: Lancer International, 1986.

Doubleday, Veronica. *Three Women of Herat.* London: Jonathan Cape, 1988.

Dupont, Beatrice. *Unequal Education: A Study of Sex Differences in Secondary-School Curricula.* Paris: UNESCO, 1981.

Dupree, Louis. *Afghanistan.* Princeton: Princeton University Press, 1973.

———. "Afghanistan Continues Its Experiment in Democracy: The Thirteenth Parliament Is Elected." *AUFS Reports* 15:3 (July 1971): 1–15.

———. "Constitutional Development and Cultural Change, Part III: The 1964 Afghan Constitution (Articles 1–56)." *AUFS Reports* 9:3 (September 1965): 1–29.

———. "Cultural Determinants of the Afghan Resistance to the Saur Revolution of 1978." In *Soviet-American Relations with Pakistan, Iran, and Afghanistan,* Hafeez Malik (ed.), pp. 355–365. Houndmills, Basingstoke, Hampshire: Macmillan Press, 1987.

———. "An Informal Talk with Prime Minister Daoud." *AUFS Reports* 3:3 (September 1959): 1–4.

———. "It Wasn't Woodstock, But: The First International Rock Festival in Kabul." *AUFS Reports* 20:2 (May 1976): 1–11.

———. "A Note on Afghanistan: 1971." *AUFS Reports* 15:2 (July 1971): 1–35.

———. "A Note on Afghanistan: 1974." *AUFS Reports* 18:8 (September 1974): 1–23.

———. "Population Dynamics in Afghanistan." *AUFS Reports* 14:7 (April 1970): 1–11.

Dupree, Louis, and Nancy Hatch Dupree. "Afghan Refugees in Pakistan." In *World Refugee Survey: 1987 in Review,* 13th-anniversary issue, pp. 17–21. Washington, D.C.: U.S. Committee for Refugees, 1988.

Dupree, Nancy H. "The Afghan Refugee Family Abroad: A Focus on Pakistan." *The Afghanistan Studies Journal* 1:1 (Spring 1988): 29–47.

———. "The Demography of Afghan Refugees in Pakistan." In *Soviet-American Relations with Pakistan, Iran, and Afghanistan,* Hafeez Malik (ed.), pp. 366–394. Houndmills, Basingstoke, Hampshire: Macmillan Press, 1987.

———. "Revolutionary Rhetoric and Afghan Women." In *Revolutions and Rebellions in Afghanistan,* M. Nazif Shahrani and Robert L. Canfield (eds.), pp. 306–340. Berkeley: University of California Press, 1984.

———. *The Women of Afghanistan.* Office of the UN Coordinator for Afghanistan, 1998.

Edwards, Anne. *Throne of Gold: The Lives of the Aga Khans.* New York: William Morrow, 1995.

Ellis, Deborah. *Women of the Afghan War.* Westport, Conn.: Praeger, 2000.

Emadi, Hafizullah. "Afghanistan in United States-Soviet Politics." *World Review* 28:3 (September 1989): 17–21.

———. *Afghanistan's Gordian Knot: An Analysis of National Conflict and Strategies for Peace.* Honolulu: East-West Center, 1991.

———. "Afghanistan's Struggle for National Liberation." *Studies in Third World Societies* 27 (March 1986): 17–42.

———. "Break the Silence." *Horizons* 1:1 (1986): 37.

———. "Breaking the Shackles: Political Participation of Hazara Women in Afghanistan." *Asian Journal of Women's Studies* 6:1 (2000): 143–161.

———. *China's Foreign Policy Toward the Middle East.* Karachi: Royal Book Company, 1997.

———. "An Historical Perspective of the Durand Line and the Future of Afghanistan and Pakistan Relations." *World Review* 30:1 (March 1991): 5–12.

————. *Politics of Development and Women in Afghanistan.* New York: Paragon House, 1993.

————. *Politics of the Dispossessed: Superpowers and Development in the Middle East.* Westport, Conn.: Praeger, 2001.

————. "Rebuilding Afghanistan." *Contemporary Review* 278:1623 (April 2001): 200–208.

————. "Resettlement Pattern: The Afghan Refugees in Pakistan." *Cultural Survival Quarterly* 12:4 (Fall 1988): 20–23.

————. "State, Modernization, and Rebellion: U.S.-Soviet Politics of Domination of Afghanistan." *Economic and Political Weekly* 26:4 (January 26, 1991): 176–184.

————. "State, Modernization, and the Women's Movement in Afghanistan." *Review of Radical Political Economics* 23:3-4 (1991): 224–243.

————. *State, Revolution, and Superpowers in Afghanistan.* New York: Praeger, 1990.

Emmanuel, Arghiri. *Unequal Exchange: A Study of the Imperialism of Trade.* New York: Monthly Review Press, 1972.

Engels, Fredrick. *The Origin of the Family, Private Property, and the State.* New York: International Publishers, 1967.

Farhang, Mir Mohammad Siddiq. *Afghanistan dar Panj Qarn-e-Akhir* [Afghanistan in the Last Five Centuries]. Vols. 1–3. Peshawar, Pakistan: Author, 1373/1994.

Farid, F. R. "The Modernization of Afghanistan." *Afghanistan* 17:3 (July–September 1962): 7–22.

Fayzzad, Mohammad Alam. *Jirgaha-e-Bozurg-e-Milli Afghanistan, Loya Jirgah, wa Jirgaha-e-Namnihad Tahti Tasalut-e-Kamunistha wa Rus* [Grand National Assemblies of Afghanistan, Loya Jirgah, and So-Called Jirgahs Held Under Communists and Russians]. Islamabad, Pakistan: s.n., 1368/1989.

Frank, Andre Gunder. "The Development of Underdevelopment." *Monthly Review* 18:4 (September 1966): 17–31.

Freilich, Morris. "Introduction: Is Culture Still Relevant?" In *The Relevance of Culture*, Morris Freilich (ed.), pp. 1–26. New York: Bergin and Garvey, 1989.

Fry, Maxwell J. *The Afghan Economy: Money, Finance, and the Critical Constraints to Economic Development.* Leiden: E. J. Brill, 1974.

Gankovsky, Yuri V., et al. *A History of Afghanistan.* Translated from the Russian by Vitaly Baskakov. Moscow: Progress Publishers, 1985.

Gannon, Kathy. "Fleeing Afghans Overwhelming Pakistan Camps." Associated Press, *The Seattle Times*, January 10, 2001.

General Union Afghanischer Studenten im Ausland (GUAFS). *Bistu Say-e-Saur.* March 1982.

General Union of Democratic Students and Patriotic Afghans (GUDSPA). *Afghanistan-e-Azad* [Independent Afghanistan]. No. 3 (October, 1980).

Gharghasht, Mohammad Nasir. *Rahnuma-e-Kabul* [Kabul's Guide]. Kabul: Government Press, 1345/1966.

Ghubar, Mir Ghulam Mohammad. *Afghanistan dar Masir-e-Tarikh* [Afghanistan in the Path of History]. Qum, Iran: Payam-e-Muhajir, 1359/1980.

———. *Afghanistan dar Masir-e-Tarikh.* Vol. 2. Herndon, Va.: Hishmat Khalil Ghubar, 1999.

Ghufran, Nasreen. "Afghan Refugee Women in Pakistan." Paper presented at the International Conference on "Refugees, Internally Displaced Persons, and Stateless People: The Humanitarian Challenge." Hanns Seidel Foundation, Germany, April 12–13, 1999.

Girardet, Edward R. *Afghanistan: The Soviet War.* New York: St. Martin's Press, 1985.

Girardet, Edward, and Jonathan Walter (eds.). *Afghanistan: Essential Field Guides to Humanitarian and Conflict Zones.* Geneva: Crosslines Communications, 1998.

Glukhoded, Vladmir. "The Economy of Independent Afghanistan." In *Afghanistan: Past and Present,* Oriental Studies in the USSR no. 3. Moscow: Academy of Sciences, 1981.

Gobar, Asad Hassan. "Suicide in Afghanistan." *The British Journal of Psychiatry* 116:534 (May 1970): 493–496.

Goodwin, Jan. *Caught in the Crossfire.* New York: E. P. Dutton, 1987.

———. *Price of Honor: Muslim Women Lift the Veil of Silence on the Islamic World.* Boston: Little, Brown, 1994.

Goulet, Denis. "Development . . . or Liberation?" In *The Political Economy of Development and Underdevelopment,* 3rd ed., Charles K. Wilber (ed.), pp. 461–467. New York: Random House, 1984.

Gregorian, Vartan. *The Emergence of Modern Afghanistan: Politics of Reform and Modernization, 1880–1946.* Stanford, Calif.: Stanford University Press, 1969.

Griffiths, John C. *Afghanistan: Key to a Continent.* Boulder, Colo.: Westview Press, 1981.

Grimes, Barbara F. (ed.). *Ethnologue: Languages of the World.* 13th ed. Dallas, Tex.: Summer Institute of Linguistics, 1996.

Habibi, K. "A Glance at Literature: A Box of Jewels." *Kabul Times* 3:75 (1967): 3.

Habibullah, Amir. *My Life: From Brigand to King, Autobiography of Amir Habibullah.* London: Octagon Press, 1990.

Hazzard, Virginia. *UNICEF and Women: The Long Voyage—A Historical Perspective.* New York: UNICEF, 1987.

Helsinki Watch and Asia Watch Committees. *To Die in Afghanistan: A Supplement to Tears, Blood, and Cries: Human Rights in Afghanistan Since the Invasion, 1979 to 1984.* New York: Helsinki Watch and Asia Watch Committees, December 1985.

Helsinki Watch Committee. *Tears, Blood, and Cries: Human Rights in Afghanistan Since the Invasion, 1979–1984.* New York: Helsinki Watch Committee, December 1984.

Higgins, Benjamin. *Economic Development: Principles, Problems, and Policies.* New York: W. W. Norton, 1968.

Higgins, Benjamin, and Jean Downing Higgins. *Economic Development of a Small Planet.* New York: W. W. Norton, 1979.

Hollmann, Anneliese. "Islamic Republic of Iran: Host to over Two Million Afghan Refugees." *Refugees* no. 38 (February 1987): 10–12.

Howard-Merriam, Kathleen. "Afghan Refugee Women and Their Struggle for

Survival." In *Afghan Resistance: The Politics of Survival,* Grant M. Farr and John G. Merriam (eds.), pp. 104–125. Boulder, Colo.: Westview Press, 1987.

Howland, Courtney W. (ed.). *Religious Fundamentalism and the Human Rights of Women.* New York: St. Martin's Press, 1999.

Huldt, Bo, and Erland Jansson (eds.). *The Tragedy of Afghanistan: The Social, Cultural, and Political Impact of the Soviet Invasion.* London: Croom Helm, 1988.

Hunte, Pamela A. "Indigenous Methods of Fertility Regulation in Afghanistan." In *Women's Medicine: A Cross-Cultural Study of Indigenous Fertility Regulation,* Lucile F. Newmen (ed.), pp. 43–75. New Brunswick, N.J.: Rutgers University Press, 1985.

———. *Women and the Development Process in Afghanistan, 1978.* Project for the U.S. Agency for International Development (USAID). USAID, 1978.

Hyman, Anthony. *Afghanistan Under Soviet Domination, 1964–91.* 3rd ed. London: Macmillan Press, 1992.

Indra, Doreen (ed.). *Engendering Forced Migration: Theory and Practice.* New York: Berghahn Books, 1999.

Inkeles, Alex. *Exploring Individual Modernity.* New York: Columbia University Press, 1983.

Inkeles, Alex, and David Horton Smith. *Becoming Modern: Individual Change in Six Developing Countries.* Cambridge: Harvard University Press, 1974.

International Labor Organization (ILO). *Yearbook of Labour Statistics.* Geneva: ILO, 1975, 1976, 1982.

International Labor Organization (ILO) and UN High Commissioner for Refugees (UNHCR). *Tradition and Dynamism Among Afghan Refugees: Report of an ILO Mission to Pakistan (November 1982) on Income-Generating Activities for Afghan Refugees.* Geneva: ILO, 1983.

Jamal, Arafat. "Dark Side of the Moon." *Refugees* no. 108 (II-1997): 10.

Jaquette, Jane S. "Women and Modernization Theory: A Decade of Feminist Criticism." *World Politics* 34:2 (1982): 267–284.

Kabul New Times. January 5, 1980; March 9, 1980; March 16, 1980.

Kabul Times. February 14, 1977; June 14, 1977; May 9, 1979; October 23, 1979; November 17, 1979.

Kakar, Hasan. *Government and Society in Afghanistan: The Reign of Amir Abd al-Rahman Khan.* Austin: University of Texas Press, 1979.

Kaldor, Kathryn. "Assisting Skilled Women: Personal Observations and Considerations Regarding Implementation of Income-Generating Projects for Female Afghan Refugees." *The Afghanistan Studies Journal* 1:2 (1988): 21–33.

Kamali, Mohammad Hashim. *Law in Afghanistan: A Study of the Constitutions, Matrimonial Law, and the Judiciary.* Leiden: E. J. Brill, 1985.

Kaplan, Robert D. *Soldiers of God: With the Mujahidin in Afghanistan.* Boston: Houghton Mifflin, 1990.

Kerr, Graham. *Population and Family Planning in Afghanistan: Social Implications of the Data from Afghan Demographic Studies.* Amherst: Council on International Studies, State University of New York, 1978.

Khan, Badruddin. "Not-So-Gay Life in Karachi: A View of a Pakistani Living in Toronto." In *Sexuality and Eroticism Among Males in Moslem Societies,* Arno

Schmitt and Jehoeda Sofer (eds.), pp. 93–104. New York: Haworth Press, 1992.

Knabe, Erika. "Afghan Women: Does Their Role Change?" In *Afghanistan in the 1970s*, Louis Dupree and Linette Albert (eds.), pp. 144–166. New York: Praeger, 1974.

———. "Women in the Social Stratification of Afghanistan." In *Commoners, Climbers, and Notables: A Sampler of Studies on Social Ranking in the Middle East*, C. A. O. Van Nieuwenhuijze (ed.), pp. 329–343. Leiden: E. J. Brill, 1977.

Kramer, Harry. "Out of Isolation: Afghanistan Is Pushing Toward the Twentieth Century with Bold Spending Plan, but Tribesmen Resist." *The Wall Street Journal*, September 2, 1977.

Le Vine, Steve. "The War Within the War." *Newsweek*, January 22, 1990.

Lessing, Doris. *The Wind Blows Away Our Words, and Other Documents Relating to the Afghan Resistance*. New York: Vintage Books, 1987.

Lindisfarne, Nancy. "Women Organized in Groups: Expanding the Terms of the Debate." In *Organizing Women: Formal and Informal Women's Groups in the Middle East*, Dawn Chatty and Annika Rabo (eds.), pp. 211–238. Oxford: Berg, 1997.

Majrooh, Sayed Bahaouddin, and Sayed Mohammad Yusuf Elmi. *The Sovietization of Afghanistan*. Peshawar, Pakistan: Afghan Information Center, 1986.

Malikyar, Helena. "Development of Family Law in Afghanistan: The Roles of the Hanafi Madhhab, Customary Practices, and Power Politics." *Central Asian Survey* 16:3 (1997): 389–399.

Marsden, Peter. "Repatriation and Reconstruction: The Case of Afghanistan." In *The End of Refugee Cycle: Refugee Repatriation and Reconstruction*, Richard Black and Khalid Koser (eds.), pp. 56–68. New York: Berghahn Books, 1999.

———. *The Taliban: War, Religion, and the New Order in Afghanistan*. Karachi, Lahore, Islamabad: Oxford University Press; London and New York: Zed Books, 1998.

Marwat, Fazal-ur-Rahman. *The Evolution and Growth of Communism in Afghanistan, 1917–1979: An Appraisal*. Karachi: Royal Book Company, 1997.

Matinuddin, Kamal. *The Taliban Phenomenon: Afghanistan 1994–1997*. Karachi, Pakistan: Oxford University Press, 1999.

Mertus, Julie. *War's Offensive on Women: The Humanitarian Challenge in Bosnia, Kosovo, and Afghanistan*. Bloomfield, Conn.: Kumarian Press, 2000.

Mills, Margaret A. "Of the Dust and the Wind: Arranged Marriages in Afghanistan." In *Everyday Life in the Muslim Middle East*, Donna Lee Bowen and Evelyn A. Early (eds.), pp. 47–56. Bloomington: Indiana University Press, 1993.

Moghadam, Valentine M. *Modernizing Women: Gender and Social Change in the Middle East*. Boulder, Colo.: Lynne Rienner, 1993.

Nazaar, Fazil M. *Development, Modernization, and Leadership Styles in Afghanistan: A Human Simulation in Politics*. Ph.D. thesis, University of Hawaii–Manoa, 1972.

Nida-e-Enqilab [Voice of Revolution]. Organ-e-Tiyurik wa Siyasi-e-Hastaha-e-Enqilabi-e-Kamunistha-e-Afghanistan [Theoretical and political organ of revolutionary cells of Afghanistan's communists]. Vols. 4–5. 1365/1986.

Nizamnamah-ye-Arusi, Nikah, wa Khatnasuri, 20 Aqrab 1302, 1 Sunbula 1303 [Laws Concerning Engagements, Marriages, and Circumcisions, November 11, 1923; August 23, 1924].

Nizamnamah-ye-Asasi-e-Dawlat-e-Aliyah-e-Afghanistan, 20 Hamal 1302 [Constitution of Afghanistan, April 9, 1923]. In *Reform and Rebellion in Afghanistan, 1919–1929: King Amanullah's Failure to Modernize a Tribal Society,* Leon B. Poullada, pp. 277–291. Ithaca, N.Y.: Cornell University Press, 1973.

Nyrop, Richard F., and Donald M. Seekins. *Afghanistan: A Country Study.* Foreign Area Studies, the American University. Washington, D.C.: U.S. Government Printing Office, 1986.

"Ockenden Venture Projects for Afghan Refugee Women." *Refugees* no. 31 (July 1986): 40.

O'Connor, Robert (ed.). *Managing Health Systems in Developing Countries: Experiences from Afghanistan.* Lexington, Ky.: Lexington Books, 1980.

Oudenhoven, Nico Van. "Common Afghans: Street Games and Child Development." *Afghanistan Journal* 7:4 (1980): 126–138.

"Pakistan and Iran." *Refugees* no. 36 (December 1986): 27–28.

Patrick, Reardon J. "Modernization and Reform: The Contemporary Endeavour." In *Afghanistan: Some New Approaches,* George Grassmuck, Ludwig Adamec, and Frances H. Irwin (eds.), pp. 149–203. Ann Arbor: University of Michigan Press, 1969.

Pazhwak, Ahmad. *Modern Afghanistan.* Kabul: Kabul University, 1965.

Poladi, Hassan. *The Hazaras.* Stockton, Calif.: Mughal, 1989.

Pomonoti, Jean-Claude. "Baluchistan: One Refugee for Every Seven Inhabitants." *Refugees* no. 29 (May 1988): 18–19.

Portes, Alejandro. "On the Sociology of National Development: Theories and Issues." *American Journal of Sociology* 82:1 (July 1976): 55–85.

Poullada, Leon B. *Reform and Rebellion in Afghanistan, 1919–1929: King Amanullah's Failure to Modernize a Tribal Society.* Ithaca, N.Y.: Cornell University Press, 1973.

Quarterly Economic Review: Pakistan, Bangladesh, Afghanistan, nos. 2, 3, 1976 Annual, 1977 Annual. London: Economist Intelligence Unit, 1967, 1974, 1976, 1977.

Rahimi, Fahima. *Women in Afghanistan.* Liestal: Stiftung Foundation, Stiftung Bibliotheca Afghanica, 1986.

Rahimi, Wali M. *Status of Women: Afghanistan.* Bangkok: UNESCO, Principal Regional Office for Asia and the Pacific, 1991.

Rahmani, Maga. *Purdah Nishinan-e-Sukhangoy* [Songs of the Caged Birds]. Kabul: Anjuman-e-Tarikh, Matbaa-e-Omumi, 1331/1952.

Revolutionary Association of Women of Afghanistan (RAWA). *Ashar wa Surudha-e-Jamiat-e-Enqilabi Zanan-e-Afghanistan* [Poems and Songs of the Revolutionary Association of Women of Afghanistan]. Bonn: Published by supporters of RAWA who live abroad, Fall 1981.

———. *Barnama, Wazayif wa Asasnama-e-Jamiat-e-Enqilabi Zanan-e-Afghanistan* [Policy, Responsibility, and Platforms of the Revolutionary Association of Women of Afghanistan]. Summer 1980.

———. *Payam-e-Zan* [The Message of Women] 2:1 (December 1989).

———. *Shabnamaha-e-Jamiat-e-Enqilabi Zanan-e-Afghanistan* [Underground Letters of the Revolutionary Association of Women of Afghanistan]. Bonn: Published by supporters of RAWA who live abroad, Fall 1981.

Richter, Linda Clark. "The Impact of Women of Regime Change in Afghanistan." *Journal of South Asian and Middle Eastern Studies* 7:2 (Winter 1983): 58–68.

Rostow, W. W. (Walt Whitman). *The Stages of Economic Growth: A Non-Communist Manifesto.* Cambridge: Cambridge University Press, 1990.

Roulet-Billard, Annick. "First Person Feminine." *Refugees* no. 70 (November 1989): 24–26.

Rubin, Barnett R. "The Fragmentation of Afghanistan." *Foreign Affairs* 68 (Winter 1989–1990): 150–168.

Sa'di, Muslihuddin. *Sharh-i Bustan.* Muhammad Khaza'ili. Tehran: Sazman-i Intisharat-i Javidan, 1362/1983.

Safi, Batinshah. "Afghan Education During the War." In *The Tragedy of Afghanistan: The Social, Cultural, and Political Impact of the Soviet Invasion,* Bo Huldt and Erland Jansson (eds.), pp. 113–118. London: Croom Helm, 1988.

Saleh, Ghulam Omar. "The Economical Geography of Afghanistan." *Afghanistan* 19:3 (July–September 1963): 37–43.

———. "The Economical Geography of Afghanistan." [part 2] *Afghanistan* 19:1 (January–March 1964): 15–22.

———. "The Economical Geography of Afghanistan." [part 3] *Afghanistan* 19:2 (April–June 1964): 37–41.

"Sarnawishti Wahshatnaki Biwaha-e-Afghani" [The Horrible Fate of Afghan Widows]. *Akhbari Hafta* (Kabul) 42 (October 1989): 2–3.

Schmitt, Arno, and Jehoeda Sofer (eds.). *Sexuality and Eroticism Among Males in Moslem Societies.* New York: Haworth Press, 1992.

Shalinskly, Audrey C. "Learning Sexual Identity: Parents and Children in Northern Afghanistan." *Anthropology and Education Quarterly* 11:4 (Winter 1980): 254–265.

———. *Long Years of Exile: Central Asian Refugees in Afghanistan and Pakistan.* Lanham, Md.: University Press of America, 1994.

———. *Reason, Desire, and Sexuality: The Meaning of Gender in Northern Afghanistan.* East Lansing: Michigan State University Press, 1986.

Shindandi, G. "Matboat-e-azad dar Afghanistan bad az infazi qanun-e-assasi jadid" [Free Press in Afghanistan after the Promulgation of the New Constitution]. B.A. thesis, Kabul University, Faculty of Law and Political Science, 1348/1969.

Shpoon, Saduddin. "Paxto Folklore and the Landey." *Afghanistan* 20:4 (Winter 1968): 40–50.

Sliwinski, Marek. "Afghanistan: The Decimation of A People." *Orbis* 33:1 (Winter 1989): 39–56.

Smith, Harvey H., David E. Smith and others (eds.). *Area Handbook for Afghanistan.* Washington, D.C.: U.S. Government Printing Office, 1973.

"Standpoints of the Afghanistan Liberation Organization on a Number of Key Issues." www.geocities.com/tokyo/ginza/3231. Accessed at various dates in early 2000.

Stucki, Anneliese. "Horses and Women: Some Thoughts on the Life Cycle of Ersari Turkmen Women." *Afghanistan Journal* 5:4 (1978): 140–149.

Surkha [Sazman-e-Rahaye Bakhshi Khalqha-e-Afghanistan, or Organization for the Liberation of the People of Afghanistan]. *Chegunagi-e-Paydaish wa Rushdi Bourgeoisie dar Afghanistan* [The Process and Development of the Bourgeoisie in Afghanistan]. Berlin: Ayendagan Press, 1981.

Taniwal, Hakim K. "The Impact of Pushtunwali on Afghan Jihad." *WUFA* (Writers' Union of Free Afghanistan) 2:1 (January–March 1987): 1–24.

Tapper, Nancy. "Acculturation in Afghan Turkistan: Pushtun and Uzbek Women." *Asian Affairs* 14:1 (February 1983): 35–44.

———. *Bartered Brides: Politics, Gender, and Marriage in an Afghan Tribal Society.* Cambridge: Cambridge University Press, 1991.

Taraki, Noor Mohammad. "Basic Lines of the Revolutionary Duties of the Government of DRA." In *Democratic Republic of Afghanistan Annual, 7 Saur 1358,[1979]* pp. 62–70. Kabul: Government Printing House, 1979.

Tavakolian, Bahram. "Women and Socio-Economic Change Among Sheikhanzai Nomads of Western Afghanistan." *The Middle East Journal* 38:3 (Summer 1984): 433–453.

Tetreault, Mary Ann (ed.). *Women and Revolution in Africa, Asia, and the New World.* Columbia: University of South Carolina Press, 1994.

Thomas, Lowell. *Beyond Khyber Pass: Into Forbidden Afghanistan.* New York: Grosset and Dunlap, 1925.

Todaro, Michael P. *Economic Development in the Third World.* 3rd ed. New York: Longman, 1985.

United Nations (UN). *Demographic Yearbook 1987.* New York: UN Department of International Economic and Social Affairs, Statistical Office, 1989.

———. *Report of the United Nations Interagency Gender Mission to Afghanistan.* November 12–24, 1997. New York: Office of the UN Special Adviser on Gender Issues and Advancement of Women, 1997.

———. *Statistical Yearbook 1982.* New York: UN Department of International Economic and Social Affairs, Statistical Office, 1985.

United Nations Educational, Scientific, and Cultural Organization (UNESCO). *Basic Facts and Figures, 1954.* Paris: UNESCO, 1954.

———. *Statistical Yearbook, 1968, 1977, 1988, 1990, 1999* (Paris: UNESCO, 1968, 1977, 1988, 1990; and New York: UNESCO, 1999).

United Nations International Children's Emergency Fund (UNICEF). *Statistical Profile of Children and Mothers in Afghanistan.* Kabul: UNICEF, 1978.

United Nations International Drug Control Program. "Afghanistan: Community Drug Profile no. 2: Opium and Problem of Drug Use in a Group of Afghan Refugee Women." December 1999.

U.S. Agency for International Development (USAID). *Helping People.* Kabul: USAID, April 1976.

U.S. Central Intelligence Agency (CIA). *The World Factbook 2000.* Washington, D.C.: CIA, 2000.

U.S. Committee for Refugees. *Afghan Refugees: Five Years Later.* Washington, D.C.: U.S. Committee for Refugees, 1985.

Vafai, Gholam H. *Afghanistan: A Country Law Study.* Washington, D.C.: Library of Congress, 1988.

Vine, Steve Le. "The War Within the War: Rebel Infighting Gives Relief to the Afghan Regime." *Newsweek*, January 22, 1990.

Vollmann, William T. *An Afghanistan Picture Show, or How I Saved the World*. New York: Farrar, Straus, and Giroux, 1992.

Wallerstein, Immanuel. *The Capitalist World Economy*. Cambridge: Cambridge University Press, 1979.

Warren, Bill. *Imperialism: Pioneer of Capitalism*. Edited by John Sender. London: NLB, 1980.

Weinbaum, Marvin G. "Afghanistan: Non-Party Parliamentary Democracy." *The Journal of Developing Areas* 7:1 (October 1972): 57–74.

———. "Legal Elites in Afghan Society." *International Journal of Middle East Studies* 12:1 (August 1980): 39–57.

———. "The Politics of Afghan Resettlement and Rehabilitation." *Asian Survey* 29:3 (March 1989): 287–307.

Wilber, Charles K. *The Political Economy of Development and Underdevelopment*. 3rd ed. New York: Random House, 1984.

Wilson, Andrew. "Inside Afghanistan: A Background to Recent Troubles." *Royal Central Asian Journal* 47:3–4 (July–October 1960): 286–295.

Women's International Network (WIN). *News* 2 (Spring 1988), 16 (Winter 1990).

Yacoobi, Sakena. "Women Educating Women in the Afghan Diaspora: Why and How." In *Religious Fundamentalism and the Human Rights of Women*, Courtney W. Howland (ed.), pp. 229–235. New York: St. Martin's Press, 1999.

Yunas, S. Fida. *Afghanistan: Jirgahs and Loya Jirgahs, the Afghan Tradition, 977 A.D. to 1992 A.D.* Peshawar, Pakistan: S. Fida Yunas, 1997.

———. *Afghanistan: Organization of the Peoples' Democratic Party of Afghanistan/Watan Party, Governments, and Bibliographical Sketches, 1982–1998*. Vols. 1–2. Peshawar, Pakistan: S. Fida Yunas, 1998.

Yusufi, Mohammad Qasim. "Effects of the War on Agriculture." In *The Tragedy of Afghanistan: The Social, Cultural, and Political Impact of the Soviet Invasion*, Bo Huldt and Erland Jansson (eds.), pp. 197–216. London: Croom Helm, 1988.

Zahidi, Badruddin. "Relief Assistance to Refugees and Displaced Women and Children in Pakistan." Paper submitted to Expert Group Meeting on Refugee and Displaced Women and Children, Vienna, July 2–6, 1990.

Zekrya, Mir-Ahmed B. "Planning and Development in Afghanistan: A Case of Maximum Foreign Aid and Minimum Growth." Ph.D. thesis, Johns Hopkins University, 1976.

Ziai, A. Hakim. "General Development of Afghanistan up to 1957." *Afghanistan* 16:3 (July–September 1961): 38–55.

Zulfacar, Maliha. *Afghan Immigrants in the USA and Germany: A Comparative Analysis of the Use of Ethnic Social Capital*. Munster: Lit Verlag, 1998.

Index

About the Author

HAFIZULLAH EMADI is a development consultant. After receiving his Ph.D. from the University of Hawaii, Manoa, Emadi taught in the University of Hawaii system, joined the East-West Center's International Relations Program as a Fellow in 1990, and was awarded a fellowship at the Woodrow Wilson Center in 1999.